CANAL GUIDES
Sculpture

Renzo Salvadori
Toto Bergamo Rossi
VENICE
SCULPTURE
from the origins to the 20th century

CANAL GUIDES
SCULPTURE

Photographs
Alinari Archives, Florence
Canal *&* Stamperia Archives, Venice
Correr Museum, Venice
Fotoattualità, Treviso
G.F. Spinazzi, Venice
Guggenheim Foundation, Venice
J.E. Bulloz, Paris
Museum of Modern Art, Ca' Pesaro, Venice
Oreste Cagnato, Venice
Osvaldo Böhm Archives, Venice
Veneto Archeological Superintendency, Padua
Save Venice Inc.
Società Sansovino
Superintendency for the Artistic and Historic
Heritage of Venice

Editing
Francesca Ferrari Bravo

Layout
Andrea Camazzola e Pietro Menozzi

Translation
Marlene Klein

© 1997
CANAL *&* STAMPERIA EDITRICE srl
Venice

ISBN 88-86502-21-4
EAN 9788886502214

VENICE

GUIDE
TO SCULPTURE
FROM THE ORIGINS
TO THE 20TH CENTURY

RENZO SALVADORI
TOTO BERGAMO ROSSI

CANAL & STAMPERIA EDITRICE

Acknowledgements

The publisher and the authors would like to thank the American Committee of Save Venice Inc. and the Böhm photographic archives, which furnished most of the photographic material reproduced in this volume.
Renzo Salvadori is grateful to Guido Perocco and Wolfgang Wolters for the initial idea behind this work and for the advise they offered, though the authors claim sole responsibility for the choice of materials.
Toto Bergamo would like to thank Maria Teresa Rubin de Cervin for encouraging his choice of profession, Anne Markham Schulz for her precious advice and useful information, and Marta Coin for her support.

Preface

This guidebook is unusual in being entirely dedicated to sculpture. Although guidebooks to the painting of particular cities have existed since the seventeenth century, the sculpture of Venice has had to wait till now for a guide of its very own. This long wait is surely due to the greater effort of the imagination needed to apprehend and appreciate sculpture. Sculpture in general, but statuary especially is abstract in its want of color, in its concentration on the single figure, and in its lack of a naturalistic setting. Yet its very abstractness, along with its durability – indeed, the survival of renowned examples from antiquity – the expense of its material and transport, and the labor and skill involved in its manufacture has always conferred on sculpture a nobility and prestige that far exceeded that of painting. In Venice sculpture was the preferred medium for the symbolization of civic virtue and the commemoration of great men and deeds. It is, in large part, the special dignity of sculpture that explains the Porta della Carta, the equestrian Monument of Bartolomeo Colleoni, and the series of ducal tombs which span half a millenium.

This book is intended to introduce the interested amateur to the principal monuments of a splendid but undervalued art. Renzo Salvadori, careful and studious connoisseur of art and Venetian history, has availed himself of the contribution of Toto Bergamo, an esteemed restorer of stone sculpture. It is important for the reader to understand that this contribution is not that of someone who has studied Venetian sculpture through binoculars or from photographs, but of a man who has had almost as intimate a contact with the art about which he writes as its creators – a man who has not only seen numerous Venetian monuments from a scaffold and under intense illumination, but has learned through touch to know the quality of carved surfaces of every kind. Toto Bergamo's training and experience have disposed him to recognize and appreciate the range of techniques available to Venetian sculptors and the virtue of the different materials they used. This happy and meaningful collaboration makes this volume uniquely qualified to guide the reader in his survey of Venetian sculpture.

Anne Markham Schulz

Table of Contents

Introduction

Upon entering St Mark's basin from either the lagoon or the Grand Canal, an entire population of statues comes to life. They tower over us from above the domes and Palladian tympanums of San Giorgio, from the churches of the Zitelle and the Redentore, from the baroque volutes of the Salute, and from the golden sphere of the Dogana. The *Angel* on the campanile and the winged symbols of the lagoon city beckon us towards the Piazzetta, where the imposing four-teenth-century groups of Palazzo Ducale come toward us from the highest peaks of the "Marciana plateau". There they are answered, on the other side, by the aerial procession of figures on the library. This crowd of statues becomes even more tumultuous on the late-Gothic crowning of the basilica, whose five entrance portals make up the most vast, complete, and refined series of medieval Italian sculpture, which concludes in the final, superb, and surprising master-stroke of the gilded quadriga on the church facade.

These statues are like actors appearing on the scene, like visual captions that make the different building functions more explicit. St Mark's basin is only a small part of the overall ensemble that richly ornaments the entire city. Statues, bas-reliefs, crenellation, and friezes embellish buildings of every type, from every epoch – palazzi, churches, bridges, wells, city walls, and canal banks – rendering both the architecture and the surrounding area communicative. Sculpture becomes urban decor, a theatrical back-drop to public space. The patere aligned on the Veneto-Byzantine facades; the legendary animals on the thirteenth-century arches; the marble icons on the spires and choir screen that close the courtyards and *calli* (the narrow Venetian streets); the saints, prophets, and virtues erected between the dazzling fifteenth-century portals and windows; the Renaissance and baroque masks on the most sumptuous palazzi; the well-curbs at the center of the *campi* (the small Venetian squares); and the more humble "capitals" where the *calli* intersect – all of these merge together in a plastic *continuum* that invades every part of the city.

Venice is completely artificial, and Venice is completely adorned. The city is trimmed out like a ship, like one of the immense sculpted and gilded galleons of which the *Bucintoro* (the luxurious, ceremonial ship used by the Venetian Republic) was the most sumptuous example: a structure that acquired even move grandeur and extravagance floating out on the flat surface of the water. No other city is deco-rated and sculpted like Venice. And yet, when one speaks of Venetian art, one thinks immediately and only about paint-

Opposite page:
Monument to Doge Michele Morosini, detail of the Archangel Michael, c. 1382, church of Santi Giovanni e Paolo

ing and architecture and hardly ever about sculpture. It is almost as though the latter was a secondary, accessory product, made by anonymous artisans, without its own autonomous value. Yet the history of Venice, like that of few other Italian artistic centers, is filled with names of artists and craftsman who worked in stone, wood, and bronze: from the thirteenth-century maestros of St Mark's to Filippo Calendario, from Bartolomeo Bon to Lombardo, from Vittoria to Brustolon, from Morlaiter to Canova. These are only the most well-known names, not to mention all the works of ancient or Byzantine origin imported to decorate the public buildings or to satisfy the most secret pleasure of the city's refined collectors. All together there is an exemplary production that covers a span of more than two millenniums, practically without solutions of continuity over long periods of time. A large part of this work can still be found in its original location and leaves us a testimony that no other art form can give over so many centuries.

The Venetian plastic tradition cannot be compared to that of painting, especially if we consider the enormous influence the latter exercised over all of modern European art. Nonetheless, in certain periods, such as the thirteenth and fourteenth centuries, sculpture reached a comparable if not superior level to that of painting. The characteristics of this work can be better understood by considering the particular nature of the Venetian clientele, the city's fragmentary historical development, and the plurality of influences it encompassed over time that made it unique with respect to other Italian or European centers.

It is important to remember that Venice never had a royal court, a prince who, for better or for worse, directed cultural patronage, protected artists, and invested public or private funds (usually mingled together) thereby conferring a precise characterization to a historical era. The doge was nothing more than a public official with a very limited jurisdiction, a simple president of a collective group of organs each one of which controlled the other. This system may well have served to assure political stability, nonetheless it almost certainly limited the range of public commissions.

Private patronage, that of the important families, did not escape the Venetian norm of group decision making: in Venice the "fraternity" system reigned and imposed common management of family property (evidently adopted with the goal of impeding the dispersion of the capital required for commerce). Thus the Venetians always

Pietro Lombardo and assistants, St Jerome, c. 1475-80, church of Santo Stefano

remained prudent and parsimonious merchants; they were rarely intellectuals or humanists and they generally preferred sober and traditional art, even though they showed real appreciation for craftsmanship and fine materials. In short, Venetian society was more bourgeoisie than courtly, or, if you like, more working-class than aristocratic. Thus we find erratic taste in even in the most noble commissions. Take, for example, the tombs of the two very famous doges, who succeeded one another towards the mid-fourteenth century, Bartolomeo Gradenigo (d. 1342) and Andrea Dandolo (d. 1354); both were granted the very rare honor of being buried in St Mark's in recognition of their contribution in building the Palazzo and the Marciana chapel. Nonetheless, the commissions for these monuments were entrusted to minor, evidently not very talented artists, despite the fact that sculptors of the calibre of Filippo Calendario and Andriolo De Santi were active in Venice at that time. This is a perfect example of the superficial culture of the clientele itself, despite its aristocratic origins.

If one excludes, in part, sixteenth and seventeenth century painting, the history of Venetian art cannot be broken down into coherent and majestic historical blocks that reveal contemporaneous development in the various forms of artistic expression. It cannot be compared, for example, to the Florentine tradition, from Masaccio to Michelangelo, or to that of Rome, from Bramante to Bernini and Borromini – periods of one or two centuries in which every artist was a link on a chain that received, transformed, and re-transmitted, from his predecessors to his successors, a single style, a homogeneous vision of the world. More than anything else Venetian sculpture seems to proceed in broad leaps over brief periods without creating schools that lasted more than one or two generations. Yet, in the end, its historical span is immense, from the crusades to Canova, alternating moments of great inventiveness with almost unexplainable productive voids.

Venice was the major maritime port of medieval Europe and as such was in constant contact with the most varied of worlds ranging from the Far East to northern Europe. The city's cultural and artistic life could not help but react to these solicitations in many different ways, sometimes refusing and sometimes assimilating them, to recast them later in its own very special ways.

In the early centuries of its formation Venice was a province of the Eastern Empire. Its very origins reveal a highly stylized Byzantine tradition: sculpture is more often engraved

Monument to Doge Michele Morosini, detail, c. 1382, church of Santi Giovanni e Paolo

on a flat backgrounds than carved and is subject to a graphic linearity that avoids three-dimensionality. Thus it becomes evident why the plastic and full-bodied Paduan tradition perpetuated by Antelami had difficulty penetrating this environment, even if the mighty group of the *Trades* decorating the bases of the two large columns in the Piazzetta reigned from the year 1170 onward. When the large building site for the facade of the Marciana basilica was opened (after the Fourth Crusade), these different tendencies could not help but intertwine, blending themselves with still others, to create an exceptional plurality of styles, even if the entire complex was firmly defined on a precise iconological layout. Antelami's influence is evident, first and foremost, in the group of representing *St Mark's Dream*, placed over the main door of the church: this is the central element of the entire "story" that is developed on the three other facades. Antelami's influence can also to be found in the funerary lions of the Zen chapel, the ex "door to the sea", as well as in the *Virgin and the Magi*, now in the Seminary Museum, the original project of which probably belonged to the same entrance portal. Yet, at the same time, the programmatic clarity of the late-ancient revival is also dominant, revealing the precise ideological connotations of the proto-Renaissance. It was then that the two great portal maestros began their work, the so-called Maestro of Hercules and the Maestro of the Trades. The side portals of the western facade, done by the former, are among the most refined works of Venetian sculpture. Of clear Byzantine inspiration, they create a superimposition of sinuous lines with *stiacciato* figures lightly embossed on a gold background, so as to create an illusion of "brocade". The perforated choir screens of Islamic taste complement these figurations further lightening the portal lunettes. The Maestro of the Trades, who worked at the same time on the six bands of the three large arches above the main door, defined a style that would evolve over time, beginning from a still romanesque full-bodiness to reach, in the later figures representing the *Trades*, a freedom and vigor in the realistic treatment of scenes of daily life. This acknowledgement reveals a knowledge of both the more evolved, contemporary French Gothic art and that of the Ancients, a quality that placed this Venetian maestro at a comparable level to that of Giovanni Pisano, a sculptor who was active between 1266 and 1313.

Virgin and Child, 13th century, church of San Giovanni in Bragora

Giammaria Mosca,
St John the Baptist, c. 1525,
church of Santo Stefano

Tullio Lombardo, Virtue or Saint,
c. 1490, church of Santo Stefano

Upon the completion of St Mark's in 1270, these artists seemed to vanish into thin air, creating the first void in Venetian sculpture. It was not until fifty years later, around 1320, that excellent sculptors were once again operating in Venice and the Veneto. These artists were responsible for a series of funeral monuments in which the art of portraiture suddenly took on the dignity and refinement it had carried in ancient tradition: the faces of *Bishop Salomone* from Treviso, *Enrico Scrovegni* from Padua, and *Pievano di San Simeon Grande* from Venice constitute perhaps the first real portraits in the history of European art after those of ancient art. This marked the beginning of the portrait tradition that, in every era and in every form, would attract the most excellent craftsman in Venice.

Andriolo De Santi began his activity in the 1430s and 1440s; he was a fine artist (sculptor of the magnificent entrance portal of San Lorenzo in Vicenza, 1342-44) of whose work very little remains in Venice. At the same time the work of another artist by the name of Filippo Calendario dominated; according to Wolters, he was responsible for the design of the present-day Palazzo Ducale and also sculpted the large corner groups. He dedicated his brief but intense artistic career to the great palazzo until his tragical death in 1355, when he too left the scene without leaving heirs behind him. It was not until 1380, a generation later, that another important workshop of Venetian sculptors, that of the Dalle Masegne, began to work in Venice. Like De Santi however this studio worked much more outside of Venice than in the city itself. Its true masterpiece is found in Bologna in the church of San Francesco.

Portrait of Enrico Scrovegni, c. 1320, Padua, Cappella Scrovegni

Portrait of Bishop Castellano Salomone, c. 1322, Treviso, Duomo

From 1416 on, when the actual work began on the Gothic crowning of the basilica, entire families of Tuscan and Lombard sculptors could be found in Venice. The Republic was at the height of its economic and political strength, and the city hosted swarms of "foreign" artists who took turns working on the decoration of the ducal chapel and other buildings; very little is known about actual native Venetian artists. Indeed, in the early-fifteenth century, almost all the most important sculptors of the era passed through Venice including Jacopo della Quercia, Ghiberti, and Agostino di Duccio. Donatello settled in Padua, where he began an intense ten-year period of work beginning in 1443. Nonetheless, these presences did not leave a clear imprint on contemporary Venetian artistic production.

Bartolomeo Bon was to become the first important personality of fifteenth-century Venice. Working in the years

*Francesco Laurana,
Portrait of a Woman, late-15th
century, Paris, Jacquemart-
André Museum*

*Claus Sluter, Christ on the
Cross, c. 1395, Dijon,
Archaeological Museum*

between 1423 and 1460 he defined a completely original, autonomous style in which it is difficult to trace precise influences even on the part of his older contemporaries such as Jacopo della Quercia or Donatello. It may in fact be necessary to look elsewhere to understand this sculptor better. If Argan is correct in stating that "in the late-fifteenth century the dominant problem is that of the relationship between Italian and Flemish art", then the solution to this problem was first defined in Venice by Bartolomeo Bon. And if it is true, as Argan has sustained, that the art of the greatest protagonist of northern sculpture, Claus Sluter (1340-1406), had been known by Jacopo della Quercia from his very early work onward, then, likewise, similar consonances with the "austere Bergognone plastic" can be found in Bartolomeo.

A student and collaborator of Bartolomeo Bon, Giorgio Orsini or Da Sebenico was a noteworthy and still little known Dalmatian artist, who collaborated with Bon on the Porta della Carta. His name is linked to one of the most splendid sculptures of the entire fifteenth century: the lunette of the main entrance portal of the Scuola di San Marco. After returning to his homeland in 1441, Orsini worked intensely in Sebenico and then in Ancona. It is not merely coincidence that Francesco Laurana was trained in those years in Dalmatia, which was then part of the Venetian Republic; he was to become an excellent portrait artist, whose splendid busts transposed the same needs of absolute formal perfection that can be found in Piero della Francesca. Thus, by following the itineraries of artists like Jacopo della Quercia, Bartolomeo Bon, Giorgio Orsini, Francesco Laurana, Piero della Francesca, Giovanni Bellini, and Antonello da Messina, it is possible to speak of a "Adriatic Renaissance" as the hinge between central Italy and northern Europe.

While Bartolomeo Bon was active in Venice, in the vicinity of Padua (which had been a Venetian territory since the beginning of the century), Donatello was at work on his greatest cycle of sculptures. He also formed a school that trained artists like Bartolomeo Bellano and Andrea Briosco (otherwise known as Il Riccio), who were the most well-known designers of small bronze sculptures throughout the Renaissance. The easy reproducibility of this genre granted widespread diffusion of this new artistic taste. Slightly earlier, still in Padua, Mantegna – the artist who, according to Berenson's joyful expression, "painted in Latin" – gave new life to the ideal world of antiquity granting both architecture and sculpture an increasingly privileged presence in his

*Il Riccio, Knight, bronze,
c. 1510, London, Victoria
and Albert Museum*

*Donatello, Equestrian Monument
to Gattamelata, 1446-50,
Padua, Piazza del Santo*

*Niccolò di Giovanni Fiorentino,
Tomb of Doge Francesco Foscari,
detail of a Virtue, c. 1460,
church of the Frari*

Jacopo Sansovino,
St John the Baptist, detail,
1554, church of the Frari

Tullio Lombardo, Adam, figure
from the Tomb of Doge Andrea
Vendramin, detail, 1492-95,
New York, Metropolitan
Museum

Music, Foscari Arch,
Palazzo Ducale, c. 1470

Tullio Lombardo, Tomb of Doge
Andrea Vendramin, detail,
church of Santi Giovanni e
Paolo

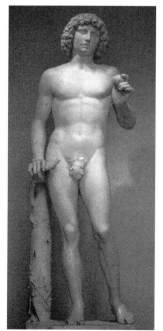

paintings.

From the latter half of the century onward, the relationship between Venice and its hinterland became closer and closer. It was a Lombard sculptor and architect, Pietro Solari, otherwise known as "Lombardo", who passing though Padua, brought the most refined rhythms of the new language of art to the lagoon, adapting it to the taste of Venetian clients. Immediately after, Antonio Rizzi, an artist from Verona, Antonio Lombardo, and his sons of Pietro and Tullio perfectly interpreted those neo-Platonic humanistic ideals that characterized the Venetian intellectual environment between the late-fifteenth and early-sixteenth century, working in perfect harmony with the most well-known architects and painters of the era, from Codussi to Giovanni Bellini, from Carpaccio to Giorgione.

When this happy parentheses of Venetian art ended with the crisis of the League of Cambrai, the cultural climate changed. Sculpture fell into another period of stasis during which, however, local production maintained a respectable level of craftsmanship (we have to exclude Alessandro Leopardi, who among other things was responsible for casting the bronze statue of *Colleoni*, Verrocchio's masterpiece). It was not until the arrival of Jacopo Sansovino in Venice in 1527 that sculpture re-assumed a certain level. A capable and well-versed architect and sculptor, Sansovino defined a style of great formal elegance that was particularly well-suited to the taste of public clients. His numerous followers, however, fell into a somewhat academic production. Alessandro Vittoria was the only one among them to distinguish himself in a clear way until, at the close of the century, he was joined by Girolamo Campagna. Vittoria is undoubtedly the greatest personality of sixteenth-century Venetian sculpture. He is distinguished above all for his portrait work where, more so than his early inspirers (Sansovino and Michelangelo) he seemed to look toward the luminosity and sanguinity of Titian or Tintoretto's work.

Analogously to what happened in painting, the panorama of Venetian sculpture of the seventeenth century is characterized by a large void, filled almost exclusively by artists from abroad, especially from the North, the most talented of which was Giusto Le Court. The most successful sculptors in Venice towards the end of the century and the beginning of the following were Filippo Parodi from Genoa and Giuseppe Mazza from Emilia, who were more neo-sixteenth century than baroque and thus defined, at a distance of more than a

Angel with holy water font in the church of the Fava, mid-18th century

Antonio Canova, Cupid and
Psyche, 1787-93, Paris, Louvre

century, the sculptural reinterpretation of the great season Renaissance season that would characterize eighteenth-century Venice and anticipated the neo-classical movement.

Despite this fragmentary development and the plurality of its influences one can still trace the thread that runs back through the entire history of sculpture and, in general, the art of Venice. It follows a basic classicism that, like a Carsican river, disappears more than once only to surface again further on limpid and fresh. Yet, this classicism hardly ever becomes academic formalism or arid intellectual research because it enriches itself as it goes along, drawing on the times, on the different artistic personalities, on the surrounding stimuli, and on the most varied expressive modes, which range from a dreamy intimacy to a sanguinary sensuality, from Apollonian refinement to the most earthly realism. It is also necessary to observe that Venice always refused the monumentality which appeared to be the other side of classicism, at least as it was understood by many Renaissance artists. Titanism and the deification of the individual, typical expressions of the Florentine and Roman courts, never took hold in Venice. The city's only "heroic" monument, dedicated to *Colleoni*, is the product of the private will of a mercenary commander who simply wanted to glorify himself and was done, in the end, by a Tuscan artist. In Venice even the most noble and grandiose forms of art are almost always corrected by a vein of realism if not irony: it is an art that goes from pure theatricality, seen as a stage game, to the most acute interiorization and psychological introspection (just think of Lotto, Titian, or Vittoria's portraiture). What prevails, in short, is always that bourgeois, concrete, realistic, and pragmatic spirit that the Venetian, as a merchant, has carried with him from the very beginning of time. The Venetians, in the words of Berenson, were indeed "the first modern population in Europe".

Classical antiquity was a constant myth of Venetian culture; it was an anchor, an element of cultural identity. According to official tradition the city of Venice was founded in 421 in an imperial era and always remained a free and independent state: it was the very same Venice that an angel had pointed out to Mark the Evangelist as his place of his "peace". Thus the Venetians felt themselves to be direct heirs to the ethical values of an ancient world, beyond that of the Christianity of its origins. It was a myth that, like all myths, had its background in historical truth: the Veneto lagoons, like the Dalmatian islands, were, after all, the only regions of Europe that did not endure barbaric invasions and passed without solutions of continuity from the ancient to the modern world, completely ignoring the feudal system. Thus it is interesting to note how this predilection for classical forms becomes evident in the various eras, even in the works of minor or anonymous artists who are always an index of an extremely widespread taste. Just consider, for example, the attractive fifteenth-century statue of *Music* on the Foscari Arch of Palazzo Ducale or the mid-seventeenth century *Angel* of the holy-water font in the church of the Fava.

The most emblematic protagonists of late-eighteenth century Venetian culture are classical, indeed neoclassical, in an absolute and visionary way as can be seen in the work of Gian Battista Piranesi and Antonio Canova, the two artists that closed the history of Italian art elevating themselves to the new developments of European culture. In the words of Hugh Honour, Canova "... studied the Ancients as a means of achieving the Ideal. He is to be credited for having broken a long tradition of servile praise to the Ancients and of having imposed the notion of 'modern' sculpture. Concentrating

Alessandro Vittoria, Stuccoes, vault of the Marciana Library staircase, c. 1555

more on form than on literary content, insisting on the importance of multiple points of view, and investigating the problem of instable balance, he went beyond the concerns of his contemporaries." The group of *Cupid and Psyche* in the Louvre, one of the heights of sculpture of all times, brings to their extreme consequence those intentions that were already clear in the early group of *Dedalus and Icarus* now in the Correr Museum and is the most extraordinary confirmation of Canova's "modernity".

Arturo Martini and Alberto Viani, the two greatest sculptors of our century who worked in Venice, can also be considered classicists in the Veneto sense of the term. Thus the 'long periods of time theorized by Braudel are once again confirmed in the history of art.

This brief illustrative guide dedicated to Venetian sculpture is intended as anthology and nothing more. It represents a choice and like all choices is evidently incomplete, though an effort has been made to include at least the most important works of all the major artists. It is a choice that attempts to document the plastic *continuum* of which we spoke at the beginning. It is a *continuum* that is entrenched in the Venetian urban environment, yet can also be seen chronologically in that it covers every epoch, even those of artistic stasis because it represents a widespread craftsmanship of considerable qualitative density that also functions in the absence of great artistic personalities.

The anthology of works proposed herein is also an anthology of quotations, retrieving some of the most significant steps of the historians that have known how to express themselves better that anyone else on many different and often little noticed subjects. Thus, we have also attempted to synthesize what has been written on the history of Venetian sculpture and, above all, to illustrate it for the first time in as complete or, in any event, as adequate a manner as possible, despite the vastness of the subject. It is attempt to review, in some way, the entire history of Venetian art from a new point of view that often presents surprising aspects. In conclusion we hope this guide can serve as an invitation to discover, or to rediscover the most sculpted city of the world: Venice.

Antonio Lombardo,
St Sebastian (?), c. 1500,
church of Santo Stefano

…N·CORNELIO
PATRI

I. Classical Heritage: A Constant Presence

"The route of the Vie Postumia and Annia is indicative of Rome's expansionist and hegemonic project that, during the second century BC, made the Veneti *socii* or 'friend' populations to be gradually inserted in their own entity" (G. Fogolari). Indeed, the two important Paduan arteries, Postumia and Annia, were constructed only a few decades after the Via Flaminia, Rome-Rimini, begun in 187 BC, and therefore underline the vital importance the Upper Adriatic played from the very beginning of the Roman conquest of northern Italy and thus that of all of Europe. Located as they were on the eastern threshold and more threatened by the Empire, the Veneti were conscious of their position, which was both one of danger and one of privilege, and border populations are always particularly jealous of their independence and cultural identity. If Aquileia, the major Roman port on the Adriatic, Padua, and Verona were the major cities of the *Tenth Regime*, which extended from eastern Lombardy to Istria including all the Veneti territories, Altino was the most important Roman center at the lagoon border. It is documented from as early as 42 BC and described by Marziale as the emulation of Baia, in Campania, due to its magnificent villas. The city was located in a key position in the complex Roman road network, on the Via Annia, which practically connected Rimini and Padua to Aquileia, and was the point of departure of the Via Claudia Augusta which united Italy to the Danubian countries. Altino was to give life to Torcello in 638, at the time of the Longobard invasions and, thus, to Venice. In the years that followed the lagoon city became the natural heir to the port functions of both Aquileia and Ravenna, a clear demonstration that its history and geography have the long and cyclically constant time frames described by Braudel.

Portrait of an Old Man, 1st century AD, Altino, Archaeological Museum

Opposite page:
Funeral stele, 1st-2nd century AD, Torcello, Provincial Museum

The Stones of Altino in Torcello

In order to escape Longobard dominion, which had by now spread in a definite way all over the Veneto mainland, the bishop of Altino decided to move the seat of the cathedral to the island of Torcello in 638. This is how the first important lagoon center was born, built in large part with the Roman stones of Altino – bricks, columns, capitals, sculptures – the very same material that would also be used a second time when Venice, from the ninth century on, would take on full development. Thus Venice is the only city constructed by a population of Roman civilization: avoiding barbarian domination after the fall of the empire, it continued the tradition of antiquity without interruption under the Byzantine protective shield. Important evidence of this continuance is found in the museums of Altino and Torcello and in the Venice archaeological museum, and is scattered in many fragments in various buildings of the city.

Arch of St Heliodorus, Roman sarcophagus, 2nd-3rd century AD., Torcello, cathedral

Cylindrical altar from the age of Augustus, Torcello, Provincial Museum

Roman Sculpture in Torcello

The archaeological section of the Provincial Museum of Torcello was instituted in 1889 by Cesare Augusto Levi as the Estuary Museum. Though of different early-Veneto, Greek, Etruscan, and Roman origins, the works exhibited here – sculptures, ceramics, epigraphs – are in large part of local origin, that is, from Altino, or in any event were found in the estuary zone. Among the latter there is a beautiful cylindrical altar decorated by fine bas-reliefs, vine garlands, and sprigs that is from the Augustan age and was discovered in the sandbank known as Monte dei Conigli. Also noteworthy is the statue of *Asclepius with the Head of Serapis*, a Roman sculpture from the first century AD, which is a copy of a Greek work from the fourth century BC. The head of Serapis, the Egyptian god of the underworld who was widely worshipped in Rome, dates back to the second century AD. There are also numerous, small bronze sculptures from the early-Veneto (5th-3rd century BC) and Etruscan periods, as well as small statues from the Roman era (1st-3rd century AD), which reproduce different divinities. The *Sarcophagus of St Heliodorus*, the first bishop of Altino, now in the cathedral of Torcello to where it was relocated in 638, is also of Roman origin (2nd-3rd century AD).

Statue of Asclepius with the head of Serapis, 1st-2nd century AD, Torcello, Provincial Museum

27

Ancient Portraits in the Torcello Museum

The Torcello museum also conserves a significant series of
Roman funerary shrines, almost
all of which are from Altino
(1st-2nd century); even if these
sculptures are schematic they
are a fascinating testimony of
how widespread the art of portraiture was among the
Romans. A woman's head dated
towards the end of the first century is also from Altino and
demonstrates the incisive characterization typical of provincial art. Among the most interesting works at Torcello there is
also a veiled head of a woman,
a fragment of a Greek funerary
stele of fifth-fourth century BC
Attic production, which shows
the influence of Phidias.

Woman's Head, 1th century AD,
Torcello, Provincial Museum

Woman's Head, Greek art, 5th-
4th century BC, Torcello,
Provincial Museum

Ancient Fragments in the City

The most ancient stones in Venice are Roman and almost always came from Torcello even if they were originally from Altino. First and foremost are the "altinelle", the thin Roman bricks that can be still be found incorporated in city's most ancient buildings. More visible fragments of Roman tomb-stones reinforce the foundations of structures such as the San Vidal campanile or the house on the corner of the Fondamenta dei Preti in Santa Maria Formosa near the Calle del Paradiso. A more appropriate use of these Altino fragments was made for the church of San Donato in Murano, where two octagonal pilasters, attractively decorated with foliage, are found on the church facade; another pilaster forms the base of the holy water font. The architect of Palazzo Mastelli in Madonna dell'Orto (also known as 'del Cammello'), a late-Gothic building from the fifteenth century, inserted a Roman altar as a sustaining column of the corner window. The stone lions that guard the Arse-nale are of even more ancient origin, despite the fact that they were brought to Venice from Greece in the seventeenth century: the most ancient, on the right of the portal, dates back to the seventh century BC and comes from Delos (the head has been re-made); the others are Hellenistic works. Last but not least, the first well-curbs in Venice were simple pieces of Roman columns, hollowed out in the center, like that of the small square of Torcello which bears the furrows produced by the cords of the water pails.

Roman altar used as a sustaining column for a window of Palazzo Camello at Madonna dell'Orto

Roman memorial tablet incorporated into a building near Santa Maria Formosa

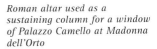

Greek lions in front of the entrance to the Arsenale

II. From the Fourth to the Twelfth Centuries: The Byzantine Matrix

The passage from imperial Roman to Byzantine administration occurred practically without solutions of continuity, so much so that the lagoon populations, like those of the Istrian and Dalmatian coasts, were the only ones in Europe that did not experience barbarian domination and, thus, the feudal system. In the words of Pertusi: "It is clear that, in the conservation of the Exarchate, the Veneti not only felt a restraint to the excessive might of the Longobards, who were uncomfortable neighbors, but also the protection of their incipient autonomy." The fall of Ravenna in 751 put Venice in a strategic position that became increasingly important for the Eastern Empire, and in the years that followed the Republic became its most faithful of ally in defending the imperial territories against Barbarian, Arab, and later Norman expansion.

Plutei, iconostasis of the cathedral of Torcello, detail

Over a span of more than eight centuries, Byzantium represented the continuity of the ancient Empire and provided the first model of Venice's civic and cultural life. Almost nothing remains in the lagoon of this period: only the basilicas of Ravenna testify to the splendor of this transition from antiquity to the Middle Ages. Indeed, Ravenna was the mother or, if the position of mother has to be left to Byzantium, the older sister of Venice.

Byzantine art represents the apex of early Christianity's artistic culture. The Church choose to ban every reference to the realism of late-classicism to create a new, non-referential art that was simpler, more didactic, and better adapted to divulging new beliefs in a world that was still continually immersed in a highly aesthetic civilization: the result, in the words of Gombrich, was "a curious amalgam of primitive and sophisticated methods".

Venice was an integral part of this world for centuries, until, beginning by at least the twelfth century, it began to open to the influence of the West. Nevertheless, as Otto Demus has rightfully observed, "the Byzantine always permeates like a perfume that penetrates everywhere, like a picturesque aroma that persists until the sixteenth century".

Opposite page:
The Tetrarchs and the Acritani Pilasters in front of Palazzo Ducale's Porta della Carta

The New Byzantium

The various works of art brought to Venice from Constantinople after the Fourth Crusade (1204) – the gilded bronze horses, the innumerable columns, and the icons meant to adorn the church of the Palazzo – were intended to make Venice into a new Byzantium, a real exhibition of imperial trophies especially on the facade towards the Piazzetta. They constitute a sculptural complex of exceptional importance in understanding the quality and meaning of the entire development of Byzantine art from the fourth century onward, even before the birth of the Venetian State. All of this was certainly a stimulus in emulating the ancient capital and also explains the artistic explosion of the thirteenth century. Yet, from what is know from that which remains, Byzantine works had arrived in Venice from the very beginning, reflecting the very quantity of what was being produced in the eastern metropolises. Even the architecture of the church of St Mark, begun in 1063, was derived directly from one of the major religious buildings in Constantinople, the church of the Twelve Apostles, erected in the sixth century during the reign of Justinian and destroyed after the Turkish conquest in 1453.

Tetrarchs in front of the Porta della Carta of Palazzo Ducale; 5th century

Trophies of the Conquest
5th-11th century
St Mark's Piazzetta

In the thirteenth century the imperial trophies brought to Venice after the conquest of Constantinople were displayed in St Mark's Piazzetta, between Palazzo Ducale's Porta della Carta and the southern entrance to the church, known as "the door to the sea" (walled in 1504 to make room for the Zen Chapel). These spoils were meant to signify that the lagoon city was by now the new Byzantium, the heir to the ancient empire.

Near the entrance of the Palazzo, we find, first and foremost, the red porphyry group of the *Tetrarchs* (the two emperors of the East and the West, and their designated successors). This fourth-century work is one of the first examples in which one can clearly note the Byzantine denial of classical realism to define a more essential, geometric, and symbolic art.
On the corner opposite the church, on the balustrade of the terrace, there was another imperial souvenir in the same style of a later date: the presumed portrait of Emperor Justinian Rino-

tometus II (d. 711), a seventh-century Syrian work now conserved in the Marciano Museum. The two so-called *Acritani Pilasters* (6th century), decorated with oriental motifs, point out the entrances to both the Palazzo and the Church, a route that was defined as a "Via Triumphalis". Finally near the Porta della Carta, on the wall of the Treasury, there is a picturesque collage of plutei (9-11th century) in which classical Byzantine art shows its propensity towards a decoration of great, exquisitely calligraphic, geometric purity.

Acritani Pilasters, detail, 6th century

Portrait of the Byzantine Emperor Justinian Rinotometus II, 8th century, St Mark's basilica

Byzantine plutei on the wall of the Treasury in front of the Porta della Carta, 9-11th century

Ivory Diptych
11th century
Archaeological Museum, room XI

This Byzantine work is part of a diptych (the other part is found in the Museum of Berlin) representing *St John Theologian* and *St Paul*. The minutely-finished, refined execution is particularly evident in the treatment of the drapery, a fundamental characteristic of all Byzantine reliefs. As Gombrich observed, it demonstrates "the way in which the folds are draped around the body and radiate around the shoulders and the knees, and the method of modelling the faces and the hands emphasizing the shadows", a quality that would have been impossible without the preceding conquests of Greek and Hellenistic art.

Ivory diptych, 11th century, Venice, Archaeological Museum

Virgin in Prayer, 11th century, church Santa Maria Mater Domini

Deesis, 10-11th century, St Mark's basilica

Deesis
10th-11th century
St Mark's Basilica, southern nave

This relief, representing *Christ between the Virgin and St John the Baptist*, is one of the most important works from Byzantium. It is notable not only for its excellent quality but also for the influence it had in training one of the major Venetian artists of the thirteenth century, the so-called Maestro of Hercules.

Virgin in Prayer
11th century, Church of Santa Maria Mater Domini

An elegant figure of the *Virgin in Prayer*, done in Constantinople, is silhouetted under an arch supported by slender, twisted, classicized columns. It constitutes the titular altarpiece of this very ancient church (10th century) and testifies to the great popularity of the marble icon in Venetian circles.

The Veneto-Byzantine Tradition

Over the course of the centuries, the cultural osmosis between Venice and Byzantium was such that the lagoon's artistic products, inspired by Byzantine prototypes and often real copies of them, were difficult to distinguish from those of metropolitan origin. It was not until the early-thirteenth century that Venetian art began to take on the characteristics that rendered it unmistakable.

Tomb of Doge Vitale Falier and His Wife Felicita Michiel
11th century
St Mark's Basilica, narthex

Only the doges that contributed to the construction or the completion of the Church or Palazzo had the honor of being buried in St Mark's. During Vitale Falier's reign (1084-96) the structure of the present-day basilica, begun by Domenico Contarini in 1063, was completed, and the tombs of he and his wife Felicita are found here. They constitute "a good example of Venetian imitations of Byzantine originals from the late-eleventh century", displaying a series of perforated screens, similar to those ornamenting the side portals of the church. In the words of Demus: "... [their] origin cannot be easily defined. In addition to undoubtedly Byzantine elements and pre-romanesque motifs, others are imported from the Islamic East or imitated from eastern models".

Tomb of Doge Vitale Falier, 11th century, St Mark's basilica,

35

Plutei

11th century, Cathedral
of Torcello

Originally intended for St Mark's, the beautiful plutei adorning the cathedral iconostasis are works by mid-eleventh century Venetian artists depicting peacocks drinking from a cantharus and lions leaning on a shaft decorated by lattice-work and leaves. They betray "certain iconographic incoherencies that reveal the Venetian tendency to derive compositional elements of the sacrophagus indiscriminately from ivories and other ancient handcrafts, reworking them according to Byzantinesque taste, infiltrated by a Venetian cursiveness which confers a pleasing sense of spontaneity and freshness and distinguishes these works from the rigorous and coherent refinement characterizing those of the metropolises" (Polacco).

Plutei, iconostasis of the cathedral of Torcello, 11th century

Patere and icons

The use of non-structural parietal decoration, which is not incorporated into the building's bearing elements, is typically Byzantine or in any event Oriental. Marble sheets, icons in very flat bas-reliefs, and especially patere – medallions in stone adorned by zoomorphic bas-reliefs, decorated by volutes, or realized in rare colored marbles – came to be widely used in Venice to embellish religious structures as well as the facades of palazzi and minor buildings.

One of the most interesting examples of this type of decoration is the twelfth-century tondo in Campiello Angaran, near the church of San Pantalon, which represents a Byzantine emperor in complete regulation attire. The first floor window of Ca' Da Mosto on the Grand Canal near Rialto conserves an uninterrupted series of patere, cornices, and marble facings done in a typical Veneto-Byzantine style (13th century). Other examples of this type of decoration are still numerous today, as can be seen on the facade of Palazzo Falier at Santi Apostoli.

Ca' da Mosto on the Grand Canal, 13th century

Patera of Palazzo Falier in Santi Apostoli, 13th century

Byzantine Emperor, 12th century, Campiello Angaran

Columns
c. 1172, St Mark's Piazzetta

The columns of the Piazzetta were erected around 1172, under the rule of Sebastiano Ziani (1172-78). Ziani was the doge who, among other things, decided to widen St Mark's Square into its present-day form and who, in the political sphere, operated as the mediator for the meeting between Pope Alexander III and Emperor Barbarossa (Peace of Venice, 1177), bringing the Republic to the rank of a European power. These two great monolithic shafts of eastern granite are crowned by Veneto-Byzantine style capitals and bear at their summit the images of *St Mark's Lion* and *St Theodore*, the city's first protector saint. They are composite works that show the open-minded eclecticism of the Venetians' use and revival of very different materials.

According to the most recent attributions, the bronze lion is a griffin-lion of early-eastern Hellenism realized by a Greek artist between the late-fourth and early-third century BC. The figure of St Theodore (placed on the column in 1329) is composed of a skillful re-use of a Roman bust from the time of Hadrian, to which the arts and the dragon were added at a later date.

From an art-historical point of view, the most interesting elements are the figures of the trades placed at the four corners

of the bases of each column. Going from north to south on the column of the "Todaro" one encounters blacksmiths, fish-mongers, basket weavers, and wine-sellers; on that of "Mark" there are fruit and vegetable vendors, butchers, meat sellers, and some unrecognizable figures. The theme of the trades would be taken up again, twice, in decorating the buildings of the square (on the central arch of the church and on the capitals of Palazzo Ducale). It is evident that Venice intended to honor its merchants, especially here, near the Piazzetta towards to mole, where for centuries the public market had been held. These figures are works of considerable artistic value and constitute the first expression of romanesque sculpture in the round in Venice: "today, the deplorable state of conservation of these works makes it difficult for us to appreciate their impressive plastic, free, and already developed sensitivity, united with a severe discipline that conserves intact the original surface of the stone block from which the groups were sculpted with a minimum of waste" (Demus).

These two majestic monoliths, erected by Nicolò Barettieri (the builder of the wooden first bridge at Rialto) are an evident imitation of the columns and obelisks that adorned the squares of Rome and Constantinople. They form a monumental entrance portal to the city, a real "door to the sea".

Columns of St Mark and St Todaro, c. 1172, St Mark's Piazzetta

III. The Thirteenth Century: A Venetian Art

The thirteenth century marks the apogee of Venice as a sea-faring Republic: the free Commune, the small city-state of merchants and navigators, became the main commercial fulcrum of the Mediterranean. After the Conquest of Constantinople in 1204, the dominion of this imperial capital extended uninterrupted from the Adriatic to the banks of the Bosporus. While the islands of Dalmatia and Greece constituted, in Braudel's fine image, "the immobile Venetian float", its traffic ranged over a much wider scale, from northern Europe (the Fondaco del Tedeschi dated from 1228) to eastern Asia (the first Polo trip to China began in 1261). This is the moment when Venice became "a truly universal economic center". While Byzantium remained the first model of its artistic life, the France of St Louis furnished

St Mark's basilica

Venice with both language (Franco-Veneto took the place of clerical Latin in the most well-known chronicles, like that of Antonio da Canal or Marco Polo) and the most refined examples of classical Gothic, the art of the new urban European civilization. In the meantime the city defined its identity in its magnificent urban spaces – Doge Ziani's St Mark's Square – and in the light and airy elegance of Veneto-Byzantine architecture. The sculptors, who gave the final decorative touch to the ducal basilica in a style that was much freer and more open-minded than that of the mosaic artists who had covered the church vaults and domes with gold for more than a century, created an incomparable ensemble in European art of this splendid epoch.

The sculptures of this period are largely destined to adorn the facades of the church of St Mark, which was renovated to render it more worthy of its new function as the chapel of an "imperial" palazzo. The artists of the thirteenth century began from the most varied solicitations of European art, from the Emilian-Lombard Romanesque to the French Gothic, from the Byzantine to late Classicism, incorporating both Islamic and Oriental elements, therein creating an art that, finally for the first time in its history, became strictly Venetian.

Opposite page:
St Mark's Horses, detail,
4-5th century BC

A Return to the Origins: The Proto-Renaissance

The renovation of the facade of St Mark's with the spoils from Constantinople gave the basilica a completely new appearance: "The three facades, with their two floors of columns, are typical works of the Venetian proto-Renaissance, comparable to the facades of Pisa and Lucca. Behind the precious exteriors of the architectural structures the forms of the eleventh century as well as those the early-thirteenth century Gothic disappeared" (Demus).

This return to antiquity had great symbolic significance for Venice: the Republic had to appear to be the legitimate heir of the early-Christian Empire (remember that, according to tradition, the city was founded in the year 420, that is, before the fall of the Empire). The columns of the ciborium are the most spectacular example of this return to the origins, which evidently took its inspiration not only from early-Christian and early-Byzantine art but also from works of classical antiquity available on site. This operation ended in 1300 with the installation of the bronze doors done by Maestro Bertuccio in Augustan style.

The exterior doors of St Mark's in bronze by Maestro Bertuccio, c. 1300

Architrave of the Porta di Sant'Alipio, St Mark's basilica, 13th century

The Horses of St Mark's

The Horses of St Mark's constitute one of the most splendid testimonies of bronze sculpture that has been handed down from antiquity, comparable in some way to Riace's well-known bronzes to which they may be contemporary. These four gilded bronze horses are slightly larger than life; the refinement of their technique and the extraordinary energy they emanate belong without a doubt to Greek art, independent of the date of their craft which remains a mystery (oscillating between the 5th-4th century BC to the 2nd-3rd century AD). A recent study by Vittorio Galliazzo proposes a fairly convincing thesis that dates the horses between the late-fourth and early-third century BC: accordingly they would belong to the school of Lysippus, the great Greek bronze artist who even worked in the court of Alexander the Great. The Marciana quadriga would be similar to that dedicated to the Sun God, or Apollo, in the famous monument in Rhodes. It would have reached Constantinople, according to two Byzantine sources, from the island of Chios, around the time of Emperor Theodosius II in the fifth century. According to other scholars, the quadriga would have been brought from Greece to Rome to decorate a triumphal arch of an emperor (probably Nero) before reaching Constantinople. From Constantinople, where it adorned the entrance to the Hippodrome, it was finally moved to Venice with the booty from the Fourth Crusade (1204) and placed above the main arch of the basilica as a symbol of triumph. Various artists, from as early as the beginning of the Renaissance – from Donatello to Verrocchio to Il Riccio – looked to these bronze horses as precious models of ancient art. In a well-known "capriccio" by Canaletto, where they are depicted high upon plinths in the center of the Piazzetta, they are interpreted as a symbol of classical or rather neo-classical perfection. Copies of the original works are now placed on the church facade, the originals are rightfully preserved in the Marciano Museum.

St Mark's Horses,
5-4th century BC

43

Ciborium Columns
5th and 13th century
St Mark's Basilica, presbytery

The Sacrifice of Isaac
13th century, St Mark's Basilica, northern facade

Traditio Legis
13th century , St Mark's Basilica, Treasury chapel

The four oriental alabaster columns of the ciborium in St Mark's illustrate the *Lifes of the Virgin and Christ* in early-Byzantine style. Criticism does not agree on the date of their origin: perhaps the fifth century, that is, of Byzantine origin, or perhaps the thirteenth, that is, a Venetian work inspired by early-Christian models. According to Demus they are probably, at least in part, fifth-century sculptures that were later re-worked by Venetian artists. A similar problem arises for the bas-reliefs on the architrave of the door of Sant'Alipio (*Christ and the Apostles,* the *Call of the Shepherds,* and the *Adoration of the Magi*); this door was the traditional entrance to the church for important holiday processions. In both cases these sculptures are positioned in particularly significant positions in the building.

The figures of this sculpture "bring us marvelously into a captured Renaissance climate, here one can no longer speak of Romanesque, Byzantine, or Gothic art ... The romanesque elements of the Italic background, reworked and inspired by the elevated lessons of France and the harmony of the early-Christian maestros, lead to the incomparable results of this relief" (Muraro). Placed side by side, the *Sacrifice of Isaac* and the *Ascent of Alexander to Heaven* (by harnessing two griffins to a chariot) (10th c.) probably form an ensemble meant to symbolize the resignation to divine will and pride.

A thirteenth century work of "rare quality" (Demus) this piece is of early-Christian inspiration or, in any event, a Byzantine work once again completely re-done by Venetian artists. It represents *St Mark* (or *St Paul*) *Presenting the Gospel to Christ,* and probably once adorned the high altar of the church. The same thing can be said for the bas-relief above, which represents *Christ in the Act of Benediction Sustained by Angels.*

Sacrifice of Isaac, 13th century, St Mark's basilica, northern facade

Traditio Legis, chapel of the Treasury, St Mark's basilica, 12th century

Left:
Columns of the ciborium at St Mark's, detail, 13th century

Temptations of the East: The Maestro of Hercules

The main facade of St Mark's is perhaps the most complete and coherent iconographic program inspired by the traditions of the great French cathedrals, the likes of which were never realized in Italy. It is an original blend of mosaic and sculptural styles and techniques, which begin from the central portal and extend to the four side entrances including the six icons between the large arches. The craftsman of the side doors, the so-called Maestro of Hercules, created this masterpiece in Byzantinesque reliefs on a gold background. It is a very refined synthesis of varied solicitations, in which the East's desire for purely abstract, decorative art, of Byzantine or Moresque origin, was fused with exquisite elegance anticipating the supple arabesques of the International Gothic or the linear purity of the *fin de siècle* of the Viennese Sezession, inspired by Byzantine art.

First side entrance of the left, detail, St Mark's, 13th century

Icons
c. 1230-50, St Mark's Basilica, main facade

The marble icons placed between the large arches of the entrance portals in pairs (*Stories of Hercules* at the extremities, the *Virgin* and the *Nuptial Angel*, *St George* and *St Demetrius*, respectively to the left and right of the main entrance) have an important symbolic significance. They represent the origins of the city, which legend tells us was founded on the day of the Annunciation, the 25th of March, and the city's protectors (*Hercules and the Warrior Saints*). Two of these reliefs are outstanding Byzantine works (part of the booty from Constantinople): *Hercules and the Erymanthian Boar* (northern corner) is from the fifth century; *St Demetrius* from the eleventh. The other four reliefs are thirteenth-century Venetian works that are the so-called Maestro of Hercules' first important attempt to interpret, if not actually copy, works of direct Greek importation to complete the facade's decorative ensemble.

*From above left:
Hercules and the Erymanthian Boar, 5th century; Hercules and the Hydra, 13th century; St Demetrius, 11th century; Virgin, 13th century; Archangel Gabriel, 13th century; St George, 13th century*

Door of Sant'Alipio

c. 1250, St Mark's Basilica, western facade

The door of Sant'Alipio was the official ceremonial entrance to St Mark's. It is the only one of the four side doors that has remained intact over time; the other three were modified at a later date. Partially figurative and partially ornamental, the reliefs that form the decoration of these entrance ways constitute the second cycle of works by Maestro of Hercules, completed after the icons of the facade. They are by far his masterpiece, no longer an imitation but rather an original work, a combination of very flat bas-reliefs on a background of golden tessurae, which produce "the effect of embroidery on golden brocade". The entire four door complex, both the volutes that border the Moresque arch and the marble lattice, and bas-reliefs of the tympanum are done with same refined techni-cal expertise. Here "we see expressed all the decorative elements that were available to the Venetians: the early-Christian reliefs, the Islamic railing, *à jour* plastic art, and mosaics create an ensemble of a very elevated decorative grace" (Demus). The only original mosaic fragment of the facade that remains is conserved in the calotte of the portal of Sant'Alipio; it represents the *Traslazione of the Body of St Mark into the Church* (c. 1260).

Second side entrance on the right, detail, 13th century, St Mark's basilica

Door of Sant'Alipio, detail, 13th century, St Mark's basilica

Icons
c. 1250, St Mark's Basilica, northern facade

The northern facade has undergone substantial modification over the course of time and, as a result, is less coherent from an iconographic point of view. Here we find a series of five icons, *Christ* and the *Four Evangelists*, placed on the western exterior wall of the Mascoli chapel, near the Porta dei Fiori,

and above the door itself. Originally, these marble icons probably decorated the ancient iconostasis (remade in the late-fourteenth century by the Dalle Masegne). The icons are among the best works done by the Maestro of Hercules and his studio. They interpret Greek classical style derived from ivories or bas-reliefs such as the *Deesis* with great confidence, adapting it to a new more fluid and rhythmic style, so much so that they

can be considered "the most solemn realization of the Byzantinesque trend" (Cocchetti-Pratesi). This is how the marble icon of the altar was created. It was used in Venice until the fourteenth century.
A similar type of relief, also done by the Maestro of Hercules or the assistants of his studio, is found in the Porta dei Fiori on the northern facade. The final result obtained here is less homogeneous.

Porta dei Fiori, 13th century, St Mark's basilica, northern facade

Icons on the exterior of the chapel of the Mascoli, 13th century, St Mark's basilica, northern facade

Influences of the West: The Maestro of the Trades

The six bands of bas-reliefs on the three arches of the main entrance to St Mark's are surmounted by the golden quadriga, the triumphant symbol of the State. They constitute the most significant work of the facade both from an artistic and from an iconographic point of view. This cycle, done or in any event managed by one artist, the Maestro of the Trades, constitutes the masterpiece of the romanesque trend, which merges here with elements of French classical Gothic. This tendency of Emilian provenience, present in Venice from the preceding century onward (the columns on the Piazzetta), is expressed in various works for St Mark's before reaching its full maturity in the large church portal where we find the *speculum mundi*. This description of the medieval universe concludes with an extremely precise and realistic representation of the Venetian trades seen "as ideal models of bourgeois behavior" (Demus).

Three large arches of the main entrance to St Mark's

49

St Mark's Dream
c. 1250, St Mark's Basilica, central portal

Another important sculpture, which seems to have been done by the same artist as that of the *Adoration of the Magi*, adorns the central entrance portal of St Mark's. It is found in the exact center of the facade, in remembrance of the realization of the angel's prophecy to the evangelist (the angel appeared to St Mark in dream while he was in an island of the estuary announcing that his remains would find their rest with the Venetian people – "Pax Tibi, Marcel").

Angel with trumpet under the main dome of St Mark's, c. 1230-40

St Mark's Dream, c. 1250 central entrance portal, St Mark's

Angels
1225-40, St Mark's Basilica, dome piers

The four *Angels* that are found in the corners of the piers that sustain the central dome of St Mark's basilica belong to the romanesque tradition and were done by an artist whose "cre-ative capacity and elegance was not much inferior to that of Antelami, and who was also more modern" (Demus). The beautiful *Censor Angel* lecturn-holder placed in the double ambo to the left of the iconostasis belongs to this group of sculptures.

Adoration of the Magi
c. 1250, Seminary Museum

These thirteenth century sculptures of Antelami's school, originally from the church of Santi Filippo e Giacomo, constitute one of the first in the round works done in Venice. Though the group is incomplete, it is of rare monumentality: only St Joseph and one of the Three Wise Men appear at the sides of the Virgin. This sculpture had to have appeared truly new in this city, where until that moment stone had been worked in a very particular way to create the very flat bas-reliefs derived from Byzantine tradition. Other works from the same era worked in a similar style include the lions and the beautiful figures of the *Prophets* found on the calotte of the Zen chapel, which at one time probably adorned the "door to the sea" that was later closed to construct the chapel.

Funeral Lion, c. 1240-50, St Mark's basilica, Zen chapel

Adoration of the Magi, c. 1250, Venice, Seminary Museum

Central Portal
c. 1230-1270, St Mark's Basilica

The six cycles of reliefs that adorn the three large concentric arches of the main entrance portal of St Mark's make up the most important ensemble of sculpture done in Venice in the thirteenth century or more precisely between c.1230 and 1270; the overall ensemble is comparable to that of Palazzo Ducale from the fourteenth century. The mosaic of the *Last Judgement* is also a part of this complex, but was completely redone in the nineteenth century (Gentile Bellini's famous canvas now in the Accademia testifies to the original). The *Last Judgement* is found between the second and the third arches and is based on an iconographic system derived from the French cathedrals, interpreted in a completely new way.

These reliefs develop themes that go from a general to an increasingly precise description of medieval life, based on those "artisanal and commercial activities capable of promoting the prosperity on which the Venetian state was based" (Polacco). Beginning with the innermost arch or underside of the first arch, we find scenes of animal fighting and fables meant to symbolize savage life; on the outer fascia, wrestling and hunting scenes, intended to compare civilized and wild life, good and evil. On the underside of the second arch we find the *Months of the Year* and the *Zodiac signs*, or the correspondence between heavenly and earthly activities; on the second outer fascia, the *Virtues* and *Beatudines*, or the ethical and religious principles that should inspire human life. Above the mosaic, the underside of the third arch presents an extraordinary celebration of the Venetian *Trades* that is "the most complete and realistic representation of daily life in medieval sculpture" (Demus): beginning on the left there are shipbuilders, wine-sellers, bakers, butchers, milkmen, brick-

layers, shoemakers, barbers, shopkeepers, carpenters, sawyers, blacksmiths and fishermen. The cycle concludes with the third outer fascia where we find, between vines and volutes, the figures of the *Prophets* and at the top the *Christ Blessing.* Various sculptors collaborated on this work, which took inspiration from both the romanesque of Antelamic origins and the French Gothic (Chartres), though elements of Byzantine taste still remain. Nonetheless, the presence of a great artistic 'director' is clear; beginning from the underside of the innermost and oldest arch he went on to express himself, especially in the later works,

with great liberty and absolute mastery of his means. By the third cycle, that of the *Months*, one already notes a skilful accuracy and liveliness in the gestures and drapery of the various figures that takes on, in the successive allegories of the *Virtues*, a clearly French elegance, reaching, finally, in the second to last fascia of the *Trades*, where the artist, called in fact the Maestro of the Trades, achieves a plastic art "animated by a realistic sense that fully grasps the vitality of daily work". Thus, with this work, it is possible to say that Venetian sculpture "imposed itself in the role of protagonist on the Italian artistic panorama" (Polacco).

Demus further notes how "especially the young faces show an intensely Roman typology making it is necessary to think that this artist had known and studied ancient portraiture, presumably from funerary stelai". Finally, in the arch of the *Prophets*, the artist reaches a level of such simplicity and grandeur or, in other words, classicism, that he must be placed alongside his great contemporaries, Nicola and Giovanni Pisano.

Details of the arches of the central portal of St Mark's, 13th century: animals fighting, men wrestling, hunting scenes, the months and Zodiac signs, the Virtues, and the Trades

Palazzo Cammello and Campo dei Mori
13th-century sculptures

The figures in Eastern attire found in Campo dei Mori in Cannaregio are curiously monumental, between the grotesque and the *naïf*, and were probably done in the late-thirteenth century. According to tradition they represent the Mastelli brothers, who belonged to a rich family of Levantine or Arab merchants. The Mastelli family owned the palazzo on Rio Madonna dell'Orto, behind the corner of the square, bearing their name but commonly known as "del Cammello". Indeed the facade of the building hosts a bas-relief depicting a camel. The corner window of this late-Gothic palazzo incorporates the Roman altar mentioned in chapter one.

Figures of Moors in Campo dei Mori, late-13th century

Bas-relief on the facade of Palazzo Cammello representing a camel

*Figures of Moors in
Campo dei Mori,
late-13th century*

IV. The Fourteenth Century: The Gothic City

The fourteenth century was both splendid and tenebrous. It was a century tormented by wars, conspiracies, and profound political changes. The lock out of the Great Council (1297) transformed Venice into a aristocratic republic or, as has been said, a collective *signoria*, and was followed by the conspiracies of Bajamonte Tiepolo (1310) and Marin Faliero (1355). Meanwhile the 100-year with Genoa raged on throughout the century devouring the Republic's energies and wealth until 1380. The demographic explosion of the city – which reached 150,000 inhabitants and became one of the great metropolises of the era – was contrasted by one of the most terrible plagues in history (1348).

P. and J. Dalle Masegne,
*Iconostasis of St Mark's, detail,
1394-97*

It was a contradictory, conservative, and aggressive century that, in artistic terms, represented a moment of ebb and flow and of extraordinary invention. The painters of the lagoon completely ignored what Giotto, Tommaso da Modena, and Altichiero were doing in the nearby areas between Padua and Treviso and continued to distill a completely Byzantine art that seemed to take inspiration from the sparkling splendors of the Pala d'Oro. Stonecutters, architects, and sculptors began to overlay decorative volutes on the simple, airy Veneto-Byzantine structures, almost in the style of art nouveau. Venetian buildings seemed "to emulate the vibrant lightness of the rush" (Coletti), and the city took on the Gothic appearance that still characterizes it today. The fourteenth century produced at least one absolute masterpiece in the history of European art: Palazzo Ducale. Still another surprising fact of this contradictory century was that the work of the important studios of Venetian sculptors, that of Andriolo De Santi and that of the Dalle Masegne, was scattered between the Veneto and Emilia, leaving very little in Venice.

Opposite page:
*Filippo Calendario (?),
Drunkenness of Noah, detail,
1341-48. Corner of Palazzo
Ducale near the bridge of the
Paglia*

57

A New Start: The First Portraits

Once the construction of St Mark's was completed between the late-thirteenth and early-fourteenth century, there was a period of stasis in Venetian artistic activity. Yet from the 1320s onward a new phenomenon took hold in Venice and especially in other centers of the Veneto, granting a completely new start in the field of funeral monuments and, in particular, in that of portraits. The portraits of *Bishop Salomone* (1322) in Treviso, *Enrico Scrovegni* in Padua, and *Rizzardo IV da Camino* in Serravalle of Vittorio Veneto, as well as those by unknown artists which seem to come from one of the Venetian studios such as that of the De Santi, are excellent works unparalleled in Europe. "It is unique," wrote Wolfgang Wolters, "that these masterpieces of portraiture (Burckhardt defined the portrait of Enrico Scrovegni as one of the first works that, since the decadence of Roman art, was worthy of being defined a portrait complete in itself) have rarely been considered. Nonetheless we search in vane among the contemporary Roman or Tuscan sculptors for such an intense rendering of the particular features of a face, a gift that seems to be typically Venetian." This tendency is reflected in the Venetian church of San Simeon Grande, which seems to be referable to De Santi's studio, one the most important Venetian sculpture workshops active towards the mid-fourteenth century particularly in Vicenza and Padua.

Icon of San Donato
1310, Cathedral of San Donato, Murano

This wooden icon done in painted relief is the only one of its kind in Venice in its blend of sculpture and painting. The sculpture represents the name saint of the church flanked by portraits of the donors, the Podestà of Murano Donato Memo and his wife. The saint is portrayed under an arcade with the pastoral and a book; the mantle, which forms a series of stylized pleats, shows the persistence of Byzantine schemes even in this fourteenth-century altarpiece. Pallucchini attributed the pictorial work to Paolo Veneziano, as his first known work. This high relief is particularly interesting in that it is still completely polychrome, as was all of the stone sculpture of that period.

Icon of San Donato, 1310, Murano, cathedral

58

St John the Evangelist Worshipped by Bartolomeo Ravachaudo
1334, Church of San Simeon Grande

The most interesting aspect of this considerably damaged relief is undoubtedly the vigorous portrait of its donor, Ravachaudo, who was one of the commissioners of the *Tomb of St Simeon*. This relief is one of the first, if not the first, portraits in the history of Venetian sculpture and is a remarkable example of the Veneto tradition of which we have spoken.

St John the Evangelist Worshipped by Bartolomeo Ravachaudo, detail, 1334, church of San Simeon Grande

Tomb of St Simeon Prophet
c. 1318, Church of San Simeon Grande

The figure of the partially-mutilated saint laid out on the sarcophagus (the feet are missing) constitutes an unprecedented work in Venice; it is signed by "Marcus Romanus" (as can be seen on the memorial tablet), an artist who evidently came from Rome and whose work revealed the influence of Giovanni Pisano. The tomb is of high quality, as can be seen from the knowledgeable treatment of the drapery and, especially, the face and the curls of hair and beard that flow freely over the forehead and around the chin. The saint's reliquaries were brought to this ancient tenth-century church dedicated to St Simeon the Prophet (named San Simeon Grande to differentiate it from the nearby San Simeon Apostolo) from Constantinople after the Fourth Crusade. This explains the exceptional nature of committee appointed to oversee the erection of the saint's tomb: it was formed by the bishops of Castello, Caorle, Torcello, and Jesolo, as well as the parish priest Bartolomeo Ravachaudo, and demonstrated, among other things, an exceptional acumen in its choice of artist.

St Simeon the Prophet, c. 1318, church of San Simeon Grande

Filippo Calendario

Some sixteenth-century chronicles report the name of Filippo Calendario as the creator of Palazzo Ducale; yet in the rare fourteenth-century documentation Calendario is cited only as a stone supplier to Baseggio (who was then the Palazzo's *protomagister* or overseer) and, in 1355, as a participant in the conspiracy of Doge Marin Faliero, for which he was condemned to death the same year. In his recent *Guide to the Museo dell'Opera at Palazzo Ducale,* Antonio Manno states: "It is only in the past two decades that historians have once again brought into the limelight an individual of whom, among other things, there does not exist a single certified work. In the lack of anything else and in virtue of the testimonies attested during the Renaissance, Calendario has become a sort of conventional name used to indicate the most capable and refined sculptor who worked on the new project for the Palazzo. He is responsible for the four capitals of the arcade (three of which are conserved in the Palazzo's museum); for the statues of the two corner groups exposed to the south, towards the Quay; and for the bas-relief depicting *Venice Personified,* visible in one of the openings of the western portico towards the Piazzetta."

Filippo Calendario (?),
Drunkenness of Noah, 1341-48

The Palazzo was erected to house the Hall of Great Council; construction began in 1341 and was completed to roof height in 1348. It is an unprecedented building that constitutes "the most admirable, sure, and ingenious structure of the civic Venetian Gothic, conceived of by one creative mind alone" (Arslan). The sculptural apparatus that adorns it is exceptional, especially for a public building.

The symbolic meaning of Palazzo Ducale is evident: in an era in which the most important Italian cities we becoming *Signorie,* the city's major building was the seat of the parliament, the real center of political power. The building itself is an enormous cubic structure that contains the hall for the more than one thousand members of the Parliament on the second floor; this hall is sustained by a double series of overlapping columns, those of the ground floor portico and those of the first floor loggia. The columns that sustain the upper part terminate in a trilobated opening giving the structure the appearance of gliding in empty space. The polychrome facing, in lozenges of white and pink marble (upper part), fringed above by slender crenellation of Moresque inspiration, furthers the sensation of lightness in the entire structure. Groups of natural height figures clamber up the corners: *Adam and Eve* and the *Drunkenness of Noah,* at the level of the portico, and two *Archangels,* on the loggia. Once the works for Palazzo Ducale were completed, there was a period of stasis that protracted through the latter half of the century until the studio of the Dalle Masegne began operating in Venice.

Corner Group
1341-48, Palazzo Ducale

On the southeastern corner of the Palazzo, near the bridge of the Paglia, facing the entrance of the port, one finds the group representing the *Drunkenness of Noah* and, on the floor above, that of the *Archangel Raphael*, protector of the weak and of travellers. This sculptural complex can be seen as a symbol of human fragility and tolerance. The old Noah appears to stagger under the trunk of a vine, his two sons at his side: Cam, who has discovered his father naked and drunk, has an gesture of

disapproval and contempt; the other son, who holds a cloth to hide the nudity of the old man, imposes silence on his brother; the third son looks upon the scene with surprise from the other side of the arch. On the opposite corner towards the Piazzetta and the columns, which was also the site of capital executions, there is another marble group representing *Adam and Eve* and, higher up, *Michael*, the archangel of the Last Judgement, representing sin and punishment. Here the action is expressed through clear gestuality: the couple is represented under a fig tree,

from one side, Eve, observed by the serpent, points out her companion with her finger; on the other Adam, who is gathering the fruit, makes a gesture of hesitation with his other hand. As in the case of Noah, the two nudes are represented with considerable realism, demonstrating the sculptor's mastery of anatomical rendering.

Filippo Calendario (?), Adam and Eve, 1341-48

Filippo Calendario (?), Venice as Justice, c. 1350

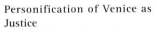

Personification of Venice as Justice
c. 1350, Palazzo Ducale, facade towards the Piazzetta

A majestic representation of *Venice* who for the first time in sculpture takes on the form of Justice: a tondo with the feminine figure who holds the sword in her right hand and is seated between two lions. The following is written on the background is written: "Venecia" and "Fortis Iusta Trono Furias Mare Sub Pede Pono". At the feet of *Venice* there is a portrayal of two "furies" or vices, probably *Wrath* and *Pride*, and a stylization of the waves of the sea, the city as the seat of good government and ruler of the sea.

Capitals
1341-48, Palazzo Ducale

The column capitals Palazzo Ducale's arcade (of which 24 out of 36 belong to the original building, now partially substituted by excellent nineteenth-century copies) were sculpted when the building was constructed – one of them bears the date 1344 – and show the styles of various artists. The most refined have to be the work of Calendario, in particular, starting from the corner near the bridge of the Paglia, the third, representing the *Family of the Crusade*, the sixth, a *Woman's Head*, the eighteenth, on the corner near the Piazzetta, the *Creation of Adam* and the *Planets and Signs of the Zodiac*. The twenty-fourth, which is perhaps the most well-known and the last of the series before the building's extension towards the Piazzetta in 1424, is the so-called *Love* capital that narrates the story of a young couple in eight episodes from their courtship to the birth of a child.

The themes of the other capitals are also varied: the *Emperors* (5); the *Virtues and Vices* (12); the *Human Race* (16); the *Philosophers* (17), bearing the date of 1344; the *Trades* (21), the *Nations* (22), *Animals*, *Birds*, etc. After the Palazzo's extension along the Piazzetta in the following century another twelve capitals were sculpted to imitate those of the preceding years. All in all the grandeur and quality of this complex is unique among the Italian municipal buildings of this epoch.

Filippo Calendario (?), the Capital of Love, 1341-48, and the corner capital with the birth of Adam and the Zodiac signs, Palazzo Ducale

Tomb of Doge Marco Corner
1368, Church of Santi Giovanni e Paolo, presbytery

The tomb of this doge is composed of two parts: the coffin of the deceased, a modest work by a Venetian artist, and the statue of the *Virgin with Two Saints and the Angels* at the sides, placed inside a Gothic frame in the upper part. From what has been written this series of sculptures appears to come from the workshop of Nino Pisano; thus the particularly elegant and sinuous figure of the *Virgin* could be one of the last works of this Tuscan maestro, who died in 1368. According to Gnudi it is possible that one of the Dalle Masegne collaborated of the figures of the deacon angels.

Tomb of Doge Marco Corner, 1368, church of Santi Giovanni e Paolo, detail.
Above right: *Virgin attributed to Nino Pisano*

Tomb of Doge Michele Morosini
c. 1382, Church of Santi Giovanni e Paolo, presbytery

This particularly magnificent funeral monument was the collaborative effort of sculptors, painters, and mosaic artists. The figures of the doge and the deacons on the side are refinely done, whereas a less expert hand was responsible for the sculptures in the side pillar niches. The mosaic found between the pillars and the arch, done in very minute tesserae, presents the portraits of the doge and his wife at the sides of Christ on the cross. It is a fine work that unites Venetian characteristics with Tuscan influences. The underside of the arch of the baldachin is decorated with stars in relief, and as Wolters observed: "A few years later, under the rule of Doge Michele Steno, the ceiling (the 'sky') of the Hall of the Great Council in Palazzo Ducale was decorated with stars carved in wood." A recent restoration (1996) brought to light the original polychrome of the stone apparatus and a splendid sinopite, probably done by Altichiero from Padua.

Tomb of Doge Michele Morosini, 1382, church of Santi Giovanni e Paolo, presbytery

The Workshop of the Dalle Masegne

The studio of the brothers Pierpaolo and Jacobello Dalle Masegne was the most important workshop that operated in Venice between 1380 and the early-fifteenth century. This studio was also very active outside Venice, especially in Bologna and in Mantua, with a production of unequalled quality and numerous collaborators. Experts find it difficult to distinguish between the style of the two brothers, who almost always signed their works together and who seemed to have been influenced by both the Tuscan sculpture of Nino Pisano and that of the Lombard school. Their two projects in Venice were done for major city buildings: the iconostasis for St Mark's and the balcony towards the basin for Palazzo Ducale.

Tomb of Jacopo Cavalli
1385, Church of Santi Giovanni e Paolo

Jacopo Cavalli (d. 1385) was a "ground commander" of the Republic and rose to the rank of nobility for his service during the war of Chioggia against the Genovese. He is remembered by this beautiful monument attributed to Paolo di Jacobello, who is held to be the son of Jacobello Dalle Masegne. "The semi-hidden face of the deceased," writes Wolters; "recedes into the background, behind this martial pomp, while the two 'lions', constrained to the ground by the weight of his head and helmut, further accent the warrior aspect of the ensem- ble; we seem to see not only the tomb of the deceased but rather the celebration of a trade." The polychrome is still well con- served and makes the precious quality of the reliefs stand out.

Tomb of Jacopo Cavalli, 1385, church of Santi Giovanni e Paolo; above: *detail*

Portrait of Doge Antonio Venier
1380-90, Correr Museum

Doge Antonio Venier (1382-1400), under whose rule the Dalle Masegne began work on the Palazzo balcony, is represented kneeling and, originally, was to have been holding a banner in his hands, in keeping with the tradition of official portrait which saw the doge kneeling in front of St Mark, symbol of the State. It is a small but well modelled sculpture that is attributed to Jacobello and probably once adorned the interior doorway to the Palazzo.

P. and J. Dalle Masegne Iconostasis of St Mark's
1394-97

The iconostasis of the presbytery of St Mark's is the only work in Venice signed and dated (1394) by Pierpaolo and Jacobello Dalle Masegne. (The two side iconostasis in the chapels of St Peter and St Clement - the latter dated 1397 - are also attributed to Dalle Masegne brothers).
The iconographic system – the statues of the twelve *Apostles*, the *Virgin* and *St Mark* with the *Redeemer* in the center – appears to have been inspired by the ancient eighth-century choir screen of St Peter's in Rome. This important sculptural complex, which recalls the studio's masterpiece in Bologna, the icon of the church of San Francesco (1388), shows a more northern style than the preceding works and must have been done by Jacobello, even if he received ample assistance from his collaborators.

Pierpaolo and Jacobello Dalle Masegne, Iconostasis in St Mark's 1394-97

Portrait of Doge Antonio Venier, 1380-90, Correr Museum

P. and J. Dalle Masegne
Balcony of Palazzo Ducale
1400-05

Doge Antonio Venier commissioned Pierpaolo Dalle Masegne to do the large balcony of the Hall of the Great Council in 1400, at the time of the building's completion by Calendario. Originally, it was a fourteen sculptural complex that, iconographically speaking, echoed the church facade and anticipated the Porta della Carta, which would be started a few decades later by Bartolomeo Bon. On the sides at the height of the balcony there are two statues of the warrior saints, *St Theodore* and *St George*; in the upper part, around the central tondo (now occupied by a sixteenth-century statue of *Charity*) are the six virtues. The portrait of the *Doge Kneeling before the Lion of St Mark* was once once found above the tondo; it was destroyed after the fall of the Republic. The niches of the central fastigium still contain the figures of *St Peter, St Mark,* and *St Paul.* Finally, at the top, one finds the statue of *Venice* "in the form of Justice" remade by Vittoria in 1579. Overall this ensemble of architecture and sculpture recalls the two tabernacles in the presbytery of St Mark's, which are also attributed to Pierpaolo. Independent of the various loses and substitutions, all of the pieces are not of the same quality: the work was in fact completed after the death of Pierpaolo in 1403.

Pierpaolo Dalle Masegne, balcony of Palazzo Ducale near the Basin, 1400-05

Calle del Paradiso, details of the arch, 15th century

Calle del Paradiso

The Calle del Paradiso constitutes a characteristic complex of medieval Venice: two parallel bodies of buildings with stores on the ground floor and barbicans sustaining the upper wall are bounded at the extremities by Gothic arches. Thus the space of the *calle* (a narrow Venetian street) becomes a semi-public and semi-private urban environment. Towards the bridge the arch carries a late-fourteenth century image of the *Virgin*.

V. The Fifteenth Century: From International Gothic to Early Renaissance

The conquest of the mainland at the beginning of the fifteenth century marked an important turning-point in Venetian politics. The sea-faring republic was transformed into a continental power, partially compensating for its loses in the Mediterranean at the hand of the Turks (Constantinople fell in 1453). After six centuries the city returned to its most ancient origins and once again began to be a part of the Veneto: indeed from this point on it is necessary to speak of Veneto rather than Venetian art. A new epoch – the Renaissance – began and the artists operating in the lagoon city interpreted it in their own style. The beginning of the fifteenth century also marked one of those moments of stagnant local production typical of the cyclical character of Venetian art history. The city was very rich and attracted artists from every part of Italy: Gentile da Fabriano, Guariento, and Pisanello decorated the interiors of Palazzo Ducale; Andrea del Castagno and Paolo Uccello were called upon to work at San Zaccaria and St Mark's; and in the early decades of the century entire families of Tuscan and Lombard sculptors were busy completing the Gothic crowning of the ducal chapel and adapting it to the Palazzo's new style. Though Donatello worked in Padua for a decade, his influence on Venetian sculpture was indirect. The most important sculptor in Venice towards in the mid-century was Bartolomeo Bon, an artist of Gothic formation sensitive to the values of the Renaissance, but of that early transitional Venetian Renaissance that fell at equal distance between the Tuscan and Flemish currents. Immediately after, Antonio Rizzo and Pietro Lombardo arrived in Venice. A new season of extreme elegance began with Tullio and Antonio Lombardo who brought into sculpture that exquisite refinement, balance, and perfection of style that we find in the paintings of Bellini, Carpaccio, or Giorgione.

Antonio and Tullio Lombardo and assistants, pilaster base of the central arch, detail, 1481- 89, church of Santa Maria dei Miracoli

Opposite page:
Nanni di Bartolo, Judgement of Solomon, corner of Palazzo Ducale towards the Porta della Carta, c. 1435

Tuscan and Lombard Influences

The presence of foreign sculptors in Venice was more and more prevalent between the late-fourteenth and early-fifteenth century, echoing the city's nature as a true "sea port". Venice's lack of raw materials, marble or stone, determined the arrival of foreign workers in the city. Indeed, from the fourteenth century onward, French, Flemish, German, or English sculptures were far more numerous in Venice than one can imagine, and the same could be said for paintings, especially Flemish works. Opportunities for work were not lacking, even for public commissions, such as the completion of the Gothic crowning of St Mark's, originally entrusted to Tuscan artists, or, from 1424 on, the extension of the facade toward the Piazzetta. In the same years construction began on the most splendid private palazzo of the Gothic period, Ca' d'Oro, which was done by Lombard and Venetian craftsman. It was with Ca' d'Oro that the Venetian workshop of the Bon family, the most important late-Gothic *tajapiera* (stone cutters), also entered the scene.

St Paul	Sant'Alvise	St Michael
c. 1440, Church of San Polo, apse	c. 1440, Church of Sant'Alvise, portal	c. 1430, Island of San Michele, convent portal

The statue of *St Paul* that is found in an exterior niche of the nineteenth-century apse of the church of San Polo probably once adorned the side entrance, attributed to Bartolomeo Bon's studio-workshop. Of ancient origin, this work was re-adapted to represent the saint: the head, the right foot, and the right arm were done in Istrian stone; the original classical sculpture is in marble.

This statue of *Sant'Alvise* (as St Louis of Toulouse was known in Venice) is yet another testimony of the popularity of this Franciscan saint, son of Charles II, Lord of Provence and King of Naples, and thus the nephew of St Louis King of France. At times the sculpture has been attributed to Bartolomeo Bon's circle; at others to Tuscan artists active in Venice in the mid-fifteenth century.

This elegant sculpture on the portal at the entrance to the cloister of the convent at the Island of San Michele (now the cemetery of the city of Venice) represents St Michael vanquishing the devil; a still-gothicizing work that seems to be inspired by the style of Jacobello del Fiore. It was probably done by one of the Tuscan artists then working on the completion of St Mark's.

St Paul, c. 1440, church of San Polo, apse

St Alvise, c. 1440, church of St Alvise, portal

St Michael, c. 1430, cloister of San Michele, portal

Gothic Crowning
c. 1384-25, St Mark's Basilica

Upon the completion of Palazzo Ducale the difference between the architecture of the new building and that of the thirteenth-century church, which was an integral part of the palazzo, became clearly evident. Thus in 1384 work began to restructure the crowning of the basilica, with the erection of the Gothic niches and spires that may have been done by Pierpaolo Dalle Masegne. The use of "figures" or statues in adorning this part of the church was not spoken of until 1415, and it seems that the first sculptor to be employed for these works was Paolo di Jacobello Dalle Masegne, who was responsible for a few of the *Prophets* and *Virtues* on the side facades. In 1416, however, he was substituted by a Florentine artist, Nicolò di Pietro Lamberti, who thus launched the twenty-year span in which Tuscan and Lombard sculptors were assured the most important works in Venice. In 1419 Pietro Lamberti, son of Nicolò, and Giovanni Martino da Fiesole were active in St Mark's; they and their collaborators sculpted some of the statues that still adorn the crowning of St Mark's: a few of the *Evangelists* in the niches of the main facade, and the decoration of the *Biblical Stories* and the *Prophets* on the fourth large arch. In 1421 the Lombard artist Matteo Raverti also intervened; he was in Venice to work on Ca' d'Oro and seems to have been responsible for the two gargoyles on the left part of the western facade. Finally, another Tuscan artist, Nanni di Bartolo, who is also called Il Rosso and who studied with Donatello, worked on St Mark's and was probably responsible for a gargoyle on the northern wall of the church. All of these works brought to Venice the first echoes of the new style that in those years was becoming known in Florence.

Anonymous, Nuptial Angel on the western crowning of St Mark's, 1415-20

Nanni di Bartolo called Il Rosso, gargoyle of the northern facade of St Mark's, c. 1423

Tomb of Doge Tommaso Mocenigo
1423, Church of Santi Giovanni e Paolo

In this period funeral monuments inside churches take on primary importance and testify, through the various ducal and other monuments, to the stylistic evolution of Venetian sculpture. Tuscan craftsman including Pietro di Niccolò Lamberti and Giovanni Martino da Fiesole were called upon to sculpt the funeral monument dedicated to Doge Tommaso Mocenigo. These craftsman had already been active in Venice for a few years and signed the base of the commemorative inscription underneath the coffin of this tomb. The architectural composition indisputably recalls the tomb of Baldassare Cossa (Giovanni XXIII), done by Donatello and Michelozzo in the Florence Baptistry. John Pope-Hennessy defined this monument "a medley of Tuscan and Venetian elements": the warrior on the right, recently attributed to Nanni di Bartolo, recalls Donatello's *St George*, now in Museo del Bargello in Florence.

Tomb of Doge Tommaso Mocenigo and detail, 1423, church of Santi Giovanni e Paolo

Portal Lunette, Corner Chapel
c. 1430, Church of the Frari

Tomb of Beato Pacifico
c. 1437, Church of the Frari

Chapel of the Mascoli, Altar
1430, St Mark's Basilica

The lunette of this exterior entrance portal depicts the *Virgin and Child* with two *Angels* at their sides. This work recalls those that were done for the Mascoli chapel and, infact, the artist of both works seems to have been same.

As Wolters rightfully observed: "Now for the first time Venetians saw works in which the mechanism of movement was rendered completely perceptible. The body stretches and pulls in such a way that the movement and drapery correspond to one another, one unveils and the other accents." The way in which Virgin's hand crosses the Child's is highly refined.

One of the most remarkable works done by a group of Tuscan artists in Venice for St Mark's is the *Tomb of Beato Pacifico*, who, according to tradition, was to have directed the construction works at the Frari in the fourteenth century. On the frescoed wall a large Gothic arch contains a lunette in polychrome terra cotta representing the *Baptism of Christ*. Below we find the sarcophagus in which the remains of Beato were conserved in 1437. This tomb has been attributed to Nanni di Bartolo due to its style and the resemblance of the sculptures to those of the *Brenzoni Monument* in San Fermo in Verona, signed by this artist.

Constructed in 1430, the chapel of the Mascoli, with its famous mosaics by Giambono and Castagno, conserves an important altar recognizable as the work of Lombard sculptors, also active in the same years in Castiglione Olona. It is an excellent work that exerted a strong influence on local sculptors. The almost fourteenth-century Gothic *Madonna* is flanked by *St Mark* on the left and *St John the Evangelist* on the right. The elegant pose of the latter figure and the movement of the drapery are particularly well-done. The angels decorating the facade of the altar are also extremely elegant.

Left: *Corner Chapel lunette, 1430 and Tomb of Beato Pacifico, 1437, church of the Frari; above: altar of the Mascoli chapel, 1430, St Mark's*

Bartolomeo Bon

Bartolomeo Bon, son of Giovanni, the *tajapiera* of which no works are certain, was probably born in Venice between 1405 and 1410. His name is documented for the first time together with that of his father for the works at Ca' d'Oro in 1423. From that date on, until the 1460s, Bartolomeo, was very active, first with his father and then on his own: his name appears in the documents of Ca' d'Oro and Palazzo Ducale, as well as those of the important churches, especially for the portals (Frari, San Giovanni e Paolo, Madonna dell'Orto, Carità), and those of two Scuole Grandi (the Misericordia and San Marco). From 1457 he is listed as the designer of Ca' del Duca, a building of which only a corner on the Grand Canal remains and which represented the city's first attempt to move away from Gothic style. Bon was attentive to both contemporary Tuscan sculpture and to that coming from the north, two schools of which Venice had abundant examples. Indeed Bartolomeo Bon's style demonstrates a few characteristics that recall northern art and that counter the most severe classical stylization and the greatest formal elegance of the Tuscan Renaissance artists, which idealizes the human figure. Thus, once again, an ancient style was continued in a new era (like the late-Gothic in the early-Renaissance, or the Byzantine in the Romanesque or early-Gothic), permitting a Venetian artist, working more on intuition than rigid stylistic schemes, to find a very personal syntheses that opened completely new paths in the development of art.

The Dalmatian artist Giorgio da Sebenico, one of the most important personalities of Renaissance art even beyond his homeland trained under Bon. He was active first in Venice and later, from 1441 onward, in Sebenico and Ancona. This Veneto-Adriatic world also trained two other important artists of Dalmatian origin: Luciano and Francesco Laurana.

Bartolomeo Bon, well-curb, 1427, courtyard of Ca' d'Oro

Bartolomeo Bon
Well-curb
1427, Ca' d'Oro, courtyard

The well-curb in the courtyard of Ca' d'Oro is without a doubt by Bartolomeo Bon. He received this commission in 1427, probably just after his twentieth birthday, or four years after his father Giovanni had begun working for the Contarini family. At the side of the red Veronese marble well, among the rich foliage, we find the figures of *Justice, Charity,* and *Strength*; four large heads decorate the corners.

The design is derived from the capitals of Palazzo Ducale, but here the figures have a completely new plastic strength, typical of all of the works attributed to this sculptor.

Lunette
c. 1440, Scuola Grande
di San Marco, entrance portal

This sculpture was rescued from the tragic fire in the Scuola Grande di San Marco. St Mark is represented in the center surrounded by a crowd of vigorously sculpted brothers who are kneeling. They are evidently portraits, among which historians have recognized the Guardian Grande, the goldsmith Zoffredo da Brazzo, in the act of kissing the saint's hand. This is an exceptional work that "at times, borders upon the concentrated power of Jacopo Dalla Quercia" (Arslan). It has been attributed to Bartolomeo Bon and Giorgio da Sebenico.

Lunette of the Scuola di San Marco entrance, c.1440

Giorgio da Sebenico
Charity
c. 1440, Scuola Grande
di San Marco, entrance portal

This work, which also belonged to the Scuola, was retrieved after the fire of 1485. It is attributed to Bartolomeo Bon, who was given the task of constructing the entrance portal in 1437. *Charity* is represented as a young mother holding two children in her arms. Some features of this group recall works by Giorgio da Sebenico in Dalmatia.

Giorgio da Sebenico (?), Portal of the Scuola di San Marco and a detail of Charity, c. 1440

Bartolomeo Bon
Porta dell Carta
1438-42, Palazzo Ducale

The Porta della Carta, the main access to the Palazzo, is the most important public work after the construction of the building by Calendario (the extension of the Palazzo towards the Piazzetta is not an exact reproduction of the facade on the basin) and completes the *Via Triumphalis* laid out in the thirteenth century with the spoils from the Fourth Crusade. This architectural project was assigned to Bon's studio in 1438, even if Bartolomeo, who placed his name of the architrave ("Opus Bartolomei"), has to be considered the real craftsman.
The tall and narrow structure, flanked by two slender pillars, takes up on the motifs of the Dalle Masegne window. An arch with mixtilinear crowning bearing the statue of Justice rises above the portal and encloses "the admirable window the proportions of which are clearly inspired by those of the nearby Palazzo, yet it is very different in the large, nervously trimmed, four-lobed perforations (where a tri-lobe is inserted in a lobe)" (Arslan).
Along with Ca' d'Oro this is one of the masterpieces of International Gothic architecture. A symbolic interpretation of the sculpture refers to the theme of justice (this is in fact the part of the Palazzo *ad jus reddendum*), a theme already introduced by the *Judgement of Solomon*. In addition to the sculpture at the peak, the four virtues – *Temperance, Strength, Prudence, Charity* – reign in the niches of the pillars. Bartolomeo was only partially responsible for this sculpture, though he can most surely be credited for the vigorous *Portrait of Doge Francesco Foscari*. This

work was saved after the destruction of the figure of the doge and the lion (the present ones are nineteenth-century copies) and is now conserved in the Palazzo museum. The other figures can be attributed to more or less gifted collaborators. The statue of *Temperance* pouring water into a bowl is particularly successful.

Bartolomeo Bon, Portrait of Doge Francesco Foscari and the Porta della Carta, 1438-42

Nanni di Bartolo
Judgement of Solomon
c. 1435, Corner near Palazzo Ducale's Porta della Carta

The *Judgement of Solomon* is one of the most elevated works of the entire fifteenth century in the Veneto. It is found on the corner of the Palazzo's extension, begun in 1424 and structurally completed around 1442. It is located near the Porta della Carta, designed shortly after by Bartolomeo Bon.
The underlying capital, attributed to the Tuscan sculptors who worked on St Mark's, is also inspired by the theme of Justice and represents the crucial moment of the King's *Judgement*. Immobile under the bal-dachin, the King lifts his left arm to block the executioner who is about to strike the child with his sword; the mother clings to him desperately to impede the execution, while the mother of the dead child stands indifferently in the background. Gnudi, who attributed this group to Jacopo della Quercia, has noted "the solemn dignity of the ancient statuary evoked but expressed with a language still rich in Gothic desinence".
Traditionally this work was been attributed to Bartolomeo Bon. However, as has been demonstrated by Anne Markham Schultz in a recent study dedicated to this artist, it appears be closer to the style of the Tuscan artist Nanni di Bartolo.

Baptismal Font
c. 1440, Church of San Giovanni in Bragora

The red marble basin of this sumptuous baptismal font decorated with rich foliage is sustained by putti in Istrian stone. It is usually attributed to the workshop of Bartolomeo Bon and Giorgio da Sebenico, yet seems to approach the style of a group of Lombard artists active in the same years in Castiglione Olona. The model for the putti can be found in the so-called *Throne of Saturn*, a sculpture from the first century which has been in Venice from the fourteenth century and is now conserved in the city's archaeological museum (see p. 103).

Baptismal font, church of San Giovanni in Bragora, c. 1440

Nanni di Bartolo, Judgement of Solomon, c. 1435, Palazzo Ducale

Medals, Marquetry, and Small Bronze Sculptures: Pisanello, Donatello, and Il Riccio

The Renaissance spread throughout Venice and the Veneto by degrees (if one excludes Padua). The ancient forms were pragmatically absorbed, without the imposition of absolute theories, in a culture that long delighted in the very precious late-Gothic with traces of the Byzantine. Antonio Pisanello (1395-1455), a Veronese International Gothic painter, was active in Venice from 1415-20. An acute drawer, he is the great maestro of the Renaissance medal, a typical product of late-fourteenth century Veneto humanism.

Perspective marquetry was another technique outside the realm of "great art" widespread in the Veneto during the fifteenth century. Among its major interpreters were Marco Cozzi from Vicenza, emulator of the well-known Canozzi brothers from Lendinara who collaborated with Piero della Francesca. Between 1455 and 1486 Cozzi decorated the choir of San Zaccaria and part of the Frari, which are among the most refined works of the fifteenth century in Venice.

In 1438 Donatello (1386-1466) carved *St John the Baptist* for the Scuola dei Fiorentini at the Frari; this is the only sculpture by this artist existing in Venice. Shortly after, in 1443, he moved to Padua for a decade, where he greatly influenced the artistic environment (think of Mantegna alone). Thus Padua became one of the major centers of bronze sculpture, especially small bronzes, and decorative or functional table objects (quill pens, lamps, etc) that rapidly spread the taste for ancient classical art among the princely courts and humanists. Bartolomeo Bellano (1435-1496,7) interpreted the most realistic and dynamic forms of Donatello, whom he worked with as an assistant. He also created an important school of bronze sculptors in Padua which trained Andrea Briosco otherwise known as Il Riccio (1470-1533), one of the most original sculptors of the early Renaissance, whose works adopted a classicism revived by a strong expressive charge.

Pisanello's Medals
1438-49, Ca' d'Oro

Ca' d'Oro conserves a considerable collection of Renaissance medals including works by Pisanello and almost all the most noteworthy medalists of the era: Bertoldo, Pollaiolo, Leoni, and, among artists of the Veneto, Matteo de Pasti, Gentile Bellini, Vittore Gambello, and Vittoria. When all these works are seen together Pisanello's great originality stands out: "his medals were small, perfect Latin compositions, epigrams of a few verses of exquisite craftsmanship" (Argan). In his first medal, representing the Byzantine Emperor *John VIII Palaeologus* (1438), both the portrait and the group of squires on the reverse side reveal the absolute precision and economy of means that give these images, despite their size, a character of classical monumentality in which portraiture achieves one of the highest peaks in its history. In the concentrated effort required by the exiguity of the space, this Gothic painter was transformed into a perfect modeler of Renaissance forms.

Pisanello's medals (1438-49) at Ca' d'Oro; left to right: Cecilia Gonzaga (reverse, 1447); the Byzantine Emperor John VIII Palaeologus (1438); Ludovico Gonzaga (reverse, 1449?)

Marco Cozzi
Marquetry
1468, Church of the Frari, choir

The art of marquetry is one of the most interesting fifteenth-century phenomena in the Veneto. These works were generally produced by wood sculptors who collaborated, especially in the perspective rendering, with the most well-versed architects and painters. Padua, Verona and Venice represented very important centers of production in the

Veneto. The choir stalls in the Frari, completed in 1468, present a significant mixture of styles: the wood structures of the choir and the bas-reliefs are Gothic and were probably done by a German maestro; the panels of the dossals, with Marco Cozzi's perfect architectural perspective in marquetry, are "exquisite demonstration of fourteenth-century 'cubism' and have to be placed alongside the art of the Lendinara brothers, disciples of Piero della Francesca" (Chastel).

Marquetry
late 15th - early 16th century
St Mark's Basilica, sacristy

Between the late-fifteenth and early-sixteenth century, there is an important cycle of marquetry on the wardrobes of the sacristy in St Mark's, which seem to have been done on cartoons by Carpaccio (Muraro). The wall panels portray the *Stories of St Mark* and a few perspectival views of considerable quality; the lower doors reproduce various objects that were probably contained in the wardrobes themselves done in trompe l'oeil. These marquetries are generally attributed to Antonio and Paolo da Mantova, Friar Sebastiano Schiavone, and Bernardino da Bergamo.

Marco Cozzi, Marquetry in the Frari choir, 1468

Lower right: *Marquetry in St Mark's sacristy, c. 1500*

Donatello
St John the Baptist
1438, Church of the Frari

In 1436 the Scuola del Fiorentini built an altar in the church
of Frari (at that time it was
placed on the wall to the left of
the main door). Two years later
Donatello was asked to sculpt a
statue of their protector saint, *St
John the Baptist* (the date, 1438,
and signature came to light
after the recent cleaning – OPUS
DONATI DE FLORENTIA ANNO
MCCCCXXXVIII). The sculpture
is done in gilded and painted
wood, in which the vigorous
naturalism of the great Tuscan
artist takes on profoundly dramatic, almost expressionist
accents, so much so as to recall
the *Magdalene* he did for the
Florence Baptistry after he
returned to his homeland from
Padua in 1453.

Donatello, St John the Baptist,
1438, church of the Frari

Portrait of a Young Man
late-15th century
Ca' d'Oro

This very elegant work is probably the portrait of a member of the Gonzaga family. It is attributed to Francesco Laurana, the great Dalmatian portrait artist who worked in various Italian cities, as well as in France, in the late-fifteenth century.

Bartolomeo Bellano
Oxen at Pasture
late-15th century, Ca' d'Oro

The small bronze sculpture representing oxen at pasture comes from the collection of Andrea Mantova Bonavides, a well-known Paduan humanist. It is an excellent example of the naturalist style that Bellano had learned from Donatello and applied in a decisive and essential way in defining form.

P.G. Alari Bonacolsi (Antico)
Apollo
late-15th century, Ca' d'Oro

This is one of the most refined small bronze sculptures by Antico, a Mantuan artist who worked in the Gonzaga court between the late-fifteenth and early-sixteenth century. It is a typical product of fifteenth-century humanism directly inspired by classical tradition.

Portrait of a Young Man, late-15th century, Ca' d'Oro

Bartolomeo Bellano, Oxen at Pasture, late-15th century, Ca' d'Oro

P.G. Alari Bonacolsi called Antico, Apollo, late-15th century, Ca' d'Oro

Il Riccio
Legend of the Cross
c. 1510, Ca' d'Oro

The four reliefs representing the stories of the legend of the Cross (the *Victory of Constantine, Constantine's Vision of the Cross,* the *Rediscovery of the Cross,* and the *Proof of the True Cross*) came from the altar by Girolamo Donà in the church of the Servi in Venice, which has since been destroyed. Dated around 1510, they belong to the artist's full maturity. They are very complex scenes in which the mass of people in the foreground contrast with the vast open spaces of the landscape. Particularly expressive is the impetuous scene of the *Victory of Constantine,* where the battle, a continuous overlapping of figures of soldiers and horses, is represented with skilful variation in modelling.

Il Riccio, Victory of Costantine and the Vision of the Cross, c. 1510, Ca' d'Oro

Il Riccio
St Martin
c. 1520, Ca' d'Oro

This relief representing *St Martin* on horseback in the act of donating part of his cloak to the poor is also by Il Riccio. Like the scenes from the *Legend of the Cross,* it came from the church of the Servi in Venice. It is a work of remarkable stylistic perfection; the re-evocation of an idealized classicism recalls Mantegna but is rendered with great energy, especially in the very beautiful horse which seems to re-make the quadriga of St Mark's, sculptures that even Donatello had certainly studied before modelling *Gattamelata.*

Il Riccio, St Martin c. 1520, Ca' d'Oro

Antonio Rizzo and the Lombardo Family

The 1560s marked the beginning of an artistic and cultural movement that would make Venice the major center of classical culture in Italy. In the words of Pope-Hennessy, "it was Venice, and not Florence, that achieved the most faithful re-creation of ancient sculpture".
In 1461 Bartolomeo Bon interrupted the works at Ca' del Duca, which were already well under way. Shortly after, Pietro Solari, otherwise known as Lombardo (1435-1515), received the commission for the tomb of *Doge Pasquale Malipiero*. It was the first of numerous works to be entrusted to the Lombard family made up of Pietro, the father, and his sons Tullio (1455-1532) and Antonio (1458-1516).
Antonio Rizzo (1430-1499) worked at the Frari and on the Foscari Arch, and later become the overseer of Palazzo Ducale. In 1468 Mauro Codussi began the construction of the church of San Michele in Isola. Once they reached Venice these Lombard or Lombard-trained artists, like Rizzo, adapted their style to the completely different requests of their Venetians clients, who were very attentive to the new humanistic needs that had to be interpreted according to local traditions with very ancient roots.
Between the late-fifteenth and early-sixteenth century sculptors, architects, and painters worked in Venice in a perfect harmony of styles, in a manner that was rarely seen in the history of European art. This is the moment in which the myth of antiquity, begun by Donatello and Mantegna in Padua, spread through the taste of collectors, who for the first time discovered the art of ancient Greece and the interpretation of Greek and Roman texts, published at that time by the Venetian printers like Jenson and Manuzio in editions that are in themselves masterpieces of visual art. It was an ancient dream with almost romantic connotations, the vision of an ideal world, perhaps an escape from reality in a moment in which Venice had to confront both the Turks and the growing hostility of the Italian and European states.

Pietro Lombardo and assistants, pilaster of the high altar, detail, c. 1471-80, church of San Giobbe

Niccolò di Giovanni Fiorentino
Tomb of Doge Francesco
Foscari
c. 1460, church of the Frari

The architectural structure of this monument alludes to the tomb of Doge Tommaso Mocenigo, predecessor to Foscari. The date of the tomb is unknown but its stylistic execution suggests a date towards the late-1450s. The unprecedented size and the unusual site – before this time the church of the Frari had not been used a a burial place for a doge – clearly explain the importance of this doge, who was sadly deposed by the Council of Ten, a week before his death. "Despite the Gothic architectural details, the Foscari tomb responds to a Renaissance aesthetic... The subjects are realized with a freedom that betrays a sculptor accustomed to modelling wax. The limbs are carved in the round, the drapery is deeply excavated, the borders undercut, and the forms seperated by voids. Even the long bands of voluminous and densely gathered folds seem to be modeled rather than carved, almost as though strips of rolled clay had been wrapped around the figures to create designs composed chiefly in curved lines. Between the bands, oval portions of apparently wet drapery adhere to the figure." (A.Markham Schulz). No document has ever been found that confirms the existence of Antonio or Paolo Bregno, normally mentioned as the sculptors of this monument. Recently, on the basis of stylistic and iconographic analogies, Anne Markham Schulz attributed the Foscari tomb to Niccolò di Giovanni Fiorentino, who, probably trained in Donatello's workshop in Padua, was certainly active in Dalmatia after 1467 (as attested by a few signed contracts for the decoration of the chapel of Giovanni Orsini in the Duomo of Traù). The art of Niccolò, who died in 1506, influenced the style of Dalmatian sculpture for almost a century.

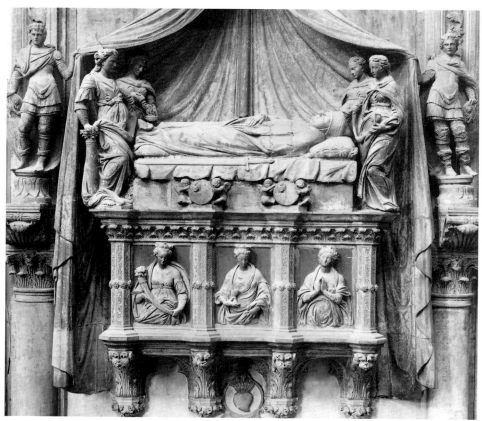

Niccolò di Giovanni Fiorentino
Monument to Vittore Cappello
c. 146, Church of Sant'Elena

Other sculptures in Venice done between 1460 and 1470 show stylistic similarities to those of the Foscari tomb. One of these is the monument to Admiral Vittore Cappello on the facade of the church of Sant'Elena; it is the city's first example of a monument surrounding a portal with columns in the round. "The artist enriched the metaphorical meaning of the group by means of this transparent allusion: like the doge, Cappello was invested as a sea captain, a function in the exercise of which he lost his life, by the titular saint of the church. As in the *Virtues* of the *Foscari*

Tomb, Niccolò gave an expressive impulse to the enlarged figures, now worked entirely in relief and freed from the conventional context, thereby transforming an icon which symbolized the relationship between the protected and the patron into a human drama" (A. Markham Schulz). In precedence this work has been attributed to Antonio Rizzo and Antonio Dentone, whose existence, like that of Antonio Bregno, has never been confirmed.

Niccolò di Giovanni Fiorentino, Tomb of Vittore Cappello, c. 1467, church of Sant'Elena

Opposite page:
Niccolò di Giovanni Fiorentino, Tomb of Doge Francesco Foscari, detail, c. 1460, church of the Frari

Antonio Rizzo
Adam and Eve
c. 1483, Palazzo Ducale

Rizzo became the overseer of Palazzo Ducale in 1483 and designed the facade on the courtyard of the east wing, including the Giant's Staircase, which is clearly his masterpiece as an architect and sculptor. Another of his most successful works is found in the figures of *Adam and Eve*, sculpted for the side niches of the Foscari Arch. (They have since been substituted by copies, and the originals are now conserved inside the Palazzo). While *Eve* still conserves a certain Gothic composure, *Adam*, in the sureness of the gesture and the anatomical perfection of the body, is one of the masterpieces of the fifteenth century.

Antonio Rizzo, Adam and Eve,
c. 1483, Palazzo Ducale

Antonio Rizzo
Tomb of Doge Nicolò Tron
c. 1476, Church of the Frari

The *Tomb of Doge Nicolò Tron*
(d. 1473) is undoubtedly the
most imposing, even if not the
most inventive, among those
realized in Venice in the fifteenth century. Here Rizzo
places himself in direct competition with Pietro Lombardo,
who in those years had moved
definitively to Venice. Though
many collaborators worked on
this tomb, Rizzo's hand is especially evident in the statues of
the lower part, with the *Doge* in
the center and the elegant por-
trayals of *Charity* and *Prudence*.
"The *Tron tomb* lacks a focal
point. The architectural elements are repeated *seriatim* and
uniformly cover the entire surface ... The figures isolated in
the niches do not communicate
amongst themselves: far from
interpreting a drama, they bear
the pure function of conventional bearers of their individual attributes. Rizzo devoted so
little attention to the tomb's
iconographic content from time
to time he repeated the same
personification or omitted their
attributes altogether. Thus this
monumentreveals at last the
absence of a coherent iconographic plan" (A. Markham
Schulz).

*Antonio Rizzo, Tomb of Doge
Nicolò Tron and detail, c. 1476,
church of the Frari, presbytery*

Antonio Rizzo
Giant's Staircase
1486-96, Palazzo Ducale

The Giant's Staircase in the courtyard of Palazzo Ducale, constructed by Antonio Rizzo between 1486 and 1496 while he was overseer of the building, is by far his true masterpiece. The staircase, located in front of the Foscari Arch, leads up twenty-seven steps of Istrian stone to the loggia on the first floor (each step is decorated in niello). At the height of the loggia a large landing opens that rests on two lateral avant-corps, occupying three arcades of the loggia itself. In 1557 Sansovino's gigantic statues of Mars and Neptune were placed here, thereby giving this exterior staircase its name. It is here on the landing of the Giant's Staircase that the official ceremony of the crowning of the doge traditionally took place. The exterior walls of the staircase are adorned with plates of crushed marble and Carrara marble pilaster strips covered by refined bas-reliefs representing trophies, body armor, helmets, and shields alongside the Marciana lions – all symbols celebrating the glories of Venice as a "second Rome". "The decoration, carved with extraordinary precision on a minute scale, is of a refinement that is usually found in goldsmith's work rather than in architecture ... no single motif is repeated" (A. Markham Schulz). The facades of the avant-corps present eight, winged Victories, on the two sides of each oculus. Each *Victory* carries a different symbol (a ducal cap, a torch, an inscription, etc.). They are figures of extraordinary elegance in which "the effect of a delicate gradation of perspective first appears in Venetian sculpture".

Antonio Rizzo, Giant's Staircase, courtyard of Palazzo Ducale, and detail of the Victories, 1486-96

The Lombardo Family Monuments in the Church of Santi Giovanni e Paolo
c. 1467-1500

In the forty years between 1467 and about 1500, the Lombardo family, first through the father, Pietro, then in collaboration with his sons, and finally and especially through Tullio constructed five funeral monuments that are found in the church of Santi Giovanni e Paolo, the Pantheon of Venice. They constitute an exceptional anthology of the artistic ideals of their epoch and are dedicated to five doges:

Pasquale Malipiero (d. 1462), Nicolò Marcello (d. 1474), Pietro Mocenigo (d. 1476), Andrea Vendramin (d. 1478), and Giovanni Mocenigo (d. 1485). The *Tomb of Pasquale Malipiero* (early-1470s), Pietro Lombardo's first work in Venice, is evidently inspired by Tuscan models (Rossellino and Desiderio da Settignano), though it is more austere in both its architectural layout and sculpture. In the following decade, towards the late-1470s, Pietro, with the collaboration of his sons, designed the *Tomb of Nicolò Marcello*, a work which, as in the preceding beau-

tiful Virtues at the sides of the sarcophagus, seems to interpret in sculptural terms the idealized faces of its counterpart in Venetian painting. The *Tomb of Pietro Mocenigo* (1476-1481) is more monumental, almost as if it were intended to complete with Rizzo's project at the Frari. Before being elected doge in 1474, Pietro Mocenigo had fought in the East against the Turks, and the monument recalls his military past with soldiers that sustain the statue of the deceased and bas-reliefs representing the *Royal Palace of Cyprus* and the *Liberation of the*

Pietro Lombardo, Tomb of Doge Nicolò Marcello, c. 1474, church of Santi Giovanni e Paolo

Pietro Lombardo, Tomb of Doge Pasquale Malipiero, c. 1467, church of Santi Giovanni e Paolo

Scutari. The other two monuments by the Lombardo family are general attributed to Tullio in collaboration with his brother Antonio: the *Vendramin Tomb*, constructed for the church of the Servi between 1492-95 and moved here in the early-nineteenth century when the two statues of *Adam and Eve* once found at the sides of the niche were eliminated. *Adam* – now in the Metropolitan Museum of New York – is considered to be Tullio's masterpiece and is perhaps the most classical work of the Venetian Renaissance. "The state of relaxation of muscles, which are not contracted, agrees with the pose of the figure, a static and unemphatic *contrapposto*, in which the divergence of the axes of the thighs and shoulders is minimal and the vertical alignment of the tense and relaxed limbs is confined within a single plane. The face, based on Roman portraits of *Antinous*, suggests a mental abstraction and withdrawal, as if the figure were listening to an interior voice" (A. Markham Schulz). Lastly, the *Tomb of Giovanni Mocenigo*, honored by the monument on the other side of the entrance portal, was also constructed by Tullio more than ten years after the doge's death, (c. 1500). It is much simpler and more austere than that of Vendramin and, in a certain sense, also more classical in its structure, of that Lombardesque classicism that means absolute perfection in technical execution, as in the inscription of Aldine type, at the center of the base, and in the bas-reliefs at the sides representing the *Baptism of Christ and of Anianus*, the cobbler miraculously cured by St Mark.

Tullio Lombardo, Tomb of Doge Giovanni Mocenigo and detail, c. 1500;
right: *Pietro Lombardo, Tomb of Doge Pietro Mocenigo, c. 1476-81*

*Tullio Lombardo,
Tomb of Doge Andrea
Vendramin and
details, c. 1492-95*

Pietro Lombardo
Church of Santa Maria dei
Miracoli
1481-89

The church of the Miracoli, defined as "one of the most beautiful among the small buildings of the world" (H. Honour), is an extraordinary retrieval of Byzantine art in a modern version (an operation that was similar to what Codussi was doing at the same time). The architectural and sculptural work is perfectly integrated: the church is entirely faced with sheets of polychrome marble in a play of marquetry in its most monumental form that represents illusory perspectives, where the element of color has a fundamental importance. The presbytery, raised and surrounded by a banister decorated with half-figures of *St Francis*, the *Nuptial Angel*, the *Virgin*, and *St Clare*, is covered by bas-reliefs sculpted with such delicacy that the stone seems to take on the appearance of alabaster.

Antonio and Tullio Lombardo, pilaster base in the presbytery and detail, 1481-89, church of Santa Maria dei Miracoli

92

Facade of Scuola Grande di San Marco
1489-95

After the fire of 1485, from which only part of the sculpture by Bartolomeo Bon's studio was saved, the reconstruction of this building was entrusted, in 1489, to the Lombardo family. In 1490 the supervision of the works passed on to Mauro Codussi, who was responsible for the mixtilinear crowning. Despite this, the building conserves an exceptional sense of unity. The sculptures that decorate the ground floor facade were done by Tullio, who used a trompe l'oeil technique to obtain various perspective layouts demonstrating, among other things, the artist's profound knowledge of both classical architecture and Donatello's reliefs in Padua. The facade is divided into two parts: on the left, at the sides of the main entrance, foreshortened views of two passages with barrel vaults open, out of which the figures of two lions appear, thereby creating the impression of a triumphal arch; on the right, in correspondence with the Sala dell'Albergo, next to the side door, the sculptor placed two arcades with a low ceiling where the scenes of the miraculous *Healing* and the *Baptism of the Anianus the Cobbler* are found. The various areas are clearly differentiated through the use of perspective, emphasized by different colored marbles. The overall effect is of two connected but distinct theatrical scenes.

Pietro Lombardo, Scuola Grande di San Marco, 1489-95, facade

Tullio Lombardo, Miracle of Anianus, 1489-95, Scuola Grande di San Marco, facade

Tullio Lombardo
Double Portrait
c. 1500, Ca' d'Oro

The *Double Portrait* of Ca' d'Oro (c. 1500), which recalls the more famous contemporary relief of *Bacchus and Ariadne* now in Vienna, represents one of the culminating moments of Tullio's career. This sculpture demonstrates the artist's perfect knowledge of Greek and Roman art. In the words of Charles Seymour Jr., "the authentic forms of classical antiquity are sought after and re-created with remarkable ability without ever even a minimal risk of suggested academicism".

Tullio Lombardo
Coronation of the Virgin
1500-02, Church of
San Giovanni Crisostomo

This altarpiece representing the *Coronation of the Virgin with the Apostles* (1500-02) is found in the left side chapel of San Giovanni Crisostomo. It is one of Tullio Lombardo's most "neoclassical" works, in the spirit of the early-Venetian Renaissance, which has some of its highest manifestations in this church. We see it first in the architecture, in Coducci's (1497-1504) neo-Byzantine style, then in the high altarpiece depicting *St John Chrysostom and Saints*, one of the few works by Sebastiano del Piombo (1509-11) in Venice, completed shortly before his departure for Rome, and, lastly, in Giovanni Bellini's great masterpiece of 1513, completed after the artist's eightieth birthday. The latter – *Saints Jerome, Christopher, and Louis of Toulouse* – is found in the chapel on the right.

Tullio Lombardo, Double Portrait, c. 1500, Ca' d'Oro

Tullio Lombardo, Coronation of the Virgin, 1500-02. Church of San Giovanni Crisostomo

94

Bronze Sculptures and Sculptors in Venice: Verrocchio and Leopardi

Bartolomeo Colleoni, a captain of the Republic's ground forces, died in 1475 leaving the Republic a fabulous bequest of 100,000 ducats on the condition that a monument be erected to him in front of St Mark's. (This request was interpreted to mean the Scuola and not the church.) Following a competition to which many artists were invited, the *Signoria* selected, in 1481, a project by Andrea Verrocchio (1435-1488). After Donatello's death, Verrocchio was the most well-known Tuscan sculptor and the owner of a large studio, which worked for the Medici family and from which emerged artists like Leonardo and Perugino. Verrocchio died before being able to finish casting the bronze, and its completion was entrusted to Alessandro Leopardi, a forger at the Venetian mint, who carried it through successfully. Indeed it was the largest most complicated bronze ever made in Venice. Leopardi was then commissioned to cast the flag stendards in St Mark's Square and probably also the statue of the *Virgin* of the Clocktower. Another forger at the Mint, Paolo Savin, did the figures of the *Moors*, who strike the hour on the terrace of the Tower. Savin and Antonio Lombardo later designed the bronze sculpture of the Zen Chapel in St Mark's. This is how a school of bronze sculptors came to be formed in Venice, one that was to receive new impulses with Sansovino's arrival in 1527.

Andrea Verrocchio
Colleoni Monument
1481-96, Campo Santi Giovanni e Paolo

In modelling this spectacular equestrian monument, Verrocchio had three great models: *Gattamelata*, cast in Padua by Donatello thirty years earlier; *Marcus Aurelius* in the Campidoglio; and the Marciana *Horses*, all three of which were examples of the classicism Venetians sought in all art forms at that time. Verrocchio, a very capable bronze sculptor, had been trained as a goldsmith and conserved the preciousness of this technique. Here he created much more than a portrait of the ideal image of a soldier: the figure of the captain imposes itself with a theatrical torsion of the bust, while the horse advances with an aggressive impetus on the high pedestal.

Andrea Verrocchio, Colleoni Monument, 1481-96, Campo Santi Giovanni e Paolo

The Clocktower
and the Stendards
c. 1500, St Mark's Square

The Clocktower, which seems to have been designed by Codussi, is one of the first significant Renaissance projects in St Mark's Square. The structure resembles a triumphal arch, indicating the main entrance to the city and the 'road' leading from the city's political hub to Rialto. At the top the self-propelled figures that strike time, the so-called *Moors* (apparently symbols of the good 'savage' in service of a higher civilization), are vigorous bronze sculptures cast in 1497 by Ambrogio dell'Anchore on a project attributed to Paolo Savin. The gilded and embossed cooper figure of the *Virgin with Putto*, in the middle, is attributed to Alessandro Leopardi. Immediately after Leopardi designed the three bronze stendards for the flags in 1505, they were placed to mark the boundaries of the space in front of the basilica and to indicate the route towards to tower; their function was the same as that of the Acritani Pilasters in relation to the entrance to Palazzo Ducale, to designate the routes that had an important ritual significance during public ceremonies.

Of Lombardesque inspiration, Leopardi's elegant bas-reliefs on the central standard portray Justice and the elephant, symbols of strength and prudence, that is, of good government; those on the side, the shellfish born by Nereids and Tritons, on the stendard near the basin, and, on the other, the earth, and the grapevines, offered by a satyr to Triton. This is how the process of celebrating the State began, to be completed later by projects done under dogeship of Andrea Gritti (1523-38).

Clocktower and a detail of one of the Moors, 1497-1505

Alessandro Leopardi, central stendard in St Mark's square, 1505

Bronze Sculptures
early-16th century,
St Mark's Square

In 1501 Cardinale Giambattista
Zen, a relative of Pope Paul II,
died. As a legate of the Republic
his was conceded the honor of
having a chapel in St Mark's in
the atrium of the "Porta da
Mar", which was closed off at
that time. The bronze figures of
Virgin and of the *Child* were
done by Antonio Lombardo,
those of *St Peter* and *St John the
Baptist* are attributed to Paolo
Savin, as is the sarcophagus and
the figure of the cardinal, all of
which were done between 1504
and 1521. The most remarkable
bronze works of this chapel are
without a doubt those of the
Virgin and Saints, inspired by
Donatello's altar in Padua.

*Effigy of Cardinal Giambattista
Zen, 1504-21, St Mark's
basilica, Zen chapel*

*Altar of the Zen chapel, detail,
1504-21, St Mark's basilica*

VI. The Sixteenth Century: Celebration of the State

When the hostilities ended in 1517, sculptural work began in Venice once again. Commissions for funeral monuments and altars increased, prompting the arrival of numerous stone-cutters from the hinterland. Giammaria Mosca was among these artists: "The virtuosity with which Mosca carved very low relief and undercut paper-thin marble was no less than that of Antonio Lombardo" (A. Markham Schulz). The small, recently-restored statue of St John the Baptist found in the center of the holy water font at the entrance of the church of Santo Stefano is an excellent example of his technique.

Giammaria Mosca,
St John the Baptist, c. 1525,
church of Santo Stefano

When Jacopo Tatti alias Sansovino arrived in Venice after the Sack of Rome in 1527, the Republic was at the height of its political power. The crisis of the League of Cambrai that had put all of Europe in a coalition against the Republic was surpassed, and the Myth of Venice, the ideal Republic, the State of Liberty and Justice reigned. Venice began to celebrate itself in every way and with every art possible, and the arts become an instrument of political propaganda aimed at making Venice a new Rome. All the artists of the era, from Titian to Veronese to Tintoretto, were invited to collaborate on this project, so wisely formulated under the dogeship of Andrea Gritti (1523-1538). Yet it was above all Sansovino who became the great 'director' in architectural, urban, and cultural terms. Renovating St Mark's Square (Library, Mint, Loggetta, and the Procuratie Nuove) and in part the Palazzo itself, he successfully imposed a completely new style, adapting the precise architectural synthesis he had learned in Rome to Venetian tradition and incorporating into the city's buildings sculpture of every type: in the round, bas-relief, and stucco. Sansovino's elegant and balanced style of attenuated mannerism faithfully interpreted the climate of restoration and self-celebration that was widespread throughout the city's dominant political class. The school that formed around his workshop became a real academy. Indeed, most of the sculpture produced in Venice in the sixteenth century was academic and thus can not be compared to its counterparts in the fields of painting and architecture. The most original sculptor was by far Alessandro Vittoria, whose portraits show a vigorous and intense realism that is close to that of the work of Tintoretto and Titian. They are, for the most part, official portraits of political men on whose faces we find impressed not only personal traits but also those of the public virtues that were most respected at that time: "prudence, wisdom, self-control" (Pope-Hennessy). Vittoria's portraits are by far the most authentic celebration of the Veneto State.

Opposite page:
Jacopo Sansovino, Mars, Giant's
Staircase, courtyard of Palazzo
Ducale, 1554

Giambattista Bregno
Angel
Church of Santi Giovanni e Paolo

Antonio Lombardo's departure for Ferrara in 1506 and Tullio's involvement in important architectural projects created an artistic void that was filled by the brothers Giambattista and Lorenzo Bregno, relatives of Antonio Rizzo, whose works in Treviso, Padua and Cesena are quite remarkable. The very beautiful copy of the *Angels* now divided between the church of Santi Giovanni e Paolo and the Berlin Staatliche Museen was once part of the altar of the Verde della Scala in the church of Santa Maria dei Servi, destroyed in 1812. It was later moved to the church of Santi Giovanni e Paolo. This sculpture is a very beautiful example of this artist's mature work.

Giambattista Bregno, Angel, c. 1511, church of Santi Giovanni e Paolo, Sacristy

The Grimani Collection and the Archaeological Museum

The Archaeological Museum of Venice was founded in 1523, when Cardinale Domenico Grimani, a well-know humanist, donated to the Republic his collection of ancient marbles coming from both from excavations on his own properties in Rome and directly from Greece.

The collection was further enriched in 1593 by the bequest of Giovanni Grimani, patriarch of Aquileia and nephew of the first donor, as well as a very important personality in sixteenth-century Venice, who commissioned, among other things, the facade of San Francesco della Vigna from Palladio. This collection of ancient marbles was initially placed in Palazzo Ducale and later on in the sixteenth century, moved to the Anteroom of the Marciana Library, which was then being completed by Scamozzi. Here it was to form what can be considered one of the first, if not the first, public archaeological museums in Europe. Above all, it was the first collection of antiquity of the Renaissance that included Greek originals: indeed at that time Greek art was only known through Roman copies. Over the following centuries, other donations were added to the Grimani collection (Contarini, Morosini, Pasqualigo, Farsetti, Nani, Zulian, Molin, Weber), giving this museum a dual importance: first for the quality of the works exhibited, and then as testimony of the highly selective taste of the Venetian collectors, which influenced the development of Venetian art itself from at least the fifteenth century onward.

Greek funeral relief,
5th century BC

Greek Art of the Classical Period (5th-4th century BC)

Rooms IV and V of the Archaeological Museum exhibit major Greek works from the classical period, coming in large from the Grimani collections. The series of acephalous female statues is from the fifth century BC; attributed to the school of Phidias, it shows strict analogies with the well-known *Erechtheum Caryatides*. They are probably votive statues that once belonged to various Greek sanctuaries. Here, it is interesting to note the ability with which the drapery is treated; it seems to reproduce light, transparent fabrics that let the body forms and movement show through, demonstrating the perfect anatomical knowledge possessed by Greek artists.

The fragment of the funerary relief found in room V is from the same period, that is, the epoch of the Parthenon metope; it represents a youth on horseback reaching the world of Hades, where he is awaited by two feasting heroes. The horse is very attractive and reveals the same superb elegance of the Marciana quadriga (Weber collection). The statue of *Hera* (room IV) is an excellent sculpture of the era of Praxiteles (4th century BC), when Greek art returned to a less idealized but still classical style. In room V there is an interesting head of *Athene*, crowned by a large helmut; this is another important Greek original from the fourth century that has been attributed to an artist working in the circle of Scopas.

Head of Athene, 4th century BC

Acephalous female statue, 5th century BC and statue of Hera, 4th century BC

Hellenistic and Roman Sculpture (1st century BC - 1st century AD)

The altar exhibited in room VI is typical of the late-Hellenistic period (1st century BC); it is decorated by refined reliefs representing bacchanal scenes treated with the virtuosity of a cameo. It is considered to be one of the most famous pieces of the Grimani collection. Similar scenes of bacchanal dances appear on the base of the triangular candelabra (room III) from the Augustan age, the corners of which are decorated by festoons of fruit. In room VIII there is a Roman copy of a Hellenistic sculpture from the Pergamene school representing the figures of *Leda and the Swan,* a subject as widely diffused among the artists of antiquity as those of the Renaissance. Finally, two among the museum's most interesting reliefs once belonged to a *Throne of Saturn*; they represent Cupids with Saturn's scepter and scythe and once decorated a throne dedicated to this god, originally from Ravenna (room XI). These reliefs have been Venice since the fourteenth century and were the property of Oliviero Forzetta (d. 1369). Bartolomeo Bon studied them was he was working on the Porta della Carta.

Leda and the Swan, Roman copy of a Hellenistic sculpture from the school of Pergamene

Throne of Saturn, Roman work, mid-1st century AD

Roman Portraits (1st century BC - 2nd century AD)

Rooms IX and X of the Museum present an exceptional series of Roman busts from the first century BC to the third century AD. Roman portraiture was one of the highest expressions of ancient art and had a very important influence on Renaissance artists, especially in Venice. The Museum has an excellent copy,

from the time of Claudius, of a portrait of *Pompey* (c. 61 BC), done when the Roman general was at the height of his fortune, after constituting the first triumvirate with Caesar and Crassus (room IX). The presumed portrait of *Vitellius* (15-69) represents the emperor who succeeded Nero and remained in power for only ten months; this bust was brought to Venice in 1523 as a part of the first Grimani collec-

tion (room X). The Museum also displays one of the best remaining portraits of *Trajan* (53-117), successor to Nerva in 97, who is remembered for the conquest of the well-known Dacia in the great column in Rome (room IX). There is also a male bust from the Republican age (room IX). All these portraits have been in Venice since the sixteenth century and once belonged to the Grimani collection.

Unknown portrait, late-Republican age, 1st century BC

Portrait of Pompey, copy from the age of Claudius

Presumed portrait of Vitellius, 1st century AD

Portrait of Emperor Trajan, 1st century AD

Jacopo Sansovino

Jacopo Sansovino (1486-1570) was already well-known as an architect and sculptor when he reached Venice at the age of forty. His fame was such that he was immediately entrusted the commission to restore the dome of St Mark's, and in 1529 he was nominated overseer of the Basilica. Over the long span of his career he probably produced more buildings and sculptures that any other artist in the city's history: in addition to public buildings in St Mark's and at Rialto (the Fabbriche Nuove), he also constructed the churches of San Geminiano, San Francesco della Vigna, San Martino, and San Giuliano; the Corner and Dolfin palazzi on the Grand Canal; the seat of the Scuola Grand dell Misericordia and that of Ca' di Dio; Villa Garzoni at Ponte Casale, and other numerous monuments.

He very soon became one of the most listened to counsellors of the *Signoria*, along with Titian and Aretino, who in addition to being very famous artists were also experts in the halls of political power both in Venice and abroad. Thus, while the Venetian Republic was moving toward an increasingly exclusive oligarchical structure under the rule of Doge Andrea Gritti (1523-1538), Sansovino, Titian, and Aretino formed a small 'princely' court in a way that had never before been seen in Venice. A dense swarm of sculptors worked in Sansovino's studio-workshop including Alessandro Vittoria, Danese Cattaneo, Girolamo Lombardo, Tiziano Minio, Francesco Segala, and Tiziano Aspetti. With the exception of Vittoria, all of these artists were rather conventional, as were their painting counterparts at the end of the century (Palma Giovane and Aliense). Collectively they expressed the void that was being created in the Venetian culture and would be passed on to the following century.

Jacopo Sansovino, Loggetta of the Campanile, 1537-59

Sansovino in St Mark's Square and Palazzo Ducale
1537-59

Sansovino received his most important commission from the Republic in 1537: the Marciana Library. This building was to house the extraordinary bequest of Cardinal Bessarione (1468), one of the major collections of ancient codices ever gathered together by a humanist. The wealth of the building's plastic and architectural ornaments make it possible to consider it the richest monument constructed since antiquity, a re-evocation of the "great mercantile cities of the Hellenistic period: Alexandria and Antioch" (Gombrich). The building itself was also a political and artistic manifesto: heir to Byzantium, Venice now had to

Opposite page:
Jacopo Sansovino, Neptune, Giant's Staircase, courtyard of Palazzo Ducale, 1554

appear more splendid that Rome itself. The Piazzetta was to be Venice's Campidoglio, the renovation of which had been commissioned to Michelangelo at the very same time. This was to be the entrance to the city, the place where the palazzo of the Great Council rose, the center of the Republic's power.

The Library, along with the Palazzo and the church, symbolically represented one of the three fundamental aspects of the life of an ideal Republic: humanistic culture side by side with politics and religion. The function of these three buildings was rendered even more explicit by their sculpture. From 1559 on, all of the gods of Olympia shone in a magnificent marble sequence on the balustrade that crowns the Library: a work by Sanso-

vino's major collaborators including Alessandro Vittoria, Danese Cattaneo, Tiziano Minio, Bartolomeo Ammannati, etc. The allegorical cycle of Wisdom that adorns the Library is much more vast and complete both in terms of sculpture and painting, and was analyzed with great refinement by Nicola Ivanoff: first the Grand Staircase, contemporary to that of Vittoria's Golden Staircase in Palazzo Ducale (1554), with paintings by G.B. Franco; then the bas reliefs of the undersides of the arches of the exterior portico; and finally the paintings of the great hall (1556) introduced by the Titian's *Wisdom* in the vestibule.

Sansovino's masterpiece is without a doubt the Loggetta, where architecture and sculpture integrate to perfection. Begun at the

Jacopo Sansovino, Apollo and Minerva, Loggetta of the Campanile, 1540-45

same time as the Library and the Mint, it was meant to be the meeting place of the noblemen in front of the entrance to Palazzo Ducale. Here the symbolic significance is completely explicit: a triumphal arch that presents, in the niches at the side of the central forum, bronze representations (1540-45) of four ancient gods – *Minerva*, wisdom; *Apollo*, harmony; *Mercury*, eloquence and commerce, and *Peace*, an indispensable condition for social prosperity. These works are among this artist's most classically refined bronzes. On the attic there are three bas-reliefs by Sansovino's collaborators representing *Venice as Justice*, in the center, and *Cyprus* and *Candia* at the sides. The opposite terrace is from the seventeenth century. On the interior in a niche, there is a beautiful terra-cotta *Madonna* with a putto and the *St John the Child* signed by Sansovino. Thus the Loggetta became the element of meeting and the hinge between the three great ritual routes of square indicated by the Columns, when arriving by sea, by the Acritani Pilasters, towards the Palazzo, and by the flag stendard for the Church and the Clocktower, the final invention of the centuries-long process of constructing the city's political center.

Rizzo's staircase, located in the courtyard of the Palazzo directly in front of the Loggetta, was also embellished by Sansovino with the statues of the *Giants* (1554), after which it is named. *Mars* was meant to signify continental dominion, and *Neptune*, that of the sea. The latter, with its hair and a long beard tossed by the wind, is perhaps among this great maestro's most successful works.

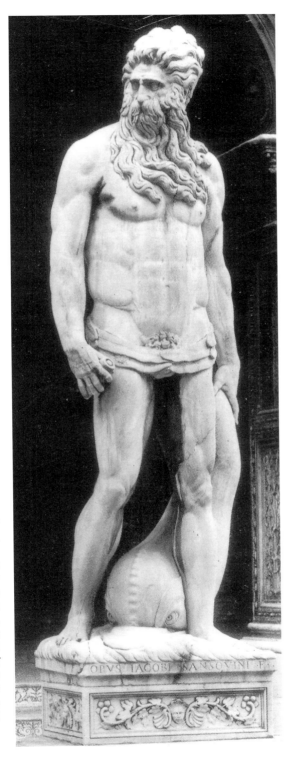

Sansovino's Bronze Sculptures in St Mark's Basilica
1537-52

While he was working on the Square, Sansovino begin an important series of bronze sculptures that were meant to decorate the presbytery of St Mark's basilica: eight bas-reliefs with the *Stories of St Mark* (1537-43) for the stalls at the sides of the choir, the door of Sacristy (1545-69), the baptismal basin (1545), and finally the small statues of the four *Evangelists* (1552) on the balustrade of the choir. All these works were done with collaboration of his assistants and reveal all the eclecticism of his style. While the reliefs in the choir-stalls, especially those on the right, appear to be a slightly artificial exercise inspired by Donatello's bronze work in Padua, those on the curved plane of the sacristy door are much freer and more elegant in the classicism of the era: the *Deposition* (below), the *Resurrection* (above), and a series of small heads of prophets in which the artist represents himself and other personalities of the era such as his friends Titian, Aretino, and Veronese (at the sides on the corners). The four small statues of the *Evangelists* demonstrate Sansovino's moment of admiration for Michelangelo.

Jacopo Sansovino, Resurrection, detail of sacristy door, St Mark's basilica, 1545-69

Jacopo Sansovino
Monument to Tommaso
Rangone
1553, Church of San Giuliano

Jacopo Sansovino
St John the Baptist
1560, Church of the Frari,
Corner chapel

One of Sansovino's latest and most successful works is the *Monument to Tommaso Rangone* on the facade of San Giuliano in the Mercerie, constructed by Sansovino in 1553. Rangone, a famous humanist and scientist from Ravenna was the Guardian Grande of the Scuola di San Marco and financed the large canvases by Tintoretto. He is depicted in his studio: his handsome face and flowing beard, cast in bronze by Giulio Alberghetti with Vittoria's assistance, are very expressive.

The *St John the Baptist* on the baptismal font in the Corner chapel at the Frari (c. 1560) is perhaps Sansovino's late masterpiece. Its proportions and technique are of rare elegance and the sculpture is a worthy re-proposal of the subject already developed by Donatello in the same church more than a century earlier.

Below: *Jacopo Sansovino, Rangone Monument, church of San Giuliano, facade, 1553;* right: *St John the Baptist, c. 1560, church of the Frari*

Alessandro Vittoria

Alessandro Vittoria (1525-1608), a sculptor from the Trento region, reached Venice in 1543 before his twentieth birthday. He immediately went to work in Sansovino's studio, where he began collaborating on the statues of the Library. Considering their different temperaments, this student-maestro relationship had to have been difficult from the very beginning, and in 1547 Vittoria left the city and moved to Vicenza. When he return to Venice definitively in 1553, he began an intense activity developing a very personal, impetuous, and inventive style, evidently modelled, ideally, after Michelangelo.

Among his major sculptural works it is important to remember - in addition to the stuccoes for the Golden Staircase, the Library (1555), and Villa Barbaro in Maser (1560) - the altars for San Francesco della Vigna, San Salvador, and San Giuliano, and various sculptures for the churches of Santi Giovanni e Paolo, the Frari, and San Zaccaria. His portraits, especially those in terra cotta in which his touch is more direct, are among the great masterpieces of the sixteenth-century. "Neither Rodin, nor Medardo Rosso were more sensitive; and do not forget that his vitalizing world arrived in Rome with Camillo Mariani, his disciple ... , leading towards Francesco Mochi, disciple of Mariani, and favorite disciple of Bernini himself" (Fiocco).

Alessandro Vittoria, stuccoes of the Marciana Library staircase, c. 1555

Alessandro Vittoria
St Jerome
c. 1565, Church of the Frari

This powerful marble statue of *St Jerome the Penitent* was once a part of the large monumental complex that included a bas-relief representing the *Assumption of the Virgin with Saints*, demolished in the eighteenth century. Only the *Saints* modelled in stucco remain at the sides of the altar. Here the sculptor's hand dominates the marble with wise mastery to achieve chiaroscural effects that recall the paintings of the same era by Titian and Tintoretto.

Alessandro Vittoria, St Jerome, 1565, church of the Frari

Alessandro Vittoria
Luganegheri Altar
c. 1600, Church of San Salvador

The altar of the Luganegheri, in the left nave of the church of San Salvador, is decorated by statues of St Roch and St Sebastian. The latter, set against the column at the side of the altar and thus incorporated into the sculpture, is represented with great mastery of the nude and shows the typical twisted figure inspired by Michelangelo. On the opposite wall one finds Sansovino's *Venier Monument* (1561), with an attractive statue of *Charity* done in the classical tradition of this artist. Sansovino also designed the altar that frames Titian's magnificent *Annunciation* (1560-65). Thus, this splendid church, a masterpiece by Giorgio Spavento begun in 1505, contains works by the three major artists that were working in Venice in the latter half of the century.

Alessandro Vittoria, St Sebastian c. 1600, church of San Salvador, Luganegheri altar

Vittoria's Portraits
Seminary Museum and Ca' d'Oro

The Seminary Museum conserves some of Vittoria's most fascinating and most elegant terra-cotta portraits, done in the artist's full maturity. Among these are representations of two important individuals, the *Bust of Doge Nicolò Da Ponte* (c. 1585), whose head rises out of the rich mantle drapery, and that of *Procurator Pietro Zen*, c. 1590), a masterpiece of psychological introspection. Another important series of Vittoria's portraits is found at Ca' d'Oro: the marble bust of *Procurator Giovanni Donà*, originally from the church of Santi Giovanni e Paolo; the terra-cotta bust of *Procurator Marino Grimani* (c. 1595), and the mighty marble portrait of *Benedetto Manzini*, parish priest of San Geminiano. The latter is one of the heights of Renaissance sculpture.

Portrait of Alessandro Vittoria c. 1590. Above: *Procurator Pietro Zen, terra cotta, Seminary Museum; Procurator Marino Grimani, terra cotta, Ca' d'Oro;* right: *Doge Nicolò Da Ponte, terra cotta, Seminary Museum;* below: *Father Benedetto Manzini, marble, Ca' d'Oro*

Girolamo Campagna
Cumaean Sibyl
1582, Church of San Sebastiano

The stucco statues done in 1582 by Girolamo Campagna for the choir of the church of San Salvador – the *Annunciation*, the *Angel*, the *Cumaean Sibyl*, and the *Erythraean Sibyl* – are among the artist's masterpieces. "In the voluminous but always gentle figures of the two sibyls, the play of light and shadow, which renders the drapery sparkling and loose, suggests an accent of grace and elegance and thus takes on an eminently decorative value" (P. Rossi).

Girolamo Campagna
High Altar
1591-93, San Giorgio Maggiore

Girolamo Campagna (Verona 1552-1626) was trained at the school of Danese Cattaneo, a collaborator of Sansovino from the Roman times. He began as a classicizing mannerist sculptor inspired by Sansovino to later open to Vittoria's influence, as in his masterpiece for the altar of the church of San Giorgio Maggiore representing the *Four Evangelists Sustaining the World under the Holy Father*. Moulded with strong mannerist accents, this imposing bronze

group forms a very effective silhouette against the white Palladian columns that make up the background of the presbytery. In the *Virgin and Child Surrounded by Angels* (1595) found in the left nave of the church, Campagna returns to the more balanced and elegant forms of the origins.

Girolamo Campagna, Cumaean Sibyl, church of San Sebastiano, 1582

Girolamo Campagna, church of San Giorgio Maggiore, high altar. 1591-93

The Sculptures at the Rialto Market

The sculptural apparatus that adorns the city's other great center at Rialto is less showy but no less significant than that of St Mark's. The bridge itself, constructed on a project by Antonio da Ponte (1588-91), presents the figures of the *Annunciation*, a very expressive work by Agostino Rubini, an assistant to Vittoria from Vicenza (on the side towards St Mark's), and *St Mark* and *St Theodore* by Tiziano Aspetti (on the other side). The overall iconological system mirrors that of the church (the *Annunciation* recalls the mythical date of the city's foundation) and the Piazzetta (the two protector saints). On the corner of Scarpagnino's palazzo (1521) designed for the Dieci Savi (the magistracy that oversaw the public taxation) is another statue of *Justice*, the central element of Palazzo Ducale's decoration. Finally, in remembrance of the market's public function, we find the other Colonna del Bando (flagstaff), also known as the *Gobbo di Rialto* because of the kneeling caryatid that sustains the steps. This work was sculpted by Pietro Grazioli da Salò, an artist of Sansovino's circle.

The sixteenth-century renovation of the city's public space could not help but affect its essential service elements: the wells. Two magnificent bronze wells, the only of their kind in Venice, are found in the courtyard of Palazzo Ducale: the one towards the Porta della Carta was done by Alfonso Alberghetti (1554-59), the other is by Nicolò Conti (1556), both of whom were master casters at the Arsenale. The two, very similar octagonal well-curbs are adorned by shields and harpies in the mannerist taste of the era. In the courtyard of the Mint there was once what was supposed to be the most monumental well in the city. It was erected on a drawing by Sansovino, with a figure of *Apollo* at the top of the arch surmounting it, done by Danese Cattaneo. This work was later moved to courtyard at Ca' Pesaro, where it is found today. The most classical of the Renaissance well-curbs is that in Campo Santi Giovanni e Paolo, from the 1510s. It was originally found in Palazzo Corner of the Ca' Grande at San Maurizio and boasts eight high-relief putti bearing festoons with fruit and one shield with the arms of the Corner around the well-curb.

Agostino Rubini, the Nuptial
Angel and the Annunciation,
Rialto bridge, c. 1590

Opposite page: *Nicolò Conti,*
bronze well-curb, 1556,
courtyard of Palazzo Ducale

Well in Campo Santi Giovanni e
Paolo from Ca' Corner at San
Maurizio, early-16th century

VII. The Seventeenth Century: Sculpture as Theater

In 1606 Venice made a last grand political gesture when Doge Leonardo Donà refused to give in to the interdict issued by Pope Paul V, which reprimanded the Venetian state for excessive independence in religious matters. Later, over the course of the seventeenth century, the Venetian aristocracy, while maintaining its monopoly of the Republic intact, no longer knew how to manage and renew itself. Abandoning every mercantile interest and investing more and more of its capital on the mainland, the aristocracy was transformed into a parasitic class of landed property owners. This withdrawal into themselves and the resultant collapse of vitality was not only political and economic but social and cultural as well. Theater alone, especially in music, witnessed a sudden and almost unexplainable splendor. In the other arts, after the extraordinary production of the preceding century, the scene was practically deserted. The most important painters working in Venice came from other cities, like Strozzi from Genoa or Luca Giordano from Naples. Only one Venetian architect, Longhena, had a truly new vision of the building arts, and almost all the sculptors were foreigners.

Baldassare Longhena, church of the Salute, 1631-81

In Catholic countries the Counter-Reform had also imposed very precise rules on the arts, rules that had to be applied with openly didactic aims: images had to be clear and realistic enough to impress and emotionally involve the congregation. Thus seventeenth-century art became increasingly more spectacular taking on the same principles as the theater. This was particularly true for sculpture: statues were like actors performing emphatically on the scene. One could say that artistic as well as religious directives were issued in Rome, and thus, in Rome, the art of Gian Lorenzo Bernini (1598-1680) imposed the aesthetic principles that had to be admired and accepted throughout Europe.

Opposite page:
*Bernardo Falcone da Lugano,
Punta della Dogana, detail,
c. 1677*

117

Foreign Sculptors: Le Court, Parodi, Barthel, and Falcone

The most prolific sculptor working in Venice from 1657 onward was also a follower of Bernini: Giusto Le Court (1627-1679), a Flemish sculptor, became the closest collaborator of Baldassare Longhena (the churches of the Salute, Tolentini, Ospedaletto, Sant'Andrea della Zirada, San Clement in Isola, San Lazzaro dei Mendicanti, etc.). Le Court was surrounded by a group of sculptors coming from all over Italy and Europe: Bernardo Falcone (Ticino), Enrico Meyring (the Netherlands), Tommaso Ruer and Melchiorre Barthel (Germany), Michele Fabris, otherwise known as Ongaro (Hungary), Clemente Molli (Bologna), and Francesco Cavrioli (Treviso).

Filippo Parodi (Genoa 1630-1702) also settled in the Veneto in 1683 after an intense period of work in his own homeland where the influence of French art was strong (Pierre Puget) and two trips to Rome. He worked in both in Padua (church of the Saint and Santa Giustina) and in Venice (*Morosini Monument* at Tolentini and *Portrait of Doge Francesco Morosini* in Palazzo Ducale). Parodi's presence represented an improvement in the quality of Venetian sculpture in as much as he imposed "the secure premises for moving decisively towards the eighteenth century, going beyond the poetics of the *neo-tenebrosi* in an increasingly more liberated apotheosis of clarity" (Semenzato). In short one could say that this sculptor occupied a similar position to that of Sebastiano Ricci in the field of painting at the threshold of the eighteenth century.

Baroque Church Facades

In the seventeenth century architecture was often a simple support for sculptural work. Numerous facades of Venetian churches were real monuments financed by wealthy families to eternalize their own personal glories. All else aside, this fashion furnished work to entire workshops of sculptors throughout the century. The most spectacular examples of this very expensive custom are, in chronological order, the facades of the church of San Salvador del Sardi (c. 1663) with sculptures by Bernardo Falconi commissioned by the merchant Jacopo Galli; Santa Giustina by Longhena (1640) with sculptures by Clemente Molli commissioned by Girolamo Soranzo; Santa Maria della Misericordia by Molli (1651-59) commissioned by Senator Gaspare Moro; the Ospedaletto by Longhena (1670-72) with sculptures by Le Court and his collaborators commissioned by Bartolomeo Cargnoni; the Scalzi by Sardi (1672-80), completely constructed in Carrara marble with sculptures by Falconi commissioned by Count Gerolamo Cavazza; Santa Maria del Giglio by Sardi (1680-83) with sculptures by Le Court on commission by the family of Antonio Barbaro, once superintendent in Dalmatia. The latter was probably the most expensive of all these projects, costing the Barbaro family the sum of 30,000 ducats.

One of the most theatrical and curious facades in Venice is that of the church of San Moisè designed by the architect Alessandro Tremignon (1668) and decorated with sculptures by Enrico Meyring, on a commission by the family of the nobleman Vincenzo Fini. Fini's bust is placed on a high central obelisk sustained by two imaginary animals, a cross between a dog and a dragon, and is bordered by an orgy of columns, festoons, and every type of figure imaginable designed with a purely scenographic function. The imaginary animals are similar to those that sustain the sacellum of the doge in the *Tomb of Doge Pesaro* at the Frari as well as that of the *Monument to the Ambassador of Argençon* in the church of San Giobbe.

Alessandro Tremignon, Facade of San Moisè decorated by E. Meyring, 1668

Giuseppe Sardi, Facade of San Salvador decorated by B. Falconi, 1663

Giuseppe Sardi, Facade of S. Maria del Giglio decorated by Le Cour, 1680-83

Giuseppe Sardi, facade of the Scalzi, 1672-80

N. and S. Roccatagliata
Antependium
1663, Church of St Moisè, sacristy

Niccolò Roccatagliata, a gold-smith from Genoa who was in Venice from 1593 on, sculpted the *antependium* of the altar in the sacristy of San Moisè (1633) with his son Sebastiano. It repre-sents the *Angels Carrying the Dead Christ* and the *Holy Father in Glory*, a bronze bas-relief clearly influenced by Sansovino. In the words of Wittkower it is: "... a work of fascinating beauty. The strange iconography would require detailed investigation, but the profound sensitivity and devotion expressed by the numerous small bronze figurines bind it tightly to the religious atmosphere of the art of the Counter-Reformation."

N. and S. Roccatagliata, Antependium, 1633, San Moisè, sacristy; opposite page: *Tomb of Doge Giovanni Pesaro, 1669, church of the Frari*

Monument to Doge Giovanni Pesaro
1669, Church of the Frari

Designed by Baldassare Longhena, this work is typical of the Venetian Baroque (1669). The complex monument frames the entire side entrance to the basilica. The gigantic marble statues were done by Melchiorre Barthel (Dresden); the two bronze skeletons and the mon-sters under the throne by Bernardo Falcone (Lugano). Four marble pedestals sustain the gigantic Moors, the Turks taken prisoner in Candia, who sustain a trabeation of trophies and triglyphs on their shoulders. Two black skeletons draped in white marble appear, in sharp contrast, between the robust Moors carry-ing a long engraved inscription. Above the trabeation four columns in grey veined marble sustain an architrave; at the cen-ter two putti uphold the Pesaro coat-of-arms. Under a rich bal-dachin of red marble imitating a brocade drape bordered by bor-dure and tassels in embossed and gilded copper, one finds the doge himself in the act of haranguing the crowd. The allegories of *Reli-gion* and *Values* (on the left), and *Good-will* and *Justice* (on the right) are placed at the sides on pedestals between the columns. Another four allegorical figures are on the cornice: a genius and three women.

The inscription is typically baroque: "Vixit anno LXX (lived 70 Years); devixit anno MDCLIX (died in the year 1659); Hic revixit anno MDCLXIX (here he lived again in the year 1669)". There have been various opin-ions on this colossal work: highly esteemed by its contemporaries, it was harshly criticized in the nineteenth century, above all by John Ruskin. After the recent restoration the monument has re-found the chromatic balance given by the sharp variations in the different marbles.

Giusto Le Court
High Altar
c. 1670, Church of Santa Maria della Salute

The Church of the Salute was constructed with public funds after the plague of 1630; it is Longhena's masterpiece. When it came time to decorate the high altar, the *Signoria* had asked Bernini to intervene, but he refused. Thus the choice fell upon Giusto Le Court, and the commission was successfully resolved. The dramatic scene on the left represents the *Virgin in*

Glory with the figure of Venice kneeling and imploring protection from the plague; that on the right depicts an *Angel* hunting after the *Plague* represented by a horrible gesticulating old woman. It is a very intense but balanced group that constitutes a powerful center of attraction upon entering into the circular space of the church. Le Court, together with Francesco Cavrioli, Tommaso Ruer, Arrigo Meyring, and other sculptors also contributed to both the interior and exterior decoration of the grandiose baroque basilica.

Filippo Parodi
Monument to Patriarch
Francesco Morosini
c. 1683, Church of the Tolentini

The magnificent *Monument to Patriarch Francesco Morosini* (d. 1678), on the left of the high altar, adorned with rich marble drapery and symbolic figures, is Francesco Parodi's most important work found in Venice. It "reunites reminiscences of Bernini with early-rococo elements" (Wittkower).
The high altar of the same period was done by Longhena in collaboration with Le Court. In the right transept there are two important seventeenth-century altarpieces by Luca Giordano and Giovanni Lyss.

Giusto Le Court, high altar, c. 1670, church of the Salute

Filippo Parodi, Monument to Francesco Morosini, detail, c. 1683, church of the Tolentini

Sculptors in Wood: Pianta, Piazzetta, and Brustolon

Francesco Pianta, dossals at the Scuola di San Rocco, late-17th century, detail of the Library and Tintoretto's caricature

At a time when sculpture is above all ornamental, considerable work was also done in Venice in wood, once almost exclusively relegated to decorative furnishings (choir stalls, wardrobes, furniture, etc.) and generally the monopoly of German artists. Piazzetta and Brustolon were the best Venetian specialists in this seventeenth-century art, as were Corradini and Marchiori in the following century. The Trevisan sculptor Jacopo Piazzetta (c. 1640 - 1705), father of the well-known painter Giambattista and owner of an important workshop, was an energetic and refined sculptor. This is evident in his best works such as his masterpiece for the chapel of the Rosary in the church of Santi Giovanni e Paolo.

Andrea Brustolon (Belluno 1662-1732), student of Parodi, is known above all as a furniture carver, a craft in which he developed his baroque-already-rococo creative impulse with great freedom, creating real sculptures in a style that demonstrated his impressive technical ability.

Francesco Pianta (1632-1692), a Venetian, was a figure apart. Only one important work of his is known, the cycle for the upper hall of the Scuola di San Rocco. It is here that this eccentric and disconcerting sculptor, who worked with a caricatured realism full of grotesque almost surrealistic inventions, created perhaps the most original expression of the Venetian Baroque.

Francesco Pianta
Dossals
late-17th century, Scuola di San Rocco

The sixteen carved caryatids on the wooden dossals of the upper hall of the Scuola di San Rocco, the major known work by Francesco Pianta, present a completely personal and hallucinated symbolism. According to the artist's own directions it has to be read beginning from the left on the wall in front of the grand staircase, where the following figures appear: *Melancholy, Honor, Greed* (with the accounts book), *Ignorance* (mule's head), *Science* (framed by books), the *Distinction between Good and Evil*, the chained *Fury, Curiosity* (in the form of a spy hidden by a cape), *Scandal, Honest Pleasure* (musical instruments), *Cicero* (as the defender of sculpture), and ending with the caricature of *Tintoretto*, which is meant to represent painting. On the walls

of the grand staircase we find *Plenty*, the *Stratagem* (in chains), the dissolute *Reproach* (with a snake twisted around it), and *Mercury* (bearing a scroll that narrates the entire cycle). The series is completed by the *Library* (64 volumes) of which *Deception* is the librarian. In his maniacal precision of detail, Pianta manages to confer an efficient and robust unity to these extravagant representations.

Giacomo Piazzetta
Dossals
c. 1680, Church of Santi Giovanni
e Paolo, chapel of the Rosary

The dossals of the chapel of the
Rosary in the church of Santi
Giovanni e Paolo are Giacomo
Piazzetta's most conspicuous
work found in Venice. They
represent the episodes of the
life of the Virgin, intercalated
by large figures in the form of
caryatids. Piazzetta's precise
and energetic engraving
underlines the shadows and
gives body to the forms in a
manner that certainly influenced the work of his son, who
is represented by the ceiling
fresco in the chapel of St
Dominic.

Giacomo Piazzetta, dossals of
the chapel of Rosario, detail,
church of Santi Giovanni e
Paolo, c. 1680

Andrea Brustolon, furniture for
Casa Venier, c. 1700,
Ca' Rezzonico

Andrea Brustolon
Furniture for the Venier
Residence
c. 1700, Ca' Rezzonico

Around 1700 Brustolon carved
an important series of furniture
for the Venier family of San Vio.
These pieces, along with those
for the Pisani family now at the
Quirinale, are among the masterpieces of wooden sculpture done
between the Baroque and the
Rococo. The artist's prodigious
ability in working ebony and
boxwood, two very hard woods,
indulges in ornamental forms
that are real sculptures in the
round. This furniture is now
exhibited at Ca' Rezzonico:
flower-stands with monumental
and boyish figures of Moors,
large chairs, allegorical groups
of the elements and the seasons
in forms of vase stands, and a
large *console*, which represents
the collection's tour de force,
sustained by a representation of
Hercules Fighting the Hydra and
Cerberus.

VIII. The Eighteenth Century: A European Capital

During the eighteenth century the port of Venice was cut back to a purely local scale, and the Republic led by an increasingly timorous and provincial political class. Yet, almost in contrast, from the beginning of the century on, the very same period saw a real explosion of creativity in the heart of the free, itinerant, and popular Venetian Republic of the arts. Painters, sculptors, architects, writers, second-rate actors, and musicians carried the vitality, optimism, and joy of living of an entire population throughout the world and once again made Venice the most inventive cultural capital of Europe. Venice began anew to export culture: Ricci, Tiepolo, Canaletto, Bellotto, Carriera, Piranesi, Vivaldi, and Goldoni were all international figures, as were Corradini and Canova. The entire Venetian artistic life was rekindled in the splendid eighteenth century, investing all forms of major and minor arts, and the Venetian Rococo imposed its taste on stuccos, furniture, and glass. It was here in Venice that the premises of a few of the most radical changes of European culture were established: Carlo Lodoli's theories, Tirali or Temanza's architecture, or Piranesi's imaginative works are at the origins of the neo-classical movement, the rational and severe expression of illuminism, of which Canova was the maximum exponent in sculpture. The great illuminist writer, Wolfgang Goethe came to Venice in 1786 to see and admire everything: buildings, works of art, theater, parties. In the highest of elogies to the city he wrote: "Everything that surrounds us is full of nobility, it is the grandiose and venerable work of human strengths joined together, it is a majestic monument not of one prince alone, but of an entire population."

Domenico Rossi, church of San Stae, facade decorated by Giuseppe Torretto, c. 1705

Opposite page:
Abbondio Stazio and Carpoforo Mazzetti Tencalla, ceiling of the Scuola Grande dei Carmini, stucco details, early-18th century

From Rococo to Neoclassicism: Torretto and Morlaiter

Eighteenth-century Venetian sculpture began under the relaxed and classicizing influence of Filippo Parodi, a sculptor from Genoa. This trend was further reinforced by two other sculptors coming from outside of Venice, Giuseppe Mazza (Emilia 1653-1741) and Pietro Baratta (Tuscany 1659-1729), who adjusted their craft to that neo-sixteenth century taste then in vogue in Venice in painting as well as architecture.

Artists of Venetian or Veneto origin, born around 1660, also became active once again in the early-eighteenth century. Among them we have to include Brustolon, of whom we spoke of earlier and who at the turn of the century was among the most inventive artists of the Rococo. Giovanni Bonazza (1654-1736) is from the same generation: he was the oldest among the Venetians and soon moved to Padua with his three sons, Antonio, Francesco, and Tommaso to decorate numerous country houses (villa Widmann, villa Pisani) as well as the gardens of the royal palace in St Petersburg with sculptures full of invention and popular realism.

Giuseppe Torretto (1661-1743) was undoubtedly the most important sculptor of his generation and the initiator of an important school where Canova trained. His works decorate numerous Venetian churches – Scalzi, San Stae, Gesuiti – with a series of figures in the round and bas-reliefs "in which the refined and measured geometry of the compositions mingles in a completely rococo impetuosity and vivacity" (Semenzato). Other artists of practically the same age, Antonio Tarsia (1662-1739), Marino Groppelli (1664-1739), and Francesco Cabianca (1665-1737), took a different approach interpreting an elegant classicism of Renaissance derivation. Anto-

Valier monument, church of Santi Giovanni e Paolo, c. 1706

nio Corradini (1668-1752) was perhaps the most successful sculptor of this period; working in Venice, Vienna, Roma, and Naples (San Severo chapel), his success can most certainly be attributed to the freely rococo style that was later continued by Morlaiter. Giammaria Morlaiter (1699-1781) was one of the most brilliant Venetian sculptors of the eighteenth century: his terra-cotta models in Ca' Rezzonico are epitomes of the refined and sensual grace of this century. Another two accomplished second-generation sculptors also worked in this vein: Antonio Gai (1686-1769) and Giuseppe Bernardi (1694-1774), Canova's maestro. Last but not least one has to mention Giuseppe Marchiori (1696-1781); initially a follower of his fellow townsman Andrea Brustolon, he was a cultured and refined sculptor who was the forerunner of that neo-classical trend that would impose itself at the end of the century.

Sculptors of the Early-18th Century
1708-30, Church of Santi Giovanni e Paolo

In 1706 Andrea Tirali designed the *Valier Family Tomb* for the church of Santi Giovanni e Paolo, presumably at the same time that Longhena working on the project for *Doge Pesaro* in the church of the Frari (sustaining Barthel's statue). Compared to the elaborate and heavy style of the latter, Tirali's design appears simple and clear, in the background drapery sustained by putti, and the sculpture has a completely eighteenth-century air of a light baroque veering toward rococo. The figures were done by different artists: *Doge Bertucci* (center) is by Baratta; *Doge Silvestro* by Tarsia; the *Dogaressa* by Giovanni Bonazza; the allegorical bas-relief representing the *Victory of the Dardanelles* (in the center of the stylobate) by Groppelli.

The nearby chapel of St Dominic is also designed by Tirali (1690-1716); the ceiling is adorned by one of Gian Battista Piazzetta's masterpieces (1727). The walls are covered by six large bas-reliefs by Giuseppe Mazza (c. 1720): five are in bronze, the first on the right is wood. These reliefs depict the *Episodes of the Life of St Dominic* in a far-reaching work of clear classical formation. The eighteenth-century reliefs decorating the walls of the presbytery of the chapel of the Rosary are more lively and varied. They were done by Vittoria in 1575 to honor the Madonna of the Rosary on whose feast day the battle of Lepanto (1571) took place.

This magnificent environment contains canvases by Veronese, sculptures by Vittoria and Campagna, and dossals by Jacopo Piazzetta; it is further embellished by high reliefs depicting the *Stories of the Life of the Virgin* (c. 1730) by Giuseppe Torretto, Giovanni and Antonio Bonazza, Alvise and Carlo Tagliapietra, and Giovanni Maria Morlaiter. It is interesting to note the difference between Bonazza's full-bodied and realistic style (*Annunciation, Adoration of the Shepherds*, and *Adoration of the Magi*) and that of more refined and self-possessed artists like Torretto (*Presentation in the Temple* and the *Nuptial Ceremony*) or Morlaiter (*Rest on the Flight into Egypt* and *Dispute with the Doctors*).

Giuseppe Mazza, Episode of the Life of St Dominic, c. 1720, church of Santi Giovanni e Paolo, chapel of St Dominic

Giammaria Morlaiter, Dispute with the Doctors, c. 1730, church of Santi Giovanni e Paolo, chapel of the Rosary

Torretto and the Early-18th Sculptors
1709-10, Church of San Stae

The church of San Stae (Sant' Eustachio) is perhaps the most complete and coherent artistic expression of eighteenth-century Venice. Construction began in 1709 on a design by Giovanni Grassi and Domenico Rossi (facade), commissioned by Doge Francesco Morosini. It was decorated in a unitary way over a brief period of time by the era's most famous sculptors (Torretto, Tarsia, Baratta, Groppelli, Cabianca, Corradini, etc.) and painters (Sebastiano Ricci, Piazzetta, Tiepolo, Amigoni, Pellegrini, etc.).

The pompous but elegant facade on the Grand Canal is dominated by Torretto's lively and easy rococo group carved in Istrian stone above the entrance portal. It is crowned by Corradini's three statues representing *Faith*, the *Saviour*, and *Hope*. Giuseppe Torretto also did the bas-relief with the *Descent from the Cross* on the antependium of the high altar and the marble *Crucifix* in the Foscarini chapel (on the left); this chapel is adorned with various busts of the Foscarini family by different sculptors, including Torretto (Antonio Foscarini), Tarsi, Baratta, and Groppelli.

Giuseppe Torretto, group of angels on the entrance to San Stae, c. 1710

Antonio Corradini at the Church of the Carmini
1721

The eighteenth century also left a significant mark on the ancient church of the Carmelites, known as 'dei Carmini'. In addition to the dome frescoes by Sebastiano Ricci (1708) and a few canvases by Ricci and Pellegrini in the central nave, the church conserves two of the six sculptures that were originally commissioned by the Scuola del Carmini from Corradini and Torretto: the figures of *Virginity* and *Gentleness* on the third altar on the right, respectively. Corradini's *Virginity* is one of the few works of this well-known artist that has remained in Venice and has all the supple elegance that characterizes his style. It was later reproduced in an etching based on a drawing by Gian Battista Tiepolo.

Giuseppe Torretto at the Church of the Gesuiti
c. 1714-29

The Gesuiti were not accepted in Venice until 1657, when they constructed, almost out of revenge, the most sumptuous church in the city. The church of the Gesuiti, which already belonged to the order of the Crutched Friars, was re-done between 1714 and 1729 on a project designed by Domenico Rossi and decorated by a numerous array of artists. The extraordinary wall covering appears like damask under the effect of the complex volutes created by antique green and white Carrara marble tessurae. The vault is covered by frescoes by Francesco Fontebasso framed by stuccoes by Abbondio Stazio. Between the splendor of the marbles and the goldwork we find the *Archangels* in white Carrara marble placed in the niches of the pilasters of the cross vault and the presbytery. These angels, so splendidly nervous and awake in the whirling of their garments and wings, are among the most imaginative of Giuseppe Torretto's works. Torretto also did the *Saviour* and the *Holy Father* on the marble globe of the high altar and the figure of the *Virgin* at the top of the facade. The statues of the *Apostles* on the facades were done by various sculptors including Groppelli, Tarsia, and Baratta, who also did the statue of St Ignatius of Loyola on the transept altar.

Antonio Corradini, Virginity, 1721, church of the Carmini

Giuseppe Torretto, Archangel Raphael, 1714-29, church of the Gesuiti

Giovanni Marchiori at the Church of the Ospizio della Pietà
c. 1753

The church of the Ospizio della Pietà, where Vivaldi taught music to the young orphans in the early years of the century, looks more like a concert hall than a religious building. It is identical in construction to the Gesuati and was designed by the same architect, Giorgio Massari (c. 1745). The church was decorated by Tiepolo, who painted the ceiling brimful of clouds and angel musicians. At the sides of the altar there are two remarkable sculptures, *St Peter* by Giovanni Marchiori and *St Mark* by Antonio Gai, both from around 1753. Marchiori's *St Peter* is a solid and composed work. It is characteristic of the trend inspired by the sixteenth century that prepared the ground for the neo-classical movement and left one of its most complete expressions in Marchiori's sculptures for the facade of the church of San Rocco and the Scuola of the same name (wooden panels with the *Stories of St Roch* on the floor above).

Giovanni Maria Morlaiter at the Church of Gesuati
1738-55

The church of Santa Maria del Rosario or the Gesuati (of the Dominican order) was constructed by Giorgio Massari between 1726 and 1736. It is another eighteenth-century jewel in which architecture, sculpture, and painting complete one another to an extreme. On the nave vault we find one of Gian Battista Tiepolo's (1737-39) most imaginative frescoes.

Giuseppe Marchiori, St Peter, c. 1753, church of the Pietà

Tiepolo also did the six canvases of the side altars (first on the right); the others are by Piazzetta (third on the right), Sebastiano Ricci (first on the left), and other artists of the era. Giammaria Morlaiter (1738-55) sculpted all the statues of the *Evangelists* and *Prophets* and the bas-reliefs of the *Episodes of the Life of Christ*. Here Morlaiter's elegant and seductive figures have the same liberty of movement and rococo grace that characterizes Tiepolo's contemporary paintings.

Giovanni Maria Morlaiter, marble altarpiece with a glory of angels, c. 1743, church of Gesuati

Giovanni Maria Morlaiter and Giuseppe Bernardi at the Church of the Fava
c. 1740-60

The church of Santa Maria della Consolazione, known as 'della Fava' offers another exceptional concentration of eighteenth-century Venetian art. It is the only religious building constructed in Venice by Antonio Gaspari (1705-15), the most baroque of the Venetian architects (in the Roman sense of the term). The church conserves two masterpieces of eighteenth-century painting, one by Piazzetta (1725-27) the other by Tiepolo (1732), and two beautiful altarpieces by Amigoni. Piazzetta himself was buried in the Albrizzi tomb. The statues of the *Saints* and *Evangelists* and the bas-reliefs representing the *Stories of the Life of St Philip Neri* along the walls of the nave are the most important work of Giuseppe Bernardi, known as Torretto, who skilfully developed the more decorative aspects of the style of his maestro Giuseppe Torretto and was Canova's maestro. In the presbytery, defined by Massari's (1750-53) elegant classical forms, the two *Angels* next to the altar are among Morlaiter's most lively and precious works. There is also a very beautiful *Angel* on the holy-water font near the entrance by an unknown artist.

Giovanni Maria Morlaiter Terra-cotta Models
Ca' Rezzonico

Ca' Rezzonico conserves the models that were once the property of Giammaria Morlaiter's workshop. They include about one hundred works in terra cotta and clay, of which about seventy can be attributed to Morlaiter himself; the others were done by different artists collaborating with the studio including Torretto, Corradini, Marchiori, etc. The success of Morlaiter's hand in modelling clay is evident, "indeed – like drawing for the painter – clay is certainly more suited to the immediacy of artifice and even involves the artistic level which is almost always higher in the models " (Elisabetta Martinelli). We find here, among the others, models of the two elegant bas-reliefs for the chapel of the Rosary in the church Santi Giovanni e Paolo, which are among the early known works by this sculptor (c. 1730).

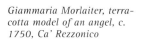

Giammaria Morlaiter, terra-cotta model of an angel, c. 1750, Ca' Rezzonico

Giammaria Morlaiter, Angel, c. 1750, church of the Fava, high altar

Baroque and Rococo Stuccoes

Venice never knew real baroque and even less rococo architecture, nonetheless "Venetians admitted rococo decoration into the intimacy of their homes, and it is there that we find *rocaille* ornaments of a delicacy and exquisiteness that is probably incomparable in Italy" (Wittkower). Indeed stucco decoration takes on increasing importance in Venetian interiors from the late-seventeenth century onward, and is done for the most part by artists from Ticino. Abbondio Stazio (1675-1757) was certainly the most famous among these sculptors, so much so that he was included in Anton Maria Zanetti's caricature "gallery", which recalls the most fashionable representatives of the Venetian art world of the era. Stazio decorated the church of the Gesuiti, the Scuola dei Carmini, Palazzo Albrizzi, and various other projects. Other notable artists from Ticino included Carpoforo Mazzetti Tencalla (a collaborator of Abbondio Stazio), Giuseppe Ferrari, and Pietro Castelli, who have been credited for mid-eighteenth century stuccoes in Palazzo Pisani Moretta at San Polo, Palazzo Pisani in Stefano, and the Venier Casino in the Mercerie, one of the most elegant interiors in Venice.

Abbondio Stazio's stuccoes: above: ceiling at Palazzo Albrizzi, early-18th century; lower left: Putto, Palazzo Zenobio; lower right: Angels, Scuola dei Carmini, early-18th century

Abbondio Stazio
Palazzo Albrizzi, drawing room
early-18th century

Abbondio Stazio transformed the ceilings of one of the rooms of Palazzo Albrizzi in San Polo into a large tent that appears to be sustained by a crowd of flying Cupids, gliding through the air in dangerous of poses; it is an invention for baroque theater realized with a light and fun-filled hand of a rococo artist. His stuccoes decorating the vault of the Scuola dei Carmini are also of great scenographic effect, whereas his ceiling for the church of the Gesuiti, which frames Fontebasso's frescoes is perfectly integrated with decoration of the most baroque of all of the Venetian churches. Other Venetian palazzi are decorated with this genre of stucco inspired by Bernini including Ca' Barbaro in Santo Stefano, Ca' Contarini in Can Beneto, and Ca' Segredo in Santa Sofia, where one reads among the decorations in the very beautiful casino the signatures of Abbondio Stazio and Carpoforo Mazzetti Tencalla.

134

Lion Cubs
St Mark's Piazzetta

In 1724 Andrea Tirali re-orga-
nized the Piazzetta del Leoncini
on the northern side of the
church: he raised it and placed
two attractive lions, sculpted by
Giovanni Bonazza in red Verona
marble, to guard the steps
toward the Piazza. The very
refined pink marble well is
adorned by modillions in Istrian
stone on a circular, three-
stepped base. The elegant bronze
gate, which closes off the
Loggetta terrace is by Antonio
Gai (1735-37).

*Giovanni Bonazza, lion in the
Piazzetta dei Leoncini, c. 1722*

Francesco Cabianca
Cloister of the Trinity
Church of the Frari (now the
State Archives)

In the same years Francesco
Cabianca sculpted all the orna-
mentation of the Trinity cloister
at the Frari: the statues of the
Angels and the magnificent central well, the most monumental
in the city, with the figures of *St
Peter* and *St Paul* (c. 1713). The
latter can be admired from both
the capitular room annexed to
the church or from the State
Archives, which now occupies
the ancient Franciscan convent.
During the great draught of 1718
almost all the wells in Venice
dried up, the only one that continued to furnish abundant
water to the entire surrounding
neighborhood was precisely this
well at the Frari. In Venice, even
when art appears in its most gra-
tuitous forms, it always empha-
sizes precise functions.

*Francesco Cabianca, Trinity
Cloister, well, church of the
Frari*

Antonio Canova

Antonio Canova was born in Possagno near Asolo (1757-1822). The son of a stone-cutter, he was trained in the school of Giuseppe Bernardi, heir to Torretto's studio. He was in fact born in the foothills that were the birthplace of numerous Veneto sculptors including Brustolon, Piazzetta, Torretto, Marchiori, and other great artists of preceding centuries such as Cima da Conegliano and Jacopo Bassano. Indeed, Veneto civilization often found its most authentic roots in the popular world, be it that of the city or of the country. Moving to Venice in 1768 when he was still very young, Canova soon claimed attention for his natural artistic gifts; at the age of sixteen he had already received his first commissions. In 1779 he took his first trip to Rome, where he became close friends with Piranesi's son and with the architects Selva and Quarenghi; two years later he settled there. In 1783 he began his first important Roman project, the *Monument for Pope Clement XIV,* which opened the way to a success that would make him known throughout Europe as the most important exponent of neo-classical sculpture. Canova was formed in the still baroque world of Torretto and Morlaiter and his sculptures conserve all the complexity of the art of that period "yet he subjected that culture to an accurate filtering operation, reducing it to the essential, boning it until its structure was evident" (Argan). On the other hand like Ingres, Poe, and Baudelaire, as Mario Praz observed, Canova was possessed by a "refined sensuality, a voluptuous emotivity, a repressed eroticism" for which "the neo-classical discipline would offer itself not as a coercion but rather as an extremely appropriate and successful vehicle". Indeed he applied the principles described by Goethe with extreme coherence, according to which the artist has to begin by studying the differences between individuals to arrive, through an increasingly greater process of abstraction, at representing the indivisible harmony *sub specie aeternitatis,* and to achieve this end has to evidently possess an absolute mastery of technique, a gift that Canova had to the highest degree. Thus, Canova, like Piranesi, though in a different way, can be considered the last great innovator in the history of Italian art, who placed himself on the path of the most advanced French and English culture of the nineteenth century.

Antonio Canova
Terra-cotta models
1787-99, Correr Museum

Museum Correr conserves terracotta models of two of Canova's most famous works: the Cupid and Psyche *couchant* (1787) now in the Louvre and the *Monument to Titian* (1791), later adapted for the *Tomb of Maria Christina of Austria* in Vienna (which in turn inspired the Frari cenotaph of Titian himself, erected by his students). The model for *Cupid and Psyche* clearly demonstrates the characteristics Canova know how to infuse in these preparatory works, which often reveal "a confidence, an immediacy, a spontaneity, and an almost palpitating vitality that seem to anticipate Rodin" (H. Honour).

Antonio Canova, Model for Cupid and Psyche, now in the Louvre, c. 1787, Correr Museum

136

Antonio Canova
Orpheus and Eurydice
1773-76, Correr Museum

The two stone statues representing *Orpheus and Eurydice* are Canova's first significant work, begun in 1773 at the age of sixteen on a commission by Senator Giovanni Falier for his villa in Asolo. *Eurydice* was the first of the two sculptures to be completed: she is portrayed in the moment in which she is grasped by the hand of Fury who emerges from the flames of Hades. *Orpheus*, which was completed immediately after, is shown in the moment when he turns and sees Eurydice disappear. While Torretto's influence is clear, especially in the figure of *Orpheus,* the exceptional technical and inventive ability of this very young artist is also immediately evident.

Antonio Canova, Orpheus and Eurydice, 1773-76. Correr Museum

Antonio Canova
Dedalus and Icarus
1777-79, Correr Museum

The group of *Dedalus and Icarus* was completed in 1779 for the Pisani family of San Polo and is clearly one of Canova's early masterpieces. The old father is portrayed setting the wings of his son with wax. The knowledgeable articulation of this group is remarkable; the artist "choose the route of idealization, developing the two figures like two opposing curves tangent to the group's vertical axis, and therein balanced or put in proportion, and not only in contrast, the two parties of light and shadow" (Argan).

Antonio Canova, Dedalus and Icarus, 1777-79, Correr Museum

IX. The Nineteenth Century: From Capital to Province

When the Republic fell in 1797, Venice was reduced from a capital to a province. It became part of the Napoleonic and then of the Austro-Hungarian empire, to be later united to the Kingdom of Italy in 1866. The revolutionary unrest that could be openly manifested during the brief democratic government of 1797 (and was passionately interpreted by Ugo Foscolo as a member of the commission for public instruction) was immediately frustrated by the Napoleonic betrayal (the Treaty of Campo Formio). Fifty years later, the city experienced a mighty explosion of popular freedom with the revolution of 1848 and the new Republic, led by Daniele Manin, resisted the Austrian siege for almost a year and a half. During the early century the city lived through a serious economic crisis: the Austrian governor of the Veneto-Lombardy favored the major cities like Milan and Trieste and the Venetian port was almost completely ignored. It did not regain strength until after the unification. Nonetheless Venetian cultural life remained discretely lively throughout century. In the field of art there was a notable level of production in painting (Caffi, Ciardi, Favretto, Nono, Brass, Milesi, etc.) and in architecture (Selva, Jappelli, Meduna, Fuin, Boito, Salvadori, and, during the period of art deco, Sullam, Torres, etc.). The foundation of the Biennale in the late-nineteenth century permitted the Commune of Venice to create one of the first international museums of modern art in Italy at Ca' Pesaro and to acquire works of major European artists.

Statue of Goldoni in Campo San Bartolomeo in a late 19th - early 20th century photo

Opposite page:
Antonio Canova, Ettore, c. 1808, Correr Museum

From Neoclassicism to Bourgeois Realism

The most successful sculptor in Venice in the early-nineteenth century was Luigi Zandomeneghi (Cologne 1778-Verona 1850). Trained under Canova, he became a teacher at the fine arts academy and was responsible for various monuments in Venice including those of *Canova* and *Titian* at the Frari, as well as the *Angel Gabriel* on the campanile of St Mark's. Other dignified followers of Canova included Antonio Bosa and Bartolomeo Ferrari. Yet the nineteenth century was above all the century of bourgeois realism, though it was also the romantic and emphatic century that invented the civic monument to national and local glories for city squares, much less suited to a city like Venice that was by nature anti-rhetorical and anti-monumental. "Oh, la belle statue! Le beau piedestal / Quoi? Les virtue à pied, le vice à cheval!" This lapidary reaction of a French poet to one of the many equestrian glories of the nineteenth century could have been inspired by the *Vittorio Emanuele* on the Riva degli Schiavoni, which is fortunately the only monument of this kind in the city and was done, evidently, after the unification. During this period Venice also had the good fortune of having at least two good sculptors: Luigi Borro (Ceneda 1826-1886) and Antonio Dal Zotto (Venice 1852-1918), who sculpted two monuments that are among the best productions of nineteenth-century commemorative statue work in Italy, one is dedicated to *Daniel Manin*, the other to *Carlo Goldoni*.

Luigi Zandomeneghi, Archangel Gabriel, 1822, St Mark's campanile

Monument to Canova
1827, Church of the Frari

The monument at the Frari dedicated to *Antonio Canova*, who died in Venice in 1822, was done in 1827 by a group of sculptors who were all students of this maestro from Possagno: Antonio Bosa, Jacopo De Martini, Bartolomeo Ferrari, Rinaldo Rinaldi, and Luigi Zandomeneghi. The monument was directly inspired by Canova's own project for *Titian's Tomb* at the Frari that was later adapted for the *Tomb of Maria Christina of Austria* in Vienna. In its realization at the Frari however the model appeared to weighed down by its excessive size. A door at the base of an imposing pyramid is flanked by St Mark's lion and the symbols of Genius and the arts.

Monument to Canova, church of the Frari, 1827

140

Antonio Dal Zotto
Monument to Carlo Goldoni
1883, Campo San Bartolomeo

Luigi Borro
Monument to Daniele Manin,
1875, Campo Manin

Antonio Dal Zotto is best known for a series of monuments of famous people interpreted in the spirit of Goldoni. These theatrical yet witty and unidealized sculptures are a good example of bourgeois realism representing figures including the Istrian musician Giuseppe Tartini, Pirano, Doge Sebastiano Venier (church of Santi Giovanni e Paolo), and Carlo Goldoni (Campo San Bartolomeo). The Goldoni monument is Zotto's masterpiece. Placed on a pedestal of reasonable height, the Venetian comedy writer participates good naturedly with utmost natural ease in the life of this center-city square.

Luigi Borro created some successful portraits (an imaginary Mirabeau, Natale Schiavone, and Doctor Catullo), all of which are now found in the Museum at Ca' Pesaro. In the words of Giuseppe Marchiori, these works "are moral portraits that were done with the acute investigation of an artist like Houdon, yet anticipated, in the midst of the Veneto province, the more individualized masks of an artist like Rodin". In the Manin Monument of 1875 Borro knew how to give this Venetian patriot a lively and dignified image that went well beyond rhetoric.

Left:
*Antonio Dal Zotto,
Monument to Carlo Goldoni,
1883, Campo San
Bartolomeo*

*Luigi Borro, Monument to
Daniele Manin, Campo
Manin, 1875*

New Sculpture at the Museum of Modern Art

"When one speaks of Ca' Pesaro, it is only natural to think about what it could have possessed in comparison to what it now owns. The Gallery was founded in 1897 with a precise mandate: to collect the most significant works from among those presented every two years in the various exhibitions of the Biennale from 1895 onward. An immense overall task with a range of selection that is perhaps unique in the world, given the international character with which the Biennale was immediately charged" (Perocco). In 1907 the Museum of Ca' Pesaro was moved to the palazzo where it is found today. It possesses an interesting though restricted number of nineteenth-century sculptures of artists of the quality of Rodin, Bourdelle, and Medardo Rosso.

Auguste Rodin
The Thinker
1880, Ca' Pesaro

Auguste Rodin (Paris 1840-1917) is represented in Ca' Pesaro by the bronze-glazed plaster cast of one of his most famous works, the *Thinker* (1880), acquired from the Biennale of 1907. Despite its vigorous classicism, this work demonstrates both an impressionistic luminance and a symbolist restlessness, the last product of romanticism at the threshold of a new century. Ca' Pesaro also possesses the plaster cast of another famous work by Rodin, the *Burghers of Calais* from 1884-86.

Auguste Rodin, Burghers of Calais, plaster, 1884-86, Ca' Pesaro

Auguste Rodin, The Thinker, glazed plaster, 1880, Ca' Pesaro

Medardo Rosso's Works at Ca' Pesaro

The Museum of Ca' Pesaro possesses eight works by Medardo Rosso (Turin 1858-1928); seven are in wax and were donated to the Museum in 1914; one is in bronze and was purchased at the Biennale. The wax works include the *Doorkeeper* (1883), one of the first sculptures that, modelled under the influence of Rodin and the impressionists, denies every pre-defined plane to find the more subtle effects of light. The bronze *Ecce Puer* (1906) was fused by Rosso himself in his Paris studio. Medardo Rosso's plastic research had to be understood in all its revolutionary implications above all by the futurists (Boccioni) and by Arturo Martini.

Medardo Rosso, "Ecce Puer", bronze, 1906, Ca' Pesaro

Medardo Rosso, Doorkeeper, wax, 1883, Ca' Pesaro

X. The Twentieth Century: Contemporary Maestros

The Venice Biennale – the first international exposition of contemporary art in Europe – was founded in 1895. In response to the rather academic nature of the early exhibitions, a group of young artists formed a Venetian "Secession", an anti-biennale that was hosted, for the first time 1908, in the rooms of the Fondazione Bevilacqua La Masa at Ca' Pesaro. Participants included artists such as Umberto Boccioni, Felice Casorati, Tullio Garbari, Arturo Martini, Gino Rossi, Pio Semeghini, and Ugo Valeri, to mention only the most well-known. Their manifestations created the most influential artistic movement in Italy at that time next to futurism, and was, therefore, at the very origins of contemporary Italian art. Arturo Martini's strong personality stands out among these artists, and he is to be considered the founder of new Italian sculpture. Another Italian artistic movement was also formed around the Venice Biennale in 1946; promoted by the Venetian critic Giuseppe Marchiori, the Fronte Nuovo delle Arti was the first important postwar movement in Italy. Some of the most representative personalities of the art of our days adhered to this movement

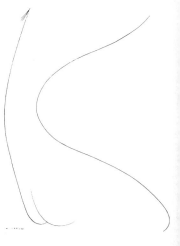

Alberto Viani, Drawing, 1956

including, from among the signers of its Manifesto, the painters, Birolli, Cassinari, Guttoso, Morlotti, Pizzinato, Turcato, Santomaso, and Vedova, and the sculptor, Alberto Viani.

The post-war exhibitions of the Biennale were also closely bound to the name of the most important contemporary Venetian architect, Carlo Scarpa. Scarpa was a complex and fascinating figure who began under the influence of the Viennese Sezession, which had, in turn, with artists like Gustav Klimt, found the inspiration for its renovation in the Byzantine tradition. And so the circle came to a close.

Before concluding it seems both right and auspicious to compare once again some of the works realized in or for Venice with those of a great private collection that has in recent years become a public museum. Like that of the Grimani four centuries ago, with the rightful differences of times and fashions, the Peggy Guggenheim collection can be seen as a testimony the modern city's will for rebirth.

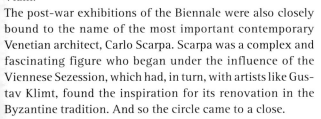

Opposite page:
Alberto Viani, Nude, Olivetti Showroom, St Mark's square

From the Biennale to Ca' Pesaro: Martini and Viani

After having worked in Nono's Venice studio, Arturo Martini (Treviso 1889-1947) met Gino Rossi in 1910 and took his first trip to Paris with him in 1912. The artists in which he showed most interest were Modigliani and Boccioni, though he also studied Canova's plaster casts in Possagno. In 1909 he exhibited for the first time at Ca' Pesaro; in 1912 he showed with Rossi, Modigliani, and De Chirico at the Salon d'Automne in Paris. "Martini had an extraordinary faculty of intercepting the aesthetic positions of the avantgarde which opened new fields to him" (Perocco). Working in sculpture and graphics, he was attentive to both the symbolist movement and to futurism, thus adhering to the metaphysical synthesis and classicist purism between the wars. He taught for a few years at the Venice arts academy, where he was succeeded by Alberto Viani (Quistello, Mantua, 1906), a maestro of abstract forms of great formal perfection based on organic, anthropomorphic structures (the magnificent *Nude* in Ca' Pesaro). In the post-war period Ca' Pesaro purchased numerous works by major Italian and foreign sculptors including Arp, Calder, Greco, Manzù, Moore, Pomodoro, Viani, Zadkine, etc. This is how, today, Ca' Pesaro completes the panorama of contemporary art of the Guggenheim Collection.

Arturo Martini
Works in Ca' Pesaro
1909-44

Ca' Pesaro possesses one of the major collections of Arturo Martini's sculptures, about fifteen works done between 1908 and 1944 in different materials (terra cotta, plaster, bronze, wood).

Some of these are works were exhibited at Ca' Pesaro during the years of the Venetian "Secession", when Martini was influenced by art nouveau and futurism. The *Young Girl at Twilight*, a plaster cast shown in the 1919 Bevilacqua La Masa exhibition reveals "sensitivity to plastic values, especially to cubism, that

is not disjoined from the classical memories of Laurana" (Perocco). There is also a plaster cast entitled *Figure* (1913) from his early works. The most remarkable works of this collection include the bronze *Sprinter* (1935) and *Woman in the Sun* (1944) and the terra-cotta *Bust of a Young Woman* (1930).

Arturo Martini, Figure, plaster, 1913, Ca' Pesaro

Arturo Martini, Sprinter, bronze, 1935, Ca' Pesaro

Alberto Viani
Nude
1950, Ca' Pesaro

Giacomo Manzù
Great Cardinal
1955, Ca' Pesaro

The marble *Nude* in Ca' Pesaro is one of this artist's finest works: the arched forms of the body, expressed through very pure volumes, take on particular significance and vigor in the clean cut at the top. Viani's vision thus re-connects "to formal models of an ideal classicism" (Mazzariol). Ca' Pesaro also conserves the bronze *Nude* from 1952, which reveals purer and more abstract forms. Another significant work by Viani is found in the Olivetti showroom at St Mark's Square.

From the large mantle to the delicacy of the barely portrayed face, Giacomo Manzù's imposing bronze statue is achieved through an extremely sensitive modelling of the material's surface, echoing the artist's knowledge of both Rodin and Medardo Rosso.

Giacomo Manzù, Great Cardinal, bronze, 1955, Ca' Pesaro

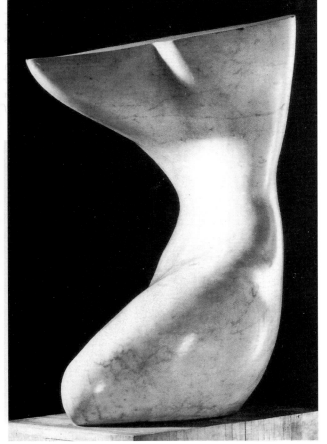

Alberto Viani, Nude, bronze, 1952, Ca' Pesaro

Alberto Viani, Nude, marble, 1950, Ca' Pesaro

The Guggenheim Collection: From Brancusi to Moore

The Peggy Guggenheim Collection is one of the major, private painting and sculpture collections of this century. Begun in Paris in the thirties by Peggy Guggenheim, it was moved to America during the war and finally established in its present-day site at Palazzo Venier dei Leoni on the Grand Canal in 1949. Today the museum is part of the Solomon R. Guggenheim Foundation along with the New York museum of the same name. Its rooms display a series of masterworks that illustrate the most significant movements of modern art from cubism to futurism, from surrealism to American abstract expressionism. The museum has noteworthy works of sculptors including Archipenko, Arp, Boccioni, Brancusi, Calder, César, Giacometti, Laurens, Marini, Minguzzi, Mirko, Moore, Pevsner, and Pomodoro.

Alberto Giacometti
Woman Walking
1932-36

Alberto Giacometti (Borgonovo, Switzerland 1901-66) studied at the Ecole des Beaux-Arts in Geneva. He visited the Venice Biennale in 1920 where he discovered the works of Cezanne and Archipenko. Of ancient art he especially admired Egyptian sculpture, Giotto, and Tintoretto. In 1922 he moved to Paris and collaborated with the the surrealists. In the thirties he began to model his sculptures in stylized forms. The plaster cast in the Guggenheim, *Woman Walking*, which seems to be derived from Egyptian prototypes is a good example: a rational almost classical work, from whose structure the series of the filiform bronze sculptures would later be derived, through an increasingly rarification of the material, the ragged and corroded contours, and the wandering and anxious shadows. The collection also possesses a very evocative example of this last phase of Giacometti's work entitled *Lion Woman* (1947), a piece that the artist cast expressly for Peggy Guggenheim.

Alberto Giacometti, Woman Walking, plaster, 1932-36, Peggy Guggenheim Collection

Costantin Brancusi
Maiastra
1912 (?)

A sculptor of Rumanian origin, Costantin Brancusi (Pestisani Gorj 1876-1957) settled in Paris in 1904, where he became friends with Rodin, Modigliani, Léger, Matisse, and Rousseau, without, however, losing contact with his homeland. The bronze *Maiastra* is inspired by Rumanian folk tradition: the arched and thin neck of bright-feathered bird of Rumanian folklore rises from its smooth and swollen body in the moment of song. The essential and geometric forms of Brancusi's sculpture reach abstraction while maintaining contact with the naturalism of the inspirational motif. The collection also conserves Brancusi's bronze *Bird in Space* from 1940.

Costantin Brancusi, Maiastra, bronze, 1912 (?), Peggy Guggenheim Collection

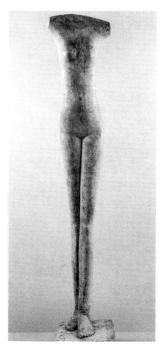

Henry Moore
Three Standing Figures
1953

Son of a an Irish miner, Henry Moore (Castleford 1898-1986) studied art in Leeds and then at the Royal College of Arts in London. Friends with Nicholson, Hepworth, and the critic Herbert Read, he made an early approach to the surrealist movement while at the same time studying ancient and classical works at the British Museum. From the thirties on he translated the human figure into forms that recalled both organic and inorganic natural elements. The Collection's *Three Figures* are typical of the artist's process: by "fusing the human figure with forms of unanimated material, like bones and rocks, the perforations through the mass of the sculpted bodies suggest the slow process of erosion by water and wind" (L. Flint).

Henry Moore, Three Standing Figures, bronze, 1953, Peggy Guggenheim Collection

**Alexander Calder
Mobile
1941**

In 1926, after completing his engineering studies, Alexander Calder (Lawnton, Pennsylvania, 1899-1976) visited Paris where he befriended Miró, Arp, Leger, and Mondrian. A pioneer in kinetic art, he created, from the thirties on, sculptures with mobile elements, which Duchamp called "mobiles": one fairly large (214 cm) example is found in the collection. "Form, size, color, space, and movement are combined and re-combined in changing and oscillating relationships that create a visual equivalent of nature's harmonious but unpredictable activity" (L. Flint). Calder also designed the silver headboard for Peggy Guggenheim's bed (1945-46), now displayed in the museum.

Alexander Calder, Mobile, 1941, Peggy Guggenheim Collection, Venice

Sculpture in the Landscape

There are an infinite number of sculptures inserted into the landscape of Venice. They have been commissioned over the years by a multitude of different clients: public entities (the *Monument to the Partisan* by the Commune), museums (Marini's *Knight* by the Guggenheim Collection), and industry (Viani's bronze sculpture by Olivetti).

Thus at the water's edge, near the bank of the Castello Giardini, we find the *Monument* dedicated the *Partisan*, a female figure in bronze by August Murer (1970). This sculpture lies connected to the bank behind in a flight of steps made of stone cubes, each isolated from the others, designed by Carlo Scarpa.

One of the most monumental works of the Guggenheim Collection, the *Angel of the City*, a visionary equestrian figure in bronze by Marino Marini (1948) was opportunely placed on the palazzo's terrace where it is very successfully inserted in the vast aqueous space of the Grand Canal.

Sculpture, architecture, urban furnishings, and ambience are integrated and exalt one another in the Olivetti showroom designed by Carlo Scarpa at the corner of the Procuratie Vecchie towards Campo San Gallo. In the foreground there is a black marble basin on whose liquid surface glides an abstract silhouette in gilded bronze by Alberto Viani (1958). The perfection of the forms and the preciousness of the material so ideally re-connects this bronze by Viani, in the spirit of the "Veneto classicism", to the Marciana quadriga we found at the very beginning of this brief anthology on the sculpture of Venice.

Augusto Murer, Partisan, 1970

Alberto Viani, Nude, gilded bronze, 1958, Olivetti showroom, St Mark's square

Marino Marini, Angel of the City, 1948

151

Bibliography

ARGAN G.C., *Storia dell'arte italiana* (3 vol.), Sansoni, Florence 1980.
ARSLAN E., *Venezia gotica*, Electa, Milan 1970.

BASSI E., *Canova*, Bergamo 1943.
BERENSON B., *The Italian Painters of the Renaissance*, Collins, London 1960.
BRANCA V., ed., *Storia della civiltà veneziana* (3 vol.), Sansoni, Florence 1979.

CHASTEL A., *La grande officina. Arte Italiana 1460-1500*, Rizzoli, Milan 1983.
–, *Storia dell'arte italiana*, Laterza, Bari 1983.
CESSI F., *Alessandro Vittoria*, Fratelli Fabbri, Milan 1966.
CIARDI DUPRE M.C., *Il Riccio*, Fratelli Fabbri, Milan 1966.

DELOGU G., *La scultura italiana del Seicento e del Settecento*, Florence 1933.
DEMUS O., *The Church of San Marco*, Harvard University Press, Cambridge 1960.

FISCOVIC C., *Juraj Dalmatinac* (Giorgio Orsini da Sebenico), Zagreb 1982.
FOGOLARI G., *I Frari e i Santi Giovanni e Paolo*, Garzanti, Milan 1949.

GALLIAZZO V., *I Cavalli di San Marco*, Canova, Treviso 1981.
GOMBRICH E.H., *La storia dell'arte raccontata*, Einaudi, Turin 1966.

HUMFREY P., *The Altarpiece in the Renaissance Venice*, Yale University Press, New Haven 1993.
HEYDENREICH L.H. and PASSAVANT G., *I Geni del Rinascimento, Arte italiana 1500-1540*, Rizzoli, Milan 1979.
HUSE N. and WOLTERS W., *Venezia. L'arte del Rinascimento*, Arsenale, Venice 1989.

La Via Annia, Arsenale, Venice 1979.
LOGAN O., *Venezia, cultura e società 1470-1790*, Il Veltro, Rome 1980.
LORENZETTI G., *Venezia e il suo Estuario*, Lint, Trieste 1963.

MANNO A., *Palazzo Ducale. Guida al Museo dell'Opera*, Canal & Stamperia Editrice, Venice 1997.
MARCIANÒ A.F., *Carlo Scarpa*, Zanichelli, Bologna 1984.
MARCHIORI G., *Scultura italiana dell'Ottocento*, Milan 1960.
MARIACHER G., *Il Sansovino*, Mondadori, Milan 1962.
–, *Antonio Rizzo*, Fratelli Fabbri, Milan 1966.
MARKHAM SHULZ A., *Niccolò di Giovanni Fiorentino and Venetian Sculpture of the Early Renaissance*, New York 1978.
–, *Antonio Rizzo*, Princeton University Press, Princeton 1983.
–, *La Scala dei Giganti*, Arsenale, Venice 1985.
–, *Saggi e memorie di storia dell'arte,* XV, Olschki, Florence 1986.
–, *Giambattista e Lorenzo Bregno*, Cambridge 1991.
–, *Nanni di Bartolo e il portale di San Nicolò a Tolentino*, Centro-Di, Florence 1997.
–, *Storia di Venezia*, Istituto Enciclopedia Italiana Treccani, 1997.
MARTINELLI E., *Catalogo delle opere di G.M. Morlaiter*, thesis, Faculty of Letters, University of Venice, 1978.
MAZZARIOL G., ed., *Proposizioni sulla città*, Neri Pozza, Vicenza 1976.
MAZZARIOL G. and PIGNATTI T., *Storia dell'arte italiana* (3 vol.), Mondadori, Milan 1977.
MCANDREW J., *L'architettura del primo Rinascimento veneziano*, Marsilio, Venice 1983.
MOLESWORTH H.D., *European Sculpture*, Thames & Hudson, London 1965.
MUNOZ A., *Antonio Canova: le opere*, Rome 1957.
MURARO M., *La vita nelle pietre*, Arsenale, Venice 1985.

PAOLETTI P., *L'architettura e la scultura del Rinascimento a Venezia*, Venice 1873.
PEROCCO G., *Le origini dell'arte moderna a Venezia*, Canova, Treviso 1972.
PEROCCO G. and SALVADORI A., *Civiltà di Venezia* (3 vol.), Stamperia di Venezia Editrice, Venice 1976.
PISCHEL G., *Storia universale della scultura*, Mondadori, Milan 1981.
PLANISCIG L., *Venezianische Bildhauer der Renaissance*, Vienna 1921.
–, *Andrea Riccio*, Vienna 1927.
POLACCO R., *La cattedrale di Torcello*, Venice-Treviso 1981.

POPE-HENNESSY R., *Italian Gothic Sculpture*, Phaidon Press, London 1955.
—, *Italian Renaissance Sculpture*, Phaidon Press, London 1958.
—, *Italian High Renaissance and Baroque Sculpture*, London 1963.
PRAZ M., *Canova*, Rizzoli, Milan 1976.

RIZZI A., *Le vere da pozzo pubbliche di Venezia e il suo estuario*, Commune of Venice, 1976.
ROMANO S., *Tullio Lombardo e il Monumento ad Andrea Vendramin*, Arsenale, Venice 1985.
ROSAND D, ed, *Interpretazioni veneziane*, Arsenale, Venice 1984.
ROSSI P., *Girolamo Campagna*, Vita Veronese, Verona 1968.
RUSKIN J., *Le pietre di Venezia*, Mondadori, Milan 1982.

SALVADORI A., *101 Architetture da vedere a Venezia*, Canal, Venice 1969.
SEMENZATO, C., *La scultura veneta del Seicento e del Settecento*, Alfieri, Venice 1966.
SEYMOUR C. JR., *Sculpture in Italy 1400-1500*, Penguin Books, Harmondsworth 1966.
SHEARD W.S., *Sanudo's List of Notable Things in Venetian Churches and the Date of the Vendramin Tomb*, Yale Italian Studies, New Haven 1977.

TEMANZA T., Vite dei più celebri Architetti e Scultori Veneziani, Venice 1778.
TRINCANATO E., *Venezia Minore*, Edizioni del Milione, Milan, 1946.
—, *Guida alla Venezia Minore*, ed. Renzo Salvadori, Canal & Stamperia Editrice, Venice 1978.

Venezia, Guide d'Italia, Touring Club Italiano, Milan 1985.

WITTKOWER R., *Arte e architettura in Italia 1600-1750*, Einaudi, Turin 1972.
—, *La scultura dall'antichità al Novecento*, Einaudi, Turin 1985.
WOLTERS W., *La scultura veneziana gotica, 1300-1450* (2 vol.), Alfieri, Venice 1976.
—, *Der Bilderschmuck Des Dogenpalastes*, Steiner, Wiesbaden 1983.

ZAVA BOCCAZZI, *I Lombardo*, Fratelli Fabbri, Milan 1966.

Museum Catalogues

FORLATI TAMARO B., *Il Museo Archeologico di Venezia*, Istituto Poligrafico dello Stato, Rome 1970.
FLINT L., *La Collezione Peggy Guggenheim*, The Solomon Guggenheim Foundation, New York 1983.
MOSCHINI V., *Le raccolte del Seminario di Venezia*, Libreria dello Stato, Rome 1943.
PEROCCO G., *La Galleria d'Arte Moderna a Ca' Pesaro*, Istituto d'Arti Grafiche, Bergamo 1959.
ROMANELLI G., *Il Museo Correr*, Electa, Milan 1984.
VALCANOVER, F., *Le Collezioni della Ca' d'Oro*, Electa, Milan 1986.
—, *Le Gallerie dell'Accademia*, Electa, Milan 1984.

Exhibition Catalogues

Italian Bronze Statuettes, The Victoria and Albert Museum, London 1961.
Leonardo e Venezia, Palazzo Grassi, Bompiani, Milan 1922.
The Age of Neoclassicism, The Arts Council of Great Britain, London 1972.
The Genius of Venice 1500-1600, The Royal Academy of Arts, London 1983.
I Cavalli di San Marco, Procuratoria di S. Marco, Venice 1977.
Carlo Scarpa 1906-1978, Gallerie dell'Accademia, Venice 1984.

Name index

Site index

Sculptures in this volume restored through funding by UNESCO - Private Committees Program for the Safeguarding of Venice

Amici dei Musei

Church of Santi Giovanni e Paolo, Tomb of Doge Marco Corner, 1984-85
St Mark's Basilica, Funerary lions in the Zen Chapel, 1984
Church of Santa Maria della Salute, high altar, 1984-85
Church of Santi Giovanni e Paolo, Tomb of Jacopo Cavalli (Pierpaolo Dalle Masegne), 1987-88

Comitato Italiano per Venezia

Ex Convent of the Frari, cloister, 1971-73

Comité Dante Alighieri de Aarau

Church of the Frari, Corner Chapel, interior and exterior sculptures, 1971

Comité Français

Church of Santa Maria della Salute, general restoration, 1970-73, in collaboration with Italian State and the Commune of Venezia

Consiglio d'Europa "Pro Venetia Viva"

Patriarchal Seminary, terra-cotta portraits (Alessandro Vittoria), 1983

Fondazione "Pro Venezia" Svizzera

Church of San Stae, general restoration, 1977-79
Church of Santa Maria del Giglio, facade, 1989-96

Fondazione Venezia Nostra

Rialto Bridge, general restoration, 1973-75

Italia Nostra

Colleoni Monument, marble base, 1976-78

Lloyd Triestino, München

Scuola Grande di San Marco, main portal lunette, 1979-82

Radio Club "Elettra Marconi"

Campo Santi Giovanni e Paolo, well-curb, 1978-79

Rallye San Marco

Campo dei Mori, statue, 1991-92
Calle del Paradiso, Arch of Paradise, 1993-94

Save Venice Inc.

Church of the Frari, St John the Baptist (Donatello), 1973
Church of San Giovanni Crisostomo, marble altarpiece (Tullio Lombardo), 1980-81
St Mark's Basilica, Zen Chapel, 1982-84
Church of Santa Maria dei Miracoli, general restoration, 1987-1997
Church of San Polo, San Paolo, exterior apse, 1988
Church of San Giobbe, pilasters (Pietro Lombardo), 1990
Church of Santo Stefano, St Sebastian (?) (Antonio Lombardo), 1990-91
St Mark's Piazzetta, Acritani Pilasters, 1991-92
Church of San Giovanni in Bragora, baptismal font, 1995
Church of Santi Giovanni e Paolo, Tomb of Doge Michele Morosini, 1996
Church of Santo Stefano, St John the Baptist (Giammaria Mosca), 1996
Church of Santo Stefano, St Jerome (Pietro Lombardo), 1996
Church of Santo Stefano, Virtue or Saint (Tullio Lombardo), 1996

Venice in Peril

Sansovino's Loggetta, structural consolidation and cleaning, 1972-74
Palazzo Ducale, Porta della Carta, 1976-79
Church of San Zulian, facade, 1990-92
Palazzo Ducale, 14-15th century capitals and columns, 1994-96
Sansovino's Loggetta, preservation monitoring, 1995-96
Fondamenta dei Mori, statue, 1996
Church of the Carmini, altar (Antonio Corradini), 1996-97

World Monuments Fund

Church of Pietà, building restoration, 1970-78
Church of San Simeon Grande, Tomb of St Simeon, 1989
Church of San Giovanni in Bragora, Virgin and Child, 1994
Colleoni Monument, preliminary studies, 1997

Printed in Italy Grafiche Veneziane
Canal & Stamperia Editrice, Venice - August 1997

ESSAYS

ESSAYS

GARETH WARDELL

GROUSE BEATER

This book is dedicated to readers who know the difference between clairvoyance and reality, despair and joy, faux freedom and liberty.

CONTENTS

PREFACE

As existence moves to the final breath, one's thoughts turn to the corpuscular: red blood cells, immune therapy, and my homeland living a half-life, the destruction of the planet, fires, floods, pestilence and poverty. You can choose to fight or stick your head in the sand. I chose to write, sedentary yet active. Writing essays began as a weekly intellectual exercise when I returned to Edinburgh from working too long in the city of fallen angels, Los Angeles. I came home a wiser person, ready to be part of the great liberating movement to restore Scotland's self-governance and free it from the suffocating shackles of Westminster rule.

I had taken my film projects to Hollywood only to discover Hollywood has gone to Scotland to make the epic *Braveheart* and a paean to simplistic honour, *Rob Roy*. I was determined not to be left on the periphery of my own country's march to independence. Frustrated at finding no way to be part of an official dialogue with fellow Scots – sticking fliers in letterboxes a waste of ability, I hit upon the unoriginal idea of writing political tracts. I eschewed blogs – an ugly word – because those I read were more or less themed diaries, or specialist platforms for specific sections of society such as mothers, cooks, or car enthusiasts. I chose the long form of prose composition to test the strengths and weaknesses in my political argument, and where necessary, do some homework.

"Have you thought about publishing your political views?" said my much missed compatriot, the Scots novelist Frederic Lindsay.

"Your polemic is sharp, and you've a fine capacity for a well-honed phrase." I laughed off his encouragement, but his remark stuck in my mind spoken as it was just days before he died. "Gareth holds opinions some might find difficult to handle," wrote my English head of department, Joe Casciani, in a letter recommending a lecturing post, adding, "But he espouses them with modesty and never with arrogance." Buoyed by the assurance of friends, the *Grouse Beater* site was born. I chose the sobriquet because a grouse is essentially a ground dwelling bird living among the aptly named *calluna vulgaris*, heather, the grouse common in Scotland, hard put upon by foreign landowners and driven out by beaters, some of them Scots. It has symbolism.

One evening I rushed six essays of various qualities in three hours and went to bed amazed I had so many topics in me to regurgitate. Next morning, ready to delete the work, I reread them astonished to discover comments had been added by members of the public. In my ignorance of computer processes – switching from an Adler typewriter to an HP desktop marvel left Tipp-Ex on the screen! – I had clicked *publish* thinking it was *record* and would remain private.

The first comment was to the point: "Yer writing is fantastic, pal, but if I was you I'd attend tae yer typos". His back-handed compliment was a spur to greater effort though I soon realised essays over two thousand words best published at weekends when people had leisure time to digest them. Brahms was asked how he organised his day. "I get up at dawn, have three cups of coffee and a cigar, and compose until midday. After lunch I remove what I composed in the morning." My day is similarly organised.

As the reader will observe, I see human endeavour as a great journey of continuous learning. I have lived an eventful life of impulse, obsessed with people and things, education, theatre, films, classical music and jazz, garden design, my wife and daughters, and finally my country. The past and the future of Scotland is the theme of this collection of essays taken from 2015 to 2021. The essays begin with all the optimism one expects from the joy of seeing a country renew itself, and end with the despair of a government fallen into moral decline. That is no reason, of course, to lose sight of the ideal: reinstatement of Scotland's civil and constitutional rights. It means more hard work and doubling effort. For the challenge I wish I was young again. It is sad to get old.

What the world will make of the brutal colonisation of Scotland once we are free from our oppressors (the anti-democratic are still scheming, still plotting), or what folk will think of the key political protagonists of these last years, is for history to judge. Time takes so damn long to make a judgement that writers are obliged to fill the gap with warnings and opinions and exhortations of fresh hope. I prefer hope backed by courage and strength of purpose. I trust readers will find both in this book.

1

THE SHAME OF THE PRESS

The British press, their hacks and minions, do their level best to defame and demean Scotland. If there's a negative to be found, the press will find it, amplify it, and then call it truth. Quite frankly, if I list the defamation published *this* week alone I'd feel tarnished.

Denigrating and ridiculing Scottish politics and the independence movement is nothing new. For some it's a life's hobby. Lying and exaggerating – an exaggeration *is* a lie – is part and parcel of today's press, working for the status quo to manufacture consent, backed by some of the wealthiest people in the land… who live abroad to avoid tax.

Many years ago my cousin worked for the *Scottish Daily Mail* when it was based in Scotland's capital. Back in the day when it was a real newspaper it was a good training ground for apprentice journalists before it became what it is today, proto-fascist, racist, peddling stereotypes, hatred, and chasing vacuous celebrities. He went on to be a respected correspondent for the *Times* and *Reuters*.

His name was Iain Christie.

Eventually he found himself covering Portugal's colonial retreat from Mozambique, a withdrawal ransacking the country as it left, slashing and burning. As I write, years after that struggle, the country still very poor, gold has been found giving some hope of limited prosperity. But that's another story. Mozambique is independent again and proud to be so.

Back in the day the liberation movement, Frelimo, was led by a smart, handsome, charismatic military commander, a statesman called Samora Machel.

As well as a respected revolutionary leader, Machel proved himself a bonnie fighter against the evils of South African apartheid. After a long, arduous and dangerous struggle, Samora won his country's independence to become its first president and an unusually resourceful politician, before a South African assassination squad downed his plane in 1988. Graca his widow went on to become the second wife of Nelson Mandela; one supposes the first woman to be First Lady of two countries.

Machel was a revolutionary socialist, one Her Majesty, Queen Elizabeth, was happy to invite to dinner at Buckingham Palace a good few times. He was, after all, a democrat. Machel was welcomed by many another head of state.

In time my cousin decided he liked the country so much he wanted to live there, Maputo, to be exact, and there he settled down to dedicate himself to Mozambique's future. He settled with his young wife. His son Conor was born and educated there as was his daughter Carol.

Iain accepted Machel's offer to head the establishment of Mozambique's broadcasting service, a considerable challenge. It barely existed. Creating a broadcasting corporation is an expensive business; you need a ton of money to create the infrastructure, from studios to radios, at a minimum. Mozambique was lost for any reasonable communication system.

His earliest programmes were staffed by energetic amateurs. Knowing the poverty he had witnessed in his own Scotland, Iain used all his innovative skills to build up a professional broadcasting service at the service of the people.

A lot of his station's output was ridding the populace of a colonial mentality, giving them confidence in their own language and culture. Occasionally he broadcast some subjects to the UK, usually detailing the murders and destruction caused by the brutality of the Portuguese colonialists.

Still working for the *Times* and *Reuters*, now freelance, broadcasting to Mozambique's population with listener access programmes and the occasional report to the BBC, the *Times* decided to dub my cousin 'Lord Haw-Haw' of Africa. No one knows quite why.

Iain specialised in reporting on the struggles waged by southern African liberation movements against colonial and racist rule. Perhaps the Portuguese ambassador had a word in the ear of the British ambassador along the lines of, wouldn't it better if your 'British' journalist toned down the anti-Portuguese news items? Or it could have been Iain's occasional report on what the white rulers of Rhodesia were up to keeping down the 'blecks'. He was the first, for example, to report that Rhodesian premier, a farmer, Ian Smith, prime minister from 1964 to 1979, was moving his herds of cattle out of the country while pretending he stood defiant against British sanctions. Whatever it was, the British government was behind the switch from treating my cousin as a respected journalist to *persona non grata*. Press duly briefed, political editors did their own switcheroo, shifting from being his former employers to scumbags.

Iain was stunned, shocked, insulted. British newspapers were playing a double game.

For those short on Second World War history Lord Haw-Haw was the nickname given to one particular journalist, William Joyce, who broadcast Hitler and Goebbels propaganda from their "*Germany Calling*" studios in the Reichssender Hamburg radio station in Bremen.

The vilification of Iain's reputation went on unabated. The *Daily Mail* joined the fray. There was a derogatory story almost every day. Remember, this was the newspaper that had trained him, and knew him to be an excellent, assiduously honest journalist.

It did not take long for hacks to discover where my cousin was born – a quick call to the *Mail* was enough – Pilton, a working class estate in Edinburgh. They tracked down his house and elderly mother who lived alone.

His mother, inexperienced in the wily ways of cheap hacks interviewing techniques, was bombarded with doorstep belligerence, but she was happy to talk of her son with pride, how he was a passionate cyclist, posters of the *Tour de France* on his bedroom walls, and a mad keen jazz fan.

The next day his mother opened the newspapers to find the front pages emblazoned with the headline: "Lord Haw-Haw a Communist!"

The BBC followed suit, never questioning a single allegation or assertion. In reality, and for the record, Iain considered himself Marxist and anarchist in the sense of someone who challenges authority, but not a communist. Then again, what does that matter? He cared about the poor and the forgotten and justice.

The Scotsman, then a reasonably respected national daily with a good circulation, was last at his mother's door, Jimmy-come-lately, you might say. The reporter found Iain's mother in tears, predictably confused and bewildered.

"I never said he was a communist," she pleaded. "Why are they doing this? Why are they telling lies?"

After listening to her tales of shock and anger the *Scotsman*'s reporter, conscience duly pricked, closed his notebook without writing a word, "If my editor calls, tell him you were out when I arrived at your door." And he left. He never printed a word about my cousin.

But the accusation of Edinburgh harbouring a commie subversive stuck. When Iain died of throat cancer in his early fifties in 2000, an habitual pipe smoker, he was given a state funeral in Mozambique – a hero of the nation, another industrious, dedicated Scot garlanded and lauded abroad, *not* in his homeland. In his homeland he was smeared.

Manuel Vetorano, head of Radio Mozambique, said at his funeral in Maputo, "Born in Scotland, Iain Christie gave us all lessons in nationalism and patriotism."

The *Scotsman* obituary repeated the claim he was a communist.

It would have been better if the original reluctant *Scotsman* reporter *had* written a column, one *denouncing* press colleagues who libelled and defamed Iain. *That* was the *honest* thing to do. **That** was the **courageous** thing.

2

MY DAYS AS A HERO

I have amassed fond memories teaching Speech and Drama in an east-end secondary school in Glasgow. The school was newly built, the teachers not long enough in it to hate their job, hence the good luck to be among them, particularly pupils happy to be in a bright, contemporary building.

As I entered the gates for the first time, I had no idea what the place would have in store for me, or how it would alter my attitude to Scottish society or how it would politicise me. The experience was the impetus to found and run Scotland's national theatre for talented youth. It exists to this day.

Filled with missionary zeal, I threw all my energies into showing teenagers from predominately poor and deprived homes (as my own was) that they had real potential, raw ability as yet untapped, something society could value when matured. Above all, they needed confidence, not to be a smarty pants, but not to fear words, to know how to use them to express oneself well.

It wasn't about being an actor, for I taught the technical side of drama too, writing, set design, oratory work, presentation techniques, and musical performance. It was about imbuing them with self-confidence, and developing language ability.

The students responded enthusiastically. I would stand at my desk as the period bell rang listening to the clatter of shoe on tile as they rushed to my classroom pitched at the end of the building, burst through the door, yelling and shouting, collapsing in heaps into seats placed around the classroom edges, the centre a stage. Schoolbags got tossed into a corner. There were no desks just seats and a few tables.

The drama class became the two-hour event of the week. Classes generally consisted of book or poetry readings, lots of improvisations to acquire skills in handling tricky real-life situations, role playing, movement work, social games that boosted communication skills, short sketches to act out, film analysis, and lots of writing. They learned how to handle everyday situations, to speak for themselves.

I wrote full-length plays for the end of term designed to the fit the pupils' ages, no adding beards or moustaches. One was set in a movie studio taken over by a gang of black suited Mafia-type hoodlums – a synonym for society taken over by fascists. (Parents spotted the inferences but not the slow-witted headmaster.) I think I must have been studying Bertolt Brecht at the time for it had resonances of '*The Resistible Rise of Arturo Ui*'.

The characters sported real Tommy guns, firing pin removed, the boxes they were packed in delicately opened by Special Branch and badly repacked to send on to the school from Bapty the theatrical armour and weapons suppliers. *Revolution Revolve* was a black comedy written two years before *Bugsy Malone* hit the big screen a similar story of kids as mock gangsters.

The headmaster saw parents arriving in droves to witness the theatrical event, parents no other school event had ever enticed across the car park. Each night saw a full house.

One incident stands out. A rather unprepossessing, squat student with warts where there ought to be none, and a head of thick hair cut by a blunt lawnmower, asked to see me. He was keen to join in the school production, but pathologically shy of being seen on a stage under spotlights. He was gauche and inarticulate. I saw the seed of ability in his pleas for participation. I was at a loss how to involve him.

I needed a gorilla for a comedy routine during the interval and hit on the idea his head behind a mask would free him of inhibition. I was right. It did the trick. He became completely animated, so good in fact, that his role was enlarged to include audience participation. He lost all physical awkwardness, became expansive in gesture, loud of voice and laughter. He was having the time of his young life.

On the way home from the production he was waiting for me in the half-light near the school gate. "Sir, have yi go' a minute?" I stopped and waited to hear what he had to say.

"Ah wanted tae thank you fir what yiv done fir me, sir. It's been great, this actin' stuff."

I told him it was all his doing. He showed he had ability. For a few moments he stayed silent trying to summon the words he wanted to express.

"An'… an' there's something else Ah need tae say. Ah've nivver been any good wi' girls, but being in yer play has well… changed tha', an'… an Ah go' a girlfriend."

Standing a few yards behind him was a coy, dark haired girl from his year, poorly dressed in a thin coat for the cold night air, clutching her mother's patent white handbag, and wearing her mother's best shoes. She shifted uneasily at my gaze.

My heart leapt into my mouth and I stuffed a £10 note into his handshake, telling them to enjoy themselves at the pictures. As a dominie, those are moments to cherish.

On another occasion, a production opening with the storming of Russia's Winter Palace and ending in a movie studio, had its red silk revolutionary flags stolen. A few days later a group of boys sported neat red handkerchiefs in the breast pocket of their blue Crombie coats, exactly one inch of fold showing, a gang emblem. The group that stole the flags had parents who were members of the local Orange Lodge, an infamous sect of unionist zealots affiliated to Northern Ireland's extremist ideology.

We're the boys wi a' the graces,
Yellow shirts an' gallus braces.
We're the boys that chib yer faces,
We're the Brigton Derry!

Years later I met one of the gang in Sauchiehall Street, or rather he met me, shouting from across the street dodging cars as he ran over to greet me in that instantly chummy way Glaswegians have of greeting old acquaintances.

'Hibby' was wearing an expensive camel hair coat, shirt and shoes. "Sir, sir! It's me – Hibby!" He pumped my hand up and down in greeting. "You wur the only teacher who thought Ah wus worth somethin'."

I grinned as I returned his handshake telling him he was exactly that. How he was dressed now proved it. He laughed at the compliment. We chatted awhile, mentioned the school plays, and with a huge smile, unsolicited; he made his confession there and then.

"Remember when yer flags went 'missin'?" I nodded. How could I forget? I paid for them out of my own pocket. Twice. "That wus us, sir. They wus perfect hankies."

With his expensive coat and fur collar, I had to ask him what he was doing for a living. "Dinnie worry about me, sir. Got a barra at Barrowland. Daein' jist fine." He changed tack. "Remember wee Eck? He's been up fir thievin' three times. Nae hope fir him. Naw, I'm daein' good."

And then he unburdened himself of another confession. "Ken Mister McTavish, yon music teacher?" I remembered him well, a pleasant old guy sent around schools to teach Glasgow's children the joys of Chopin and a few traditional Scots songs playing the piano. He had an unfortunate facial tick when he spoke. As the words were about to come out he made a clicking sound and blinked hard. After a while you got into the habit of timing him to prepare for the next click, blink, and stumbled sentence. If he knew about his affliction he never let on. Had he ambition to become a concert pianist one day, the facial tick ruined it.

"Aye, that's him, sir," said Hibby.

"We used tae get tae his class afore him and nick a tenner outa his wallet fae his jaiket hangin' in the cupboard. Then we pushed wee Eck oot the windae tae run tae the sweet shop and bring back loads o' goodies. When McTavish got tae the room we aw sat lookin' innocent, like. He had nae idea whit we were uptae, jist told us no tae eat in the classroom."

He gave a huge grin, chuckled, and added the zinger. "We did that fir ower a year an' he didnae ken a thing!" By face tick and a tenner, Mister McTavish was a two-time loser.

The headmaster retired early, a kind, considerate man devoid of a sense of humour. His excuse was genuine, a bag of shattered nerves issuing from meeting too many aggressive, heavy-weight mothers in his study complaining that their rambunctious child was bright and should be given a second chance.

He had tried his best to civilise their in-built animosity to schooling but failed. It was not his fault. They were the dispossessed, people who knew they were the downgraded. Their life was one long struggle. They had to fight for everything. He tried to show kindness to their children, in one case, saying "hello, and who are you?" to a snotty nosed three year-old mite in a pushchair. The child looked up at him and uttered the immortal rebuke, "Up yer geggy!" The poor headmaster has no idea what those words meant, but he knew it was an insult. His sigh was long and deep.

He was succeeded by the first female appointed to run a comprehensive secondary school in Scotland, a fine looking and formidable man-chewing harpy on horseback. Her raunchy aggression was sensuous as hell to some male staff. I found it imperious and intimidating.

To some of the older male staff who tried to take her on, but failed, it was wrestle Pussy Galore time in Auric Goldfinger's stable. Black gown flying open behind her like a bat cape, blood red, tight, body hugging cocktail dress underneath (more honest to say 'cock teasing' dress), she strode down corridors as if in a Byronic storm, the clatter of her killer high heels on cold concrete warning of her approach.

One day I arrived for work my chin sporting designer stubble – and have never lost the look since, freed from the pain of shaving my face with a piece of razor sharp metal. She strode by without as much as a sidelong glance speaking loudly so all around could hear, "Perfecting the professorial look, are we, Mr Wardell?" and disappeared into her bell tower, or wherever it was she hung upside down in the dark hours.

I'll give her one thing; she was ace at breaking up playground fights. Hardly would a punch be thrown, when out of nowhere she flew, pouncing down upon the throng, throwing herself into the middle of the scrummage of chanting children, she shouting "Stop! That! At! Once!" In one swift move she grabbed the perpetrators by the scruff of the neck, and hauled them limp and fearful off to her lair to be consumed at leisure.

In many respects Miss Mountebank, as I called her though never to her face, was ahead of her time, but severely imperious doesn't win friends. I could see she was a lonely person. Years later I read she had committed suicide. She lived alone.

Pupils soon learned to trust me as someone on the side of fair play and no physical punishment. I could slice an ear with a cutting remark, but would never flay skin with a length of seasoned leather from the hide of a bull. I was a hero to those young people.

They saw me as a rebel and a confidante, someone like them, against the 'establishment', the harsh reality that they knew. In time they grew to trust me absolutely, and I no longer walked in fear of out-of-work adolescent groups hanging menacingly around the local streets. I was 'the drama teacher' – "Let him past, Jakey. He's okay."

One day, while filling in my report on my last class' progress, in a period off duty, the deputy headmistress paid me a visit, closing the door behind her carefully, with a deft turn of the handle behind her back.

"Mr Wardell." Formality gets stronger the higher up the education tree you go. "Mr Wardell, do you mind if I have a chat with you about a tricky issue?" I pulled a seat to my desk and offered it to her.

"You had one girl from P3 coming to speak with you the other day... for a private chat."

This was true. The girl appeared at my door distressed and in a ten minute quiet conversation confessed things were not as they should be at home. As she talked uninhibited, she wrung her hands constantly. I was at a loss how to help her, knew she was attaching herself to me as a person she could trust.

"Well, it's not the done thing," warned the deputy headmistress. "Pupils with emotional problems should be referred to me, and I'll take it from there." The deputy head was not an intimidating woman unlike her superior. She was middle aged, hair not dyed to fool, never to be a headmistress, but she was not working class either, not the type of woman a Glasgow child would consider safe to unload private experiences.

"Couldn't I just leave the door open if they want a chat?" I replied, slightly miffed my integrity was being challenged.

"That's most certainly not the answer. Refer them to me because… you never know what the pupil, a girl especially, might accuse you off."

I realised she was warning me of unforeseen repercussions, that private chats should have two teachers present. I nodded in reluctant agreement and she left, duty done, but I felt cheated of a line of communication to young people looking for help. Only later did I recognise that the deputy head found what she had to say to me almost impossible to communicate in straight language. How's that for irony?

Life as a salaried teacher was attractive, freed from fear of an empty bank account. It seemed a good, productive life, a 'keeper', but all the while charlatan politicians concocted noises off about poor standards in education. Education is an easy target. Politicians know they can only fiddle with the edges, radical change is too costly. Scotland's internationally admired education system was "in peril". It was a gross exaggeration back then and is still so voiced today.

In a philosophical mood, wondering if I was doing any good at all, I questioned what it was students got from my drama classes. The education hierarchy saw drama as Liberal Studies, a pleasant pastime, but a diversion from 'real academic work'.

It was a very Scottish attitude to the arts, and it took decades to throw over. Years later, applying for scientific research funds, I was told in a written refusal, art was art and science was science. I replied that that attitude rendered Leonardo Da Vinci just another loser.

What did the students think? Did they understand much of it is language and how we use it? I composed a questionnaire. Here, from the pragmatic and the confused, are a few First Year student answers, poor spelling and all.

Why do you get Speech and Drama?

- "To show us that school is not all a lot of rubbish." John
- "So we can rest our bones." Angus.
- "It helps you improve your character and imagination." Mary.
- "If your school wants to raise funds you can have a drama to help." Alison.
- "To improve your mind about things you thought were not possible". Ann.
- "To make us think, to have our own opinion, not be ashamed of it." Andrew.
- "To help us speak right without getting all embarrassed." June.
- "I have no idea why we get Speech and Drama." William.
- "We get drama because it's on our timetable." Betty.
- "Because we are one of the lucky classes." Graeme.
- "To help us convist good when we convist with people and speaken right." Ian.
- "To stop us worrying. Even I can do it because it's not like work." Dennis
- "To make you learn about other people whether you like them or not." Brian.
- "It keeps me away from my younger brother." Margaret.
- "To learn about yourself and to give you currage." Mary.
- "It learns you about theatre, and plays, and costumes." Jeanette.
- "Because I am going to be a film star." Michael.

- "So when we explain things we can make them interesting." Grant.
- "To make you feel happy." Garry.
- "Because some of us need confidence. I am one of those who has not got much confidence. Please excuse the handwriting." Alistair.

Giving seven sermons a day, handling classes of twenty or more, is exhausting, a young person's task. How do elderly teachers manage? I guess that's why so many look for promotion to administrative posts, or drift out of the profession.

One old codger, who looked as if he had known Dickens' Mr Bumble in his early teaching days, had the habit of putting algebraic equations on the blackboard as the hour's work, and falling asleep at his high desk, chins resting on his fist. The surprising thing was, his classes tended to do the work on the blackboard and keep quiet so as not to waken him, or have him see Jim snogging Mary in the rear corner seat.

Teaching is an inspiring career and a killer. If a teacher today I'd probably be militant, out there on marches with the teacher's union, decrying the cant and hypocrisy of two-bit, pig ignorant politicians forever berating the profession for this and that, and having holidays they think are too long.

"The belt didn't do me any harm" says the authoritarian. Aye, is that so? It didn't do you any good either. Have you had a look at yourself lately, you chancer?

I never used corporal punishment, the tawse or belt as it was called, although there were some hairy moments when I got close to bringing out the ultimate weapon. I think a lot of harassed teachers back then were driven insane to the point of slapping a pupil, though nowadays it means instant dismissal for not being a saint.

One disturbed pupil refused to join in my classes, day after day, just sat in a corner, knees pulled up under his chin, glaring. I shall call him Tam. I never won him over. Peer pressure, bags of sweets, soft spoken words, did no good. I could tell something rotten was happening at home, if Tam had one, and it wasn't affection or caring parents. I asked but he refused to speak. The most I got out of Tam was '*nut*', meaning no. He would not do as I asked or participate. I remember him because I failed him.

Tam had his nemesis, a history teacher, a man determined to reach the teaching inspectorate one day, a burly guy with dank wet black hair, combed back like Hitler. He kept his tawse slipped over his shoulder under his sports jacket for ease of action like a gunslinger, ready to whip out in an instant and smack knuckles too slow to be retracted to jacket pockets. He belted every pupil that dared to move a muscle, even an eyelid. He was a strict disciplinarian of the old school. His classes were going to sit ramrod stiff and not speak unless spoken to, so help him God. He was chronically belt happy. He liked being cruel.

One day he flung open my classroom door and threw the terrified Tam across the floor. "Hold him down, while I belt him!" he said, strident as a Gauleiter. This was a new situation to me, a test of my will power and integrity. The boy looked up at me expecting two large grown men to beat him to a pulp. My big test had arrived.

"You've got your teacher really mad", I said, kneeling beside Tam, smiling as hard as I could to ease his fears. For a few moments I was in a panic. The geography teacher was flexing his belt, getting his stance ready, one leg back to steady him so he could bring his belt down hard on Tam's naked palm and wrist. And then I had a flash on inspiration; "Let's go to the headmaster's office", I said. "Let's see if he can sort out your differences". The head of history glared at me, ready to give me six of the best.

We duly took the hapless Tam two corridors and an echoing staircase down to the Head's office and I left them to his solution, which, it transpired, was not three of the best for silent insolence, but a call to a special care officer for troubled children. The history teacher was, naturally, furious with my limp response and made sure the next few days in the staff room were chilly. I had broken the honourable code of teacher supporting teacher against pupil.

I do not know if I passed my test by holding to my principles, but I have never forgotten the mixture of fear and rebellion in that boy's eyes. Years later a thesis I had written at university, a research study, on the efficacy and practice of corporal punishment was cited as a guide in the banning of the barbarous practice in Scottish education. I am proud of that.

I loved those children, every one, their quirks and their quick sense of humour. A geography teacher who had a bad stutter, and a long turkey neck, they daubed 'super-chicken'.

My days as a drama teacher were memorable. They were the making of me. Where are those children now? What did they do with their lives? I'm honoured to have known them. I hope they're well. I trust none joined the army for loss of a better job, and became cannon fodder. I hope they're teaching their children honesty and perseverance. I hope at least one reads this and recognises a time of fond remembrance. I hope.

3

A LETTER TO PRESIDENT JOE BIDEN

Dear President Biden,

I must begin with belated congratulations on the occasion of your election as President.

In paying tribute to you, I believe I speak for many people in Scotland relieved to see sanity return to the Whitehouse. We hope you will be bold in substance, radical in ideas, and steadfast in upholding truth and justice. I am pleased to see legislation you have passed to-date demonstrates a profound moral sense and a humanitarian creed.

You have your hands full renouncing your predecessor's anti-democratic, cruel, self-centred policies, reviving your nation's well-being, spiritually and economically brought low by the Covid pandemic. I trust, I plead, that halting wars is on your agenda. Peace and international friendship is devoutly to be wished if we are to concentrate our efforts on mitigating the worst of climate change that lies before humanity.

On the subject of international friendship, my immediate reason for writing to you is to draw your attention to the political situation Scotland finds itself in through no fault of its own. In 1707, only earls, some lawyers and clergy had the vote, and used it to sign the Treaty of Union with England. The rest of the population, denied democracy, wept in the streets, or rioted. Since then there have been many attempts to restore Scotland's self-governance, all halted by England's might one way or another. Hope is cancelled. In any other situation, this would be called sanctions imposed by an occupying power.

Your respect for your Irish-Celtic antecedents is well known. Back in the day the Irish populated Scotland, and many more fled here during the years of English rule and the Great Famine. My grandfather was Irish, Patrick Reilly from County Mayo, my mother, Maureen Constance Reilly. I was born here in Scotland's capital.

Like our Irish cousins, we Scots are a fiery, argumentative bunch, but unlike the Irish unwilling to die for our country. We die for other people's countries. Our era of Enlightenment taught us it was desirable to use the ballot box and not the bullet, but the peaceful route makes for a long, hard slog, a wearisome journey to full civil rights when your opponent insists on moving the finishing line further and further away. Liberty is a mirage.

Though there are noble exceptions, in dealings of equality, Englishmen are not generally swayed by empirical evidence and truth. An Englishman will explore every avenue until only common sense is left. Logic is not his passion. Foreigners are treated with suspicion, and in Victorian terms, governance is only for the wealthy elite. Scots are never quite English enough, told we will be classed as 'foreigners' if independent. We might become a prime minister one day, but for the United Kingdom, not for an autonomous Scotland. We got a parliament of sorts by agitating for many years, but for all the powers it has, it might as well be wampum, a string of beads for the natives.

For the last 300 years and longer, England's administration has suppressed dissent by the sword, by taxation, by censorship and by brutal policies. In Westminster today we are outnumbered twelve to one.

In 2014, Scotland's governing party offered a new relationship with England based on mutual respect, a genuine partnership of equals:

no borders, continued free trade, we keep the monarchy as head of state, cultural and scientific co-operation continued in return for our sovereignty protected. This petition of good neighbourliness rested on keeping what we earn. In swift rebuff, the new treaty was categorised as 'separatism', a slur, considering the UK registers Scotland with the United Nations as a separate country. We saw a referendum in 2014, undermined by false promise and later, pulling Scotland out of the European Union against the will of the people.

England dumping Europe is not described as separatism by our ever present vacillating neighbour. Scotland's trade is blocked to the west – Ireland and the USA, and now blocked to the east in trade to Europe. Boris Johnson's 'Internal Market', a right-wing snare, will control all our trade. We are effectively corralled. Our rights are traduced, our lives constrained, and the Highlands left as a playground for the rich, infrastructure and rewilding under-developed, land still in the hands of influential private hands, our trade and culture undermined. We are back in the 1700s, only with iPhones and cars.

You will perceive a strong movement in England to retain the UK parliament as its own. This is an understandable ambition, one many Scots support, but it is disingenuous – Westminster has *always* been England's parliament, in agenda and in foreign policy. Scotland is the subservient partner. Boris Johnson's administration is tightening the screws to hobble our Parliament more than it can bear. We live in a colonised reality.

Honour demands mention of English who live and work in Scotland. Some want our independence restored, alarmed at the resurgence of intolerance emanating from their old homeland. It would be dishonest for me to omit their hopes, for Scotland is an inclusive land where Irish, Polish, Italian, and Indian peoples have contributed to our culture for generations. Frustratingly, we make progress towards the ideal only to find new hurdles and ditches placed in our way; we experience setbacks and bereavements among our kind denied basic justice.

Every nation has a right to exercise free will and conduct itself with dignity. The soldiers of colonialism, British civil servants, press and media are fully engaged in the tactics of fear, humiliation, division and smear. English politicians are unable to grasp the imminence of their actions. The situation is intolerable and at crisis. Only the other day people in a Glasgow street stopped a Home Office van in the wee small hours from snatching and deporting two legitimate asylum seekers. The mood was rebellion, the means non-violent action. It worked. The men were released. Martin Luther King would be proud. You can see why we envy Ireland its freedoms, its advances and above all, its independent thinking.

I do not know if this letter will reach your outer office, let alone your desk. Undaunted, I ask that you look upon Scotland's honest ideals with equanimity and good will, that you dismiss the concocted complications of England's elite, the fabrications and falsehoods of Lords and Baronesses claiming Scotland is unfit to be a nation state again, an inferior sub-sect of the species Homosapien. They do not realise 'sapien' means *wise*.

Better a Scotland friendly than a Scotland coerced.

Scotland has no wish to be anything more than a normal nation state, to return to nationhood. We wish our quarrels left behind yet we are forced to reflect we are in the grip of an alien ideology. Thinking of Boston's act of rebellion, perhaps we might get more political traction if we threw crates of England's tea into Glasgow's River Clyde!

How pleasant it would have been to meet you one day to talk as two patriots with pride in our countries. I want Scotland renewed, not the biggest small nation, nor the most powerful small country, just a normal independent nation. Now a white haired old man, I ask that you respect and support Scotland's sovereignty.

I wish you well and a long life!

4

CHOOSING A CAR'S COLOUR

Choosing the correct colour for your spanking new chariot, inside and out, can be the difference between receiving praise from family and friends, or getting the shade so wrong your ability to sell it in good quick time is lost. No one wants a car if a brash shade of orange or candy pink unless an exhibitionist.

Telling a best friend their new SUV in 'Cascading Barf' livery is a shocking error of judgement will activate deep insecurities. Usually, the car dealer offers extreme coloured cars at a discount – to get rid of them. I see vivid lime green cars around, their owners oblivious they have clashing red signal lights and a bright yellow registration plate at the rear. There are the fitted kitchens whizzing around, all-white cars, outside, inside, even the steering wheel. And then there is the craze for cars the colour of burnt orange. They stand out in the crowded car park, but not for the rights reasons.

Colour choice can thoroughly bamboozle all of us without an aesthetic education, the basics of art school studies. Watching a couple at the paint shelves in a B&Q store in agonising dither is a painful sight to behold, trying to match a hue from a paint chart with a swatch of carpet or wallpaper. As for the seriously colour blind, the disability ought to be eligible for welfare assistance.

First there are shades of colours to consider, and then there is proportion to volume. Lastly, there is the quality of light, not only the light under which you scrutinise a colour, but daylight. A bright yellow sports car looks cheerful in sunny Spain, but turns a weird green in Scotland's dull winters. Colour choice is a minefield of traps.

Men who following the fashion of ordering an iridescent 'flip' paint are trying to out-do the car's designer. Flip paints, like matt colours destroy a car's lines. 'Reflective' paints, the kind you'd only ever consider for a waistcoat or a posh handbag, change the shape of body panels. The human eye is disturbed, confused.

We know if you park your car outdoors in all weathers the paint will fade in time, acid rain, sun, aphid spit from overhanging trees, bird droppings take their toll. Paint needs depth. Depth adds intensity. Some manufacturers add only one top coat. But adding more than one coat or a new coat of paint adds weight. Added weight reduces miles per gallon. Trying lifting two 5 litre tins (cans) of paint to understand what I mean. Buy a car cover.

A vehicle's cabin is a small space. Breaking it up with contrasting 'inserts', vivid colours, disintegrates visual cohesion. Avoiding disharmony isn't always easy. Manufacturers are just as tempted as we are to produce cars with interiors that look like patchwork quilts. Electric cars are civilising this by the elimination of buttons and switches, keeping surfaces clean and uncluttered. There are any numbers of people who design a car, once it has left the initial designer's sketch book, approved by the head of design.

Design staff are divided into: engineers on engine and undercarriage, body shape designers and cabin designers. The cabin is broken into seats, doors, carpet and ceiling, transmission tunnel, fascia and dash. Then there is the instrument style to think about and how they are lit. If they don't all work together they can end up creating an automotive pudding.

Good cabin designers try to alleviate funeral black or charcoal grey interiors with instrument highlights and illumination, aluminium instrument bezels, switches and door handles. The Audi TT is a good example of clear, well balanced objects to hold interest on dash, console and doors. Today, cabin designers are using ambient LED light to make a difference to an interior's gloomy space. Illumination in the foot-wells, and door handles often gives a comforting, cosy feel.

Subtle is achieved ordering car seats and door cards stitched to match the car's colour, red, blue, yellow, or white a neutral choice, or ask for a strip of bodywork colour up and over the seats. Embroidered initials or flamboyant images on seats backs are very fashionable.

Manufactures offer dash materials clad in leather, metal, textured plastics, or in the same shade as the bodywork, a choice offered to modern Fiat 500 owners. Up market there's machine turned dashes or wood veneer. Why cause visual clutter by breaking up a cabin interior with all sorts of clashing materials and colours?

Subtle instrument illumination helps. Blue, as used in Jaguars, offers a calming effect, a strong red used in BMW sport saloons is known to inflame a driver subconsciously, to make a driver aggressive, ask any Spanish bull about why bright red affects its mood, not that a bull can drive a car; it has no fingers to grip the steering wheel.

In Seventies Edinburgh the interior of a double-decker bus was grey and dark red. Passengers began complaining they felt nauseous. Corporation officials – it was not termed 'Edinburgh City Council' back then – assumed there was something wrong with the bus suspension until it was pointed out battleship grey and maroon combined in large doses makes people sick.

The best modern artists taught designers how colour and its intensity swings emotions. Mark Rothko, abstract expressionist, the greatest proponent of colour study, proved that in his giant canvases. They took years to create. He layered his canvasses with different hues. Car designers do that today to give a colour depth, as if glowing from underneath the top coat. Get it wrong, for example place modern micra paint on a classic car, and you can see how it destroys a car's visual and historical integrity.

There are as many shades of black as there are shades of white. Some colours are warm, some are cold. Warm means there's a portion of red or yellow in it, cold means a lot of black or grey. Put the two together and the eye tells us something is incompatible even if the head doesn't know why. Some shades have no intensity. No matter how bright the sun the shade won't reflect light to delight the eye. By trial and error we discover using one shade for everything doesn't guarantee uniformity. Different materials absorb colour in different ways, carpet, leather, metal, plastic, and so on.

Those who scoff at colour care are the first to admit a bright red sports car is a magnet to speed cops. And you don't have to own a Doberman Pincher to choose an expensive model in black with a chocolate brown interior. You can just be stupid. Or you can be Porsche who will sell you that exact combination for a lot of money. Choosing colour is as important as choosing the car itself. Of course, there are folk who don't care. They buy a car and don't worry what it looks like, rust, scrapes, old vinyl roof, just to get from A to B.

If you care about good aesthetics but forget everything you've just read, remember this: **Keep. It. Simple**.

5

THE SORROW AND THE SHAME

The term *ethnic cleansing* to denote over a hundred years of clearing Scots from their land is a phrase rejected by those who see Scotland's ills issuing from its weather, strange culinary habits, an odd unintelligible language, and a people a little too inclined to be pushy. Scotland, it seems, is full of vexatious people who do nothing but complain.

Using 'cleansing' is condemned as out of context, erroneously contemporaneous, too emotional because it was often Scot against Scot that did the dirty work.

Well, I have news for slimy proselytisers. It was Jewish guards given temporary preferment who hustled Jews to the gas chambers, less their belongings and clothes. They had no choice. It was a matter of do or die. Who would dare not call that barbarity a cleansing?

Evictions, deportation in all weathers cause deaths, especially of children, pregnant mothers and the elderly. Many Scots died from the vicissitudes that befell them, some from losing their wits, and more perished on the emigrant ships.

After the battle of Culloden – its repercussions I explain later – British rule arrived with a vengeance. New laws and taxes were imposed on Scotland leaving only the most rebellious prepared to protest. Clan chiefs found themselves in the invidious position of being landlords forced to report on their clan's behaviour monthly to prove they were loyal to the British Crown and keeping the peace.

The Clearances – I refer to both the Lowlands cleansing as well as the Highlands, were carried out over decades not a few intense years, too often without witness or written record. You have to search for court summonses and eviction orders, or rely on the oral tradition to find detail of village clearances.

Those who died on the journey south or out of Scotland given an unmarked pauper's grave. Keep in mind, only 7% of Scotland's population lived in large towns making it fairly easy to evict people living in remote areas, and do it without fear of reprisal.

The heartless try to tell us life was hard, houses hovels; people lived in appalling conditions, a truism of other agrarian societies in France, Italy, Spain, and most of the Balkan countries, none of which cried out for English intervention to restore them to economic health. The 'hard life' theme is the apology for clearing thousands off the land they tilled and their forefathers before them.

English rural dwellers encountered a similar fate when Westminster decided full-blown capitalism was a core principle goal of a civilised nation, workers needed for the industrial revolution, but in Scotland evictions were comprehensive, enforced, savage and relentless.

There were two distinct types of 'clearance'. The first was forced settlement on barren land usually near the sea. Homes were burnt and tenants forced to leave at the point of a sword or musket, carrying little or nothing as they headed towards an unknown fate.

Clearances of 2,000 a day were not uncommon. Forced eviction was one method, draconian rent increases another.

An absence of an official record is very convenient. It allows discounters of our history freedom to claim almost anything they want. They can describe lost communities as progress, villages '*abandoned*', not people forcibly evicted, homes torched. They can avoid the pain and suffering, they can dismiss the stench of authoritarian rule. They don't have to talk about individuals or specific families; they can talk in generalities and platitudes.

Sadly for apologists there *are* written accounts. Here is one, published in book form, (I have a copy) by the eminent geologist Sir

Archibald Geikie, an honest witness to evictions on the Isle of Skye. Readers will forgive his use of 'valley' that should be *glen*.

> *I had heard rumours of these intentions to clear people off their land but did not realise they were in the process of being carried out in effect until one afternoon, as I was returning from my ramble, a strange wailing sound reached my ears at intervals on the breeze. On gaining the top of one of the hills on the south side of the valley I could see a long and motley procession winding along the road that led north from Suishnish. It halted at the point of the road opposite Kilbride, and there the lamentation became long and loud. As I drew nearer, I could see that the minister with his wife and daughters had come out to meet the people and bid them all farewell. It was a miscellaneous gathering of at least three generations of crofters. There were old men and women, too feeble to walk, who were placed in carts; the younger members of the community on foot were carrying their bundles of clothes and household effects, while the children, with looks of alarm, walked alongside. There was a pause in the notes of woe as a last word was exchanged with the family of Kilbride. Everyone was in tears; each wished to clasp the hands that had so often be-friended them, and it seemed as if they could not tear themselves away. When they set forth, a cry of grief went up to heaven, the long plaintive wail, like a funeral coronach, was resumed, and after the last of the emigrants had disappeared behind the hill, the sound seemed to re-echo through the whole valley of Strath in one prolonged note of desolation. The people were on their way to be shipped to Canada.*

Once the Treaty of Union was signed in 1706, the Acts of Union following a year later, and after the failed resurrection against English rule at the Battle of Culloden in 1745 when 'Butcher' Cumberland committed genocide against refugee survivor and the innocent, the British authorities acted hard and decisively to suppress and disrupt clan loyalties.

British imperialism has rarely confined itself to extractor of wealth and resources. Imperial rule has to alter a non-English speaking society to its own image in order to sustain its hold over the people and the land. You enslave a people and then teach them how to play cricket to show you mean no harm, and to give the false impression they are one of you. In the case of the Clearances the tale of repression included prohibitions, brutal laws, taxation without representation, and the suppression of Gaelic and Scots languages.

1708: England increases taxes on the Scottish population to be collected by clan chiefs, the annual sum gathered to repay half the loan given to Scottish nobles who lost money on the Darien Schemes, the schemes blocked by England's trade war.

1720: The Disarming of the Clans Act forces warriors and their families to leave Scotland.

1725: Propelled by sustained unrest over the Act of Union, General Wade upgrades cattle trails to proper roads and bridges – from one English loyal garrison to another.

1730: England's demand for cattle and sheep increase ten-fold – the Highlands the place to graze them. Clan chiefs encouraged to shift their people off the best ground.

1735: Clearances begin in earnest, emigration rate rises dramatically.

1746: Post-Battle of Culloden, Highland stragglers, homeless, sent to Caribbean as slaves.

1747: Act of Proscription – wearing of tartan banned; the teaching of Gaelic banned; the gathering of clan members banned; playing bagpipes banned; hoarding weapons banned. English language made first language.

1747: Heritable Jurisdiction Act imposed – Highland landowners must accept English rule or forfeit their land. Many clan chiefs step down and move south, some to London.

1762: Clearances is full spate all over the Highlands and spreads to the Lowlands. Some Lowland villages flattened to incorporate the land into a single one-owner estate.

1782: Loch Quoich – flocks of sheep replace 500 souls forced to emigrate to Canada.

1782: Westminster decides Scotland's rebellious nature is tamed and the Proscription Act is repealed. But remaining clan members stay mere tenants.

1788: Donald Cameron of Lochiel begins clearing his lands of villagers and farmers.

1791: Records show over 7,000 people emigrated from Inverness and Ross lands.

1792: The 'Year of the Sheep' – it is estimated that there are now more sheep than people North West of Perth. Sheep deemed 'more profitable than farming'.

1792: Sir John Sinclair of Ulbster introduces vast flocks of Cheviot sheep to Caithness; 'four footed clansmen' replace people, two for one.

1800: Edinburgh and Glasgow turn cities as Highlanders and Lowlanders leave the land.

1807: Highland economy collapses. This is the excuse given for the need to reuse land for 'better' purposes. A calamity wholly man made is exploited to propel greed.

1811: Clearances begin in earnest in Sutherland under the auspices of the Duke and Duchess of Sutherland. In 1811 the scattered population was recorded at 1,574. By 1831 the number was 257, most serving the Duke's estate.

1816: Patrick Sellar, a factor who burned down cottages, walks free from court.

1820: Landlords propose 'crofting villages' as enclaves of cheap or free labour.

1846: First serious potato famine speeds up Clearances once more.

1853: Women in Gruinard village, (Greenyards) Ardgay, Strathcarron, their men absent, soldiers fighting in the Crimean war, repel Glaswegian police for weeks, by guile and ploys, attempting to evict them. Police finally succeed with bloody baton charge.

1900–1958: With two world wars concentrating the British mind, Clearances continue without pause placing great swathes of Scotland in the hands of a few wealthy owners, leaving tenants with few rights.

1960–Present: Large tracts of supposedly infertile land in the Highlands and many Islands change hands for millions of pounds, Gruinard included.

The slow, incessant crushing of Scotland as an independent state has not ceased. One can understand the fury and the despair that issues from being a perpetual colony.

What difference is there between the vengeance exacted upon Scotland after Culloden, and the reprisals enacted by Westminster now? The repercussions from that lost plebiscite on the fateful 18th of September, 2014 are barbed wire 'Made in England'.

In no special order: artificial austerity imposed on a wealthy nation, forced withdrawal from Europe, grabbing of Scotland's powers by Westminster; loss of welfare rights and pensions, forced repatriation; Scots regiments moved south, shared institutions closed in Scotland, empty shipyards where naval vessels were promised, removal of worker protection rights; bedroom tax; the drip, drip withdrawal of the Barnett Formula, theft of Scotland's oil, the swell of English xenophobia infecting British life, sustained smearing of our Parliament as a useless executive – they all amount to teaching the natives a lesson they won't forget.

The people who voted against Scotland's right to govern its self once more, those who blocked a wealthy country from its legitimate civil rights, are petty accomplices in the clearances of modern Scotland. What they missed was obvious. We are at a point where Westminster under Tory and its alter ego Labour aim to keep the populace uncertain, busy watching our backs, our tomorrows not quite guaranteed. They are imposing constant political upheaval, or as Karl Marx put it, "an uninterrupted disturbance of social conditions, everlasting uncertainty and agitation".

Liberty happiness, autonomy, individuality, spirituality, self-guided development are ideals we all are heir to. There is only one way to realise the clamour for Scotland's permanent freedom, and it isn't inviting more tourists to visit the Highlands to take picturesque snapshots of a banished civilisation. Burn the hand-me-down tattered and bloody Union Jack. Scotland is capable of creating a liberal community, 'Made in Scotland'.

6

CHIPPY HARRY McNISH

As true as I can tell it, this is the story of a Scotsman, an Englishman and a cat. The Scot was called Harry McNish. The Englishman was called Ernest Henry Shackleton, CVO OBE FRGS FRSGS, 'Sir' to you and me. The derogatory phrase 'chippy Scot' derives from Harry McNish's character. He was known to be argumentative, but usually because he was well-informed, better than his shipmates, he knew his subject, ships carpentry. The term 'chippy Scot is nowadays applied to any Scot querulous or protesting.

McNish had a cat called Mrs Chippy who is part of this story. Mrs Chippy took no insult at the name, a generous toleration considering *she* was a *he*, Mr Chippy. He went everywhere with McNish, on the harbour while McNish fixed a trawler's hull or mended a cabin, the cat knowing the hand that fed him, and without qualms near water for he had his sea legs too. That Mrs Chippy was gie adept at walking a yardarm, catching rats, or sleeping curled up atop a binnacle. The cat amazed the crew of the *Endurance* by being able to walk along the ship's inch-wide guard rails, in even the roughest seas.

He, Harry, not the cat, was born in Port Glasgow in September 1874, and died 56 years later, ill, knackered by his arduous adventures and without his teeth, forgotten in his native land. He proper name was Henry McNish. Life would have seen McNish a decent, competent local carpenter, but fate had a different role in mind.

McNish played a vital role in saving Earnest Shackleton's hapless expedition to the South Pole only to see his ingenuity and perseverance denied both praise and a medal. Actually, Shackleton was Irish-born, but of an English family from Yorkshire. His family moved to London when he was ten. In the archives of England's best universities that keep tally on their national heroes, McNish is described as 'British' not Scottish. New Zealand named a whole island after him just to remind Scotland how we are dominated by our neighbour to the point we leave it to the British cabinet and the BBC to decide who is fit for greatness and who is not.

They say all great men have a skeleton in their cupboard, sometimes with flesh on it, such as a mistress, sometimes a dark deed, sometimes a theft from which they benefited. Shackleton had a closet full of hubris. He is our second character in this story, a man who let bitterness cloud his judgement. As for McNish, finding a cupboard was very hard. The home he grew up in was so small the one cupboard held coal for the fire. McNish was the third of eleven children born to John and Mary Jane (née Wade) McNish. Finding a bed for each was often the drawer of a pine dresser.

It could be argued infancy in a wooden drawer imprinted McNish to the extent he choose carpentry as his trade. Not much is known of his youth other than he was a person who knew his own opinion and was quick to stand his ground in an argument. Living in Port Glasgow, Inverclyde, he was drawn to boats and ships, and like all Scots living in a land taken from him, he acquired the outward urge.

Our story takes place in the time of the British Empire, a time where successful men had man servants and ladies personal dressers, and the poor had food to find or lived off the land as labourers. A time too, when plucky Brits ventured forth to explore far off places no one had been to before, with plucky fortitude, and plucky courage, there to achieve greatness in the Empire's gaze and of course, claim land for Queen Victoria.

McNish was 40 years of age, widowed twice, ten years in the Merchant Navy, a skilled shipwright in constant demand for repairs on small and large boats, when he applied to join Shackleton's expedition aboard the *Endurance* set too sail to the Antarctic.

By then, McNish had acquired the Scottish habit of being judgemental of people and things, an age-old Presbyterian trait, and yet, because of his ability for hard graft, another Scots characteristic, that and his carpentry skills, he was well liked and respected by the crew.

Accomplished and certain in his own actions, he was lauded for his ability to repair and fix parts of the *Endurance* that got worn or broken. McNish proved invaluable during the time the ship was caught in the ice. He built instrument cases for the scientists aboard, constructed a chest of drawers for Shackleton's cabin, put together a windbreak for the helmsman, redesigned the crew's sleeping quarters, and, after the ship was damaged by ice pressure, constructed a cofferdam in the stern to try and stop the leak from flooding the entire ship.

Curmudgeonly as he was, McNish was in every sense a *team* player. Though crew members found Mr Chippy too quick to point out the shortcomings of others, they liked his cat a lot, the gentle side of McNish, and made a cat-sized hammock for the feline creature to sleep in.

Like any tradesman, McNish began his inspection of the damaged part of the ship by saying, "Who mended this last time? What a mess. Amateurs!"

McNish was a perfectionist. There was nothing more annoying than people who abused good workmanship, and in his mind, certain to abuse it a second time. One aspect of the ship he complained about was its inability to withstand sea ice if trapped for any length of time. In that he was to be proved profoundly correct.

In return, judging McNish harshly as a pain-in-the-arse, Shackleton expressed reservations about McNish in letters written from South Georgia in 1914 describing him as "the only man I am not dead certain of".

He is "a very good workman and shipwright, but does nothing I can get hold of", meaning, if you asked McNish to do something one way, he did it another, but got the job done to such a high specification no one could fault it.

McNish was the oldest on the expedition, an accomplished sailor, a life-long socialist and a devout member of the United Free Church of Scotland who abhorred the use of bad language. When he grumbled about the behaviour of a crew member it was never accompanied by profanity. However, you wouldn't want to challenge McNish without feeling the weight of his personality bear down upon you to remind you of how much of a fool you were not to be suffered.

As school history books tell, Shackleton failed in his attempt to chart the South Pole, and instead watch the *Endurance* crushing to pulp and twisted metal in sea ice. Unlike the Scots, the English are proud of their heroic failures, making Shackleton, a man who cared genuinely for the safety of his crew, an instant hero fit for a statue.

The flash-point came in December 1915 when, ordered to abandon ship, McNish questioned Shackleton's instruction to drag *Endurance*'s lifeboats across the pack ice following the destruction of the ship. McNish argued that dragging the boats across such rough ice would damage them beyond repair and, besides, that after leaving the ship, he wasn't legally obligated to follow any orders. The captain of the *Endurance*, Frank Worsley, couldn't manage to control McNish and sent for Shackleton.

Shackleton deployed both logic and force to counter the insurrection – reminding McNish with the aid of a brandished pistol that he had agreed to serve under him *both* on ship and ashore. Shackleton went further, denying McNish the right to salvage the timbers from *Endurance* to build a sloop to take the men home.

In the end, dragging the boats proved impossible and Shackleton and McNish right. Beaten by his obduracy, Shackleton ordered the men to turn back. In his diary, he wrote: "Everyone working well *except the carpenter*. I shall never forget him in this time of strain and stress" – his comments effectively a logging for insubordination.

McNish's skill and ingenuity in events which followed is still remembered. After 16 freezing months trapped on the ice, the men set sail in the three small boats for Elephant Island. Eight days after their arrival, one of the vessels, the 20ft whale boat *James Caird*

– the boat named after the Dundee jute magnate who donated £10,000 to Shackleton's exploration fund, was commandeered to strike out for South Georgia – a journey of 670 miles – with six men on board, including McNish. It was only possible because, during their time trapped on the ice, McNish worked tirelessly to ensure the seaworthiness of the escape craft.

In keeping with the ingenuity of a gifted mind, McNish devised his own mixture of flour, oil paint and seal blood to caulk the seams of the boats. He raised the gunwales to make them safer in the high seas and fitted small decks fore and aft to the *Caird*. The crew with him remember his inventiveness and skill with gratitude.

Up and to this point, Mrs Chippy the cat had been a comfort to the crew. They marvelled how the cat coped with the freezing conditions so well, healthy, catching the ship's vermin until the last moment of leaving, and always ready to chase a ball of yarn for a play thing. Mrs Chippy was most definitely an honourable member of the crew.

Before Shackleton, and two others, set off for the final 36-hour traverse of South Georgia's mountain ranges, McNish fashioned crampons out of the boat's two inch brass screws. "We certainly could not have lived through the voyage without it", Shackleton wrote later of his carpenter's efforts.

Without going into detail, the sailors were picked up by the Norwegian steamer *Samson* and then sent back to England directly from South Georgia, joining the cargo ship *Orwell*, which arrived in Liverpool on 3 August 1916. But that isn't the end of the story.

When Shackleton returned in 1917 from his failed mission to conquer the Antarctic, it fell within his gift to recommend his men for the Polar Medal. Of the 27 who served beneath him during the attempt to cross the continent via the South Pole, all but four had their names put forward to King George V.

The decision to leave out three trawler men – Vincent, Holness and Stephenson – was a regrettable omission, to say the least, but the omission of Harry "Chippy" McNish, has rankled with polar enthusiasts ever since and blemished the reputation of Shackleton.

Oddly, McNish expected the sleight and was never heard to complain, an unusual silence on his part.

Like Shackleton, McNish never recovered his health fully. The journey and the events that led to failure broke his strong constitution if not his spirit. He returned to the Merchant Navy but suffered severe pain brought on by the months stranded at the Pole.

After the expedition, McNish worked for the New Zealand Shipping Company, making five voyages to New Zealand. He moved there permanently in 1925 and was employed at the Wellington docks until rheumatism and a serious accident forced him to retire.

Destitute, he eventually was allowed to stay at the Ohiro Benevolent Home, until he died in a Wellington hospital in 1930. He was treated as a hero and given a funeral with full naval honours paid for by the New Zealand government. McNish Island, which lies at the east side of Cheapman Bay on the south side of South Georgia, was named in his honour.

McNish was buried at the Karori Cemetery. For many years he had an unmarked grave, but in 1959 the New Zealand Antarctic Society erected a headstone. Then, in 2004, a life-size bronze statue of Mrs Chippy was added to the grave.

And what happened to Mrs Chippy, the cat? Well you might ask. Shackleton shot Mrs Chippy for food, a callous act. McNish never forgave him. Whatever skeleton Shackleton has in his cupboard, it shares the space with a cat.

7

THE SPIRIT OF THE AGE

Like many another I am apt to shout at the television screen from time to time moved by a mendacious politician saying something that is a brazen lie. More recently I find myself booing television commercials. There was a report back in the late Nineties, research calculating we are subjected to over 3,000 advertisements a day in our daily lives. This overt mind control appears on buses, in newspapers, in street signs, on billboards, and as I write this piece, on the side of my computer screen on a communications platform that induced me to sign up on the basis I would not be troubled by multiple commercials. Joseph Goebbels would have been delighted to see so much effort put into controlling thought.

The intention of advertising is to place in our mind the need for something we do not need, what the economist Thorstein Veblen called 'fabricating wants'. It might be a product such as a vacuum cleaner or a car, or it might be black propaganda composed against a country deemed Enemy of the Month. The intention here is we should fear foreigners and protect ourselves from them by voting for our taxes spent on weapons, making amoral armament companies richer than ever. Peace among nations is not a choice we are asked to make.

A vast industry is devoted to the task of mind-bending: government policy, surveillance, immigration, crime, public relations, marketing of everything and anything, the list is endless. The task is to direct us to things that have no bearing on our existence except to unload us of earned income. A fashion is created and we are encouraged to buy it, the advertisers playing on human envy. If my neighbour has one, I ought to have one. If my neighbour has a new car, I should buy the same model but with a bigger engine and a more luxurious interior. Car makers are now so cocky they will show only the new model driven in fictionally pleasant empty streets, a vacuous slogan added in voice-over; the brand is all that matters not what benefits the new model brings.

We are 'guided' to separate ourselves from each other, seek personal gain and be selfish – "You deserve it" – and not to think for ourselves.

The American public relations industry coined the phrase "engineering consent", lately developed by intellectuals to 'manufacturing consent', a craft exploited by the reductionists of democracy. This is done for our own good, of course. The Scottish National Party had a go at crowd control when it linked arms with a unionist newspaper to condemn independence supporters who use the Internet to express honest dissent, a large 'vile' sub-sect they called 'cybernats', a derogatory sobriquet gifted by a Tory aristocrat, an enemy of Scottish self-governance. The inference desired is citizens of Scotland have no right to criticise government policy or the words and actions of politicians. The campaign to disown a swathe of the electorate was conducted as if choosing a product. Cybernats are *un*persons.

In political matters the mass of us are reduced to spectators, bewildered by the barrage of invective and counter-accusations, susceptible to doctored newspaper headlines, phony think-tank reports, media bias, and narrative of the day hand-picked by television journalists, our newspapers owned by the same oligarchs. Eventually, annoyed and outraged, someone demands a quiet life, and the advertising industry rubs its hands, minds converted, and sets to work selling holidays, super-silent lawn mowers and deck chairs.

Advertising encourages a use-and-throw-away society knowing our environment is awash, choking with discarded plastics. 'Throw-away' includes humans. Goebbels called it healthy indoctrination. "It is the absolute right of the state to supervise the formation of public opinion," said Joseph Goebbels. "And so say all of us" says the advertising industry, coining in massive profits.

8

HOW TO IDENTIFY TROLLS,
SNARK AND SOCIOPATHS

The Twitter account of 'History Woman' belongs to Jill Stephenson, a retired academic from Edinburgh University. Her specialist study was women in Nazi Germany. History Woman is a zealous anti-independence speaker. She belongs to a small group of former lecturers who see self-governance as a threat to goodness knows what. They do not make clear what they fear. Applauding the loss of the 2014 Referendum vote she said, "We have saved Scotland." 'We' is a classic hallmark of the self-aggrandiser, an allusion to an in-house, all-knowing, clique.

Ms Stephenson's prose is filled with street colloquialisms, 'nutters', 'yeah', 'you don't get it', and the fashionable shorthand for irony 'erm'. I half-expected a sarcastic 'he-llo?' followed by 'get real!' Instead she accused me of hiding behind a pseudonym to question her integrity and that was that. Apparently she has form, attracting scorn for describing a female SNP MP as 'a slut'. She refused to apologise. She has stated she'd like Holyrood Parliament shut down. I am still working out which is worse.

No academic I know with any integrity and common sense resorts to Twitter for learned discourse. Despite knowing academics whose tongue can scarify tar from a road, they would not endanger their reputation with the language of Stephenson, not in a public forum. To the relief of Edinburgh University she left their employment some time ago.

Twitter is useless for developing intellectual ideas, best for relaying brief, instant messages. Twitter is full of banter, what we used to call ribaldry. Once in a blue moon you'll see a good epigram, or sensible advice on this or that, but mostly bad grammar and shabby opinion.

The platform is a magnet for trolls. A lot of trolls are narcissists. They are easy to spot. They never answer a direct question nor defer to erudition. When accused of making banal assertion they attack the other person's intelligence, and if a good point is made, run it down with sarcasm and jeering. Abuse attended by five laughing emojis represents the author has blown their rectum inside-out laughing at the stupidity of your intelligent reply.

If a debater refuses to lower their standards and leaves the fray, the troll will accuse them of running away from the argument. They are always right even when wrong. A troll is aggressive, the equivalent of the car driver who turns homicidal if overtaken.

The opposite end of Billy Goat Troll is the sociopath. The internet has unlocked a fire door allowing in every sociopath with a jerry can and a box of matches. They are ready to tell the world their personal situation is the result of everybody's cruelty, not *their* inadequacy. *And we must all pay*! Sociologists tell us we'd be surprised at how many sociopaths are walking the streets and in broad daylight.

The sociopath is easy to identify by their inability to learn from experience. They show no moral principle, lack remorse and are remote, pathologically egocentric, have an inability to show empathy or praise, overall, poor social behaviour, simply put – a total bastard or bitch.

Like trolls, sociopaths suffer from excruciating envy, battered pride, delusions of grandeur, holding ambition way beyond ability. Their self-perception is skewed and dented. They're outsiders who want to displace insiders. The worst will do their best to **dox** your identity. Doxing/Dox is a corruption of *documents*. The verb means to search for and publish on the Internet, facts about a particular individual, and to do it with malicious intent.

Though trolls dim or vicious infest every social site, familiarity has lessened their impact. We have learned how to handle their abuse. But trolling has been overtaken by snark. Snark is cynicism on cocaine. Everybody loves being sarcastic and cynical.

Snark comes from Lewis Carroll's poem, 'The Hunting of the Snark', subtitled, 'An Agony in Eight Fits.' (*Fits* is Victorian for the Italian 'canto': in divisions.) In the poem the Snark is removed from existence, vanquished. The snarker hopes to achieve the same end for their intended victim. But the hunt never ends. It becomes an obsession. Serious snark differs from trolling in that the person using it aims to assassinate another person's character or reputation, holding on like grim death to make innuendo and fabrication stick. The intention is to have the public think there is no smoke without fire. This can sometimes slip over into libel and smear. The reputation of the unblemished, whiter-than-white, terribly perfect Mary Poppins would not stand a chance against today's snark designed to defame.

Snark imposes conformity. The unwary, the inexperienced, can be unnerved by the ferocity of attacks and knuckle-down. Indeed, there are recorded instances where a young person targeted has taken their life rather than be thought of as worthless and a laughing stock. This isn't tough cynicism we are talking about, or incisiveness. Its fatuous sarcasm and flat out cruelty. It is sadism by Internet. The malice behind snark is always palpable.

In the USA it's an internet crime to denigrate by snark if the victim can prove their reputation is harmed. Constructive harassment is a felony.

Satire is altogether a different device from snark. Satire is derived from the Latin *satura lanx* – a dish of fruits, a medley. Satire is critical of manners, vices, social conventions, and social types. The late American comedian Lenny Bruce is regarded as the originator of snark, but snark as satire that eviscerates. Our own Frankie Boyle has taken it to lengths Bruce would never have dreamed of, razor sharp one-liners, alas rarely aimed consistently or joined up. Bruce's style was more description and narration. It got him harassed by his targets and arrested by the police. Charlie Brooker, a social commentator and script writer, has made a career out of snark.

Snark was an early invention. When the Greeks and Trojans met on the battlefield they got stuck into each other with verbal insults and abuse. It could last for days until they got bored or goaded to the point of fury and battle.

I like political satire, the kind hell bent on knocking lumps out of vainglorious politicians of little brain and massive ego. The American talk show host Stephen Colbert is one of the best, a purebred satirist. He was invited to make a speech at a Whitehouse dinner when Bush Junior was president and present at the dinner. Taking a deep breath, he said this:

> *Reality is a well known liberal bias… I stand by this man. I stand by this man because he stands on things. Things like aircraft carriers, and rubble, and recently flooded city squares. And that sends a strong message, that no matter what happens to America, she will always rebound – with the most powerful staged photo opportunities in the world.*

Savage insult designed to expose contradictions is a good thing, hence there is a degree of snark that is justified. It crosses a fine line into wit.

Mid-twentieth century acerbic novelists such as Evelyn Waugh made their name with a kind of Oxbridge snark, and always following fashion when safe to do so. *Private Eye* magazine follows that tradition. When the BBC caved into the political pressure and scrapped its pioneering political punch show *That Was The Week That Was* (TW3), a cornucopia of satirical sketches on political issues of the day, we lost a chunk of the democratic spirit. A late night Saturday show, it attracted millions of viewers, and a lot of outrage from Colonel Blimps. It made the reputation of its cast, namely front man David Frost. The BBC's modern equivalent, *Have I Got News For You*, is not a better device relying as it does on sarcasm and right-wing racism – Scots we are told, hate to eat vegetables.

Snark is endemic. Most of it on Twitter is low grade stuff. The game played is 'throw some mud, see what sticks'. By its very nature, snark is philistine. It will not defer to the artistically or intellectually ambitious for it is always on the lookout for pomposity. "It is an extreme rudeness to tax any man in public with an untruth," said Queen Elizabeth's squeeze and tobacco merchant, Sir Walter Raleigh. "But all that's rude should not be met with death." He had a point. Nobody should die over slander; then again, they should not have their career or good name blighted.

On the literary side, our newspapers indulge in snark every day, rumour, gossip, slyly constructed articles implying one thing when there is no such evidence to justify it. On a loftier plain, Gore Vidal was a master of high snark. He could be savagely honest. "When a friend succeeds, something inside me dies," he once said, ruefully. Having gotten into a verbal and then physical fight with Norman Mailer, a far less able essayist, Mailer, a writer known for his excessive drinking habits and misogyny, slugged Vidal one on the jaw. As Vidal arose off the floor he said, "Words fail you, again, Norman."

This Vidal anecdote reminds me… conjecture is *not* a fact, opinion is *not* a fact, but the worst snarker thinks they are. Snark can range from a false knowingness expressed by a nonentity, to memorable wit penned by a great writer. George Orwell's essay on English mores and patriotism, '*My Country Right or Left*' is pure elevated snark.

Personally speaking, I'd rather we use our real names on the Internet; stand by our opinion and be prepared to defend it. On the other hand, if I lived under an authoritarian regime, one that suppressed dissent, I'd be relieved not to use my real name lest the knock in the night came to my door.

Opponents of truth are using the internet to spread doubt and fear, and assassinate. Snark without limit presented as personal opinion is corrosive. It narrows the debate and diverts us from the important core issues. As for the motivation for this hypothesis, 'History Woman', she's definitely a hellishly dogged conformist. She's bitter and that's unhealthy. Worse, she debases the democratic process, intent on stopping it in its tracks. If she continues along that route she knows she's cutting a path to her own extinction. Then again, by expressing my opinion of her you might determine I'm guilty of snark.

9

DEAR JK ROWLING

Dear JK Rowling,

I wish I didn't feel compelled to write this open letter because you have done so much to encourage children to return to the habit of reading books, and read them voraciously. Nevertheless, literary success is premised on some supposed superior wisdom or insight into the human condition. Overnight, a successful writer becomes a sage, and feels compelled to spray their opinion around like air freshener, boosted by cringe worthy obsequiousness shown to them for their acquired wealth.

Prior to your appearance, children were glued to computer games and television screens, the craft of reading and learning from books unfashionable. Guys like me despaired of ever getting the daughters back from a daily obsessive diet of an Aussie soap called *Neighbours*. Thankfully, they grew up.

I am certain publishers, literary agents, and booksellers are joyous you exist. For that you have a justified place in history books, although I am unsure about the dent millions of books will make on the planet's forests. Your work, your infinite success, is in great part a product of the global grip neo-liberal corporations have over economies, taxes, and free expression. Those are the self-same, self-styled 'libertarians' that cut you very large cheques, the same you think Scotland could never handle. Perhaps you don't want them regulated. They hijacked the word *libertarian*. Its original Latin means something close to free expression. They bastardised it to mean business free of regulation. They prefer small, ineffectual government ready with subsidies and grants for our captains of industry, 'welfare' to you and me.

Press and media, the Scottish Labour group in particular, elevate your utterances on Scotland's ambitions to something akin to the wisdom of a Greek sage, an embarrassing, unctuous deference to a person of infinite wealth and power.

As someone who has helped create fame for others, hollow celebrity and stardom holds little attraction. I'm witness to the private behind the public. The two rarely match. Through my writing, and from my efforts in the arts in Scotland, the UK and USA, I guess I have made a good few talented individuals gain successful careers. Personally, I would prefer the public lose interest in the lives of celebrities because undue reverence and insistent curiosity of them demotes us to second class citizens.

Anyhow, to the reason I write this letter: there are matters in life where rebellion is the only answer to right wrongs and secure justice. Some of the scorn independence supporters endure is akin to that women suffered when demanding the vote. We are a fringe group, ludicrous, fools, carrion – a term you likened us which I'll come to later.

Protest annoys those who hold power. It unsettles. They call it dissent in a pejorative sense. Looking objectively, historically and socially at Scotland's chronic lack of genuine democracy, civic revolution is the only answer to remedy Scotland's ills. Westminster will always resist unshackling constraints. But be assured, unlike disaffected Londoners rioting and looting in the streets, we use the age-old peaceful ballot box.

By praising Scotland as your adopted home I note you acknowledge you're an incomer. Pity your modesty is not sufficiently strong an inhibitor over arrogance. You feel of sufficient high social status to be given a wide hearing, and indeed you almost command the airwaves as the main headline news. Humble you aint.

Others will tell you what you know already, you are free to hold an opinion, and to donate a million pounds to the 'No' campaign. I believe it's outrageous to use wealth to undermine votes and an elected government. We all have *one* vote. Using your wealth to inculcate your fans against a democratic movement means people feel their voice is overwhelmed, the odds are stacked against them. What are you doing that is so different from the US Koch family? For one thing, if you feel there is some truth in a few medical men claiming uncertainty over retaining their research grants on the advent of autonomy it's contradictory to hand over a million pounds to a political campaign, as you did, aimed at undermining the democratic process. You could have chosen to assuaged medical men's fears by boosting their funds.

In addition, over a hundred distinguished academics, like the medical ones you cite, made public their *confidence* in a renewed Scotland and its grant awarding schemes and levels, and like those medical men, and yourself, some are incomers. They can see past slyly worded sentences mined to manufacture consent using 'might happen' and 'could happen' and 'perhaps' as a prefix to assertions of jeopardy and doom.

I would love to live in Spain, not just for its Spanish culture, but for its Roman and Moorish cultures too. I visit the south regularly staying a month or more on work, but as an *incomer* there I'd be loath to tell Catalonians they are misguided for seeking freedoms for themselves.

No matter how long one has lived in a country not your own; one never quite acquires the depth of experience of an indigenous citizen, the sense of its history and its people. One can appreciate it as an incomer after some study but never quite be fashioned by it.

From what you have had to say about your political outlook I discern you think of yourself a humanitarian, a little to the left of civilised ideology. I see you more as an old-fashioned Victorian, in the mould of a 19th century wealthy Tory philanthropist who gives to selected good causes now and again. In that regard, you're at one with the political party you support, New Labour, and your friend, Gordon Brown, bag man to the crooked banks.

The party you support and the alien government to which it is bonded is hell-bent on privatising human endeavour. They detest the "something for nothing society", as they term it. They want Scotland's welfare *state* to become a modest welfare *system*, to keep control over our democratic structures, to increase subservience, to retain a monopoly over our oil, and dictate our foreign policy. That is what you support.

When you were a struggling single parent I trust the city of Edinburgh helped you with welfare payments, a recipient of income support, as I was unemployed two painful, humiliating years. Understandably, I'm profoundly unhappy you reward Scotland's care with a rejection of its ambition to protect that care.

You also support weapons of mass destruction stockpiled in Scotland. By telling us to vote 'No' you welcome more taxpayer money spent on them. In fact, our special relationship with the USA, the same relationship you have, plans to add more. Can you stomach the thought of a generation of children wiped out in one day?

I read and reread your excuses for backing Westminster's interests. They amount to this: the intellectual faculties of the Scottish people are too immature, our economy too weak, our resilience too thin to face the complicated, big bad 21st century without intervention of a dominant neighbour state. Don't you think that something of an insult? I do.

The solution our elected administration offers keeps close ties with England, but protects our self-determination with genuine sovereignty. People power. For the life of me I cannot think why you feel that is not a good thing. You have power in abundance. You exercise it over every contract you are asked to sign, book, documentary, film, and merchandise. You have powerful lawyers to stop others cheating you. We feel manipulated, cheated *ad nauseam*.

Finally, you talk of insults levelled at you while insulting us with the term 'supremacist', a description derived from evil characters in your books, wizards called 'Death Eaters'. You dehumanise us. You castigate us as if an anonymous mass, the lumpen proletariat who have no outlet of political expression except through the perfidious internet. If Cameron and Osborne, May and Johnson are to be condemned for pontificating from Mount Olympus so can you, though you couch your opinion with meaningless good wishes for a happy outcome to Scotland's future.

The conquest of happiness is easier to achieve when a people are empowered to the degree they determine their own local and national affairs. To hold the notion Westminster, after over 300 years of exploiting Scotland and its people, will be our saviour overnight, is akin to the magic fantasy of your children's novels. I specialise in adult issues and concerns, where people lead stressful lives complicated by events they cannot control – such as bad governance. I want good governance for Scotland, for and by the people of Scotland.

You are very welcome to be part of it, but not to demoralise our idealism and our hope. Put simply, I think you have done your reputation considerable harm. Then again, being unaccountably wealthy you might answer, you don't care. You are too rich to feel insulted. You are now one of the elite.

Yours (in a sort of way),
Gareth Wardell

10

ALIMENTARY, DEAR WATSON

In the very week the world's leaders met to discuss the end days of Planet Earth, the summit held in Glasgow, and who will be remembered most of all for a statue to be erected by no one when Armageddon arrives, the British government approved the dumping of raw sewage into their southern sees and rivers. Now I know why the Scottish children's writer, A. A. Milne, named Winnie's river bridge game 'Pooh Sticks'.

There is nothing more familiar to a Scot than English politicians crapping on their own land. I suppose it makes a change from them dumping on Scotland, as they tried once, proposing their nuclear waste be hidden in the rock of Galloway's hills where it would not seep into Somerset. The loss of chemicals to purify the human waste was the result of the UK pulling out of Europe from where the liquids are dispensed; Brexit was never mentioned. Shit happens, as some wag once said. In fact, a study of restaurants discovered faecal bits, like 'bits' in cartons of orange juice, are in every batch of ice cubes dropped into our drinks. I thought it was a trick of the bartender's trade to camouflage the tiny amount of alcohol at the bottom of the glass. I no longer order ice on hot days. All this talk of arseholery shifts one's mind automatically from human excrement to cleaner stuff, toilets and toilet paper.

We pay more, much more than our American cousins for our toilet rolls. This raises an unsavoury but profound question – why do we who live in the vicinity of Holyrood pay more to attend to rear end hygiene than movie stars living in Hollywood? And why is it that the most powerful nation on the planet, the USA, has such humble demands when it comes to personal bottom cleanliness?

The worst we resort to and only in extremis, is *rumex obtusifolius*, doken leaves to you and me, ultra-careful not to include a nettle leaf when out pooing behind a bush in the countryside. Surely movie stars and other millionaires used hand-woven perforated silk and nothing less. Not so. They use cheap, thin paper and are happy.

Shopping in the Marina area of Los Angeles at Ralph's store I found myself replacing a six pack of almost transparent toilet paper back on the shelf to search for the real stuff. Nothing doing. A quick check discovered I had chosen the best. Every brand sold the same quality of paper. We Brits are extremely fussy when it comes to pampering our posteriors.

British toilet rolls are thick and soft. American toilet rolls are thin and hard. European toilet paper is also of a poor quality as I discovered the first time I found myself only able to use a primitive French loo, the one with the hole in the ground over which you squat ingloriously.

At least we don't endure the one-sheet Bronco paper, the once bane of an incontinent person's life. Bronco, for the uninitiated, was a hazard ridden, poverty-stricken excuse for rationed paper in the Fifties. Bronco – no idea why the product was given the name – was as thin as a cigarette paper but ten times larger, single sheets packed flat one on top of the other in a cardboard box, rather like Kleenex tissues, just not so luxurious. Every public convenience used Bronco except the cubicle you chose. That dispenser was always empty.

Izal toilet paper went one better and produced paper in rolls, but it too was the quality of tracing paper. Bronco, smelling competition, issued their roll of 'sanitary' paper.' In both cases, you used a mile of the stuff each occasion you sat on the throne if you were decently sanitary minded.

To an American a roll of Bronco is luxury enough. The poor used old tabloid newspaper cut into squares, held together in bunches by string, hung in the outside midden. (Privet.) You read the scrap of news while you exercised brain and bowel simultaneously.

However, British luxury comes at a price. We pay twice as much for a bog-standard bog roll than Americans. Why the discrepancy? For a start, our toilet paper is often three times as thick, textured, and the rolls are much longer. A chat with Ralph's store manager enlightens the west over the cultural difference. The brand leader, Andrex, is an American owned company. It learned decades ago the British are unwilling to get fobbed off with any old paper. We won the damn war, didn't we? We're entitled to a bit of opulence. Andrex executives researched our toilet habits and began a revolution in freedom for our arses, or as my American cousins prefer, ass. You could call it, *anus mirabulus*.

They noticed too, our keenness for coloured paper, pinks, blue, green, colours to match our bathroom tiles, and when an avocado bathroom suite was all the rage, Andrex issued avocado toilet rolls. The company gave the rolls fancy names so we could avoid the social embarrassment overheard asking for the toilet paper aisle. We asked for a pack of 'warm pink' or 'cosy peach' and stuffed it at the base of the supermarket trolley. (Carte.)

Andrex spotted we buy more rolls of twin-ply than single. In time they got ultra-smart and tripled the layers, and then quilted them for posh butts. Currently, the fashion is for white, often embossed with a pattern. Status conscious house owners still display their wealth by the thickness of the toilet paper in their contemporary bathroom designed by Porcelanosa, or Phillipe Stark.

The pendulum is swinging back again to colour, at twice the price of best white, of course. Bank on paying £10 for a three-pack. The Portuguese paper company of Renova began by selling black toilet paper, colour fast, naturally, 'sensual, absorbent, delicate', before branching out into purple, and then exploding into truly camp colours, some scented. The American attitude to personal sanitation is simple; why bother paying for expensive paper when it all goes down the toilet? The extravagance is a waste of money. What the butt can't see the eye won't grieve over.

In planning for our economic future the Scottish Parliament should not underestimate the importance of luxury toilet paper for the nation's well-being. I won't go into what psychologists think of the character of those who roll under, or roll over, or place their rolls in fancy-shmancy holders. (I drop mine onto the handle of the loo brush.) One thing is certain. Citizens of nations that have truly arrived, shop at Waitrose for 'Quilted Bathroom Paper… enriched with extracts of Cashmere.'

For all our attention to personal cleanliness we deposit our nose snot in a tissue or handkerchief and keep it in our pocket. And we park our toothbrush close to the toilet bowl the receptacle where our pet dog drinks that then licks our face. Still, we leave England to float its boat and kill its fish in a sea of brown slime.

11

AFTER INDEPENDENCE

The alternative title is, 'Things to do in Scotland before you die'. This list is by no means a comprehensive, detailed agenda of priorities to follow once Scotland reinstates its autonomy. Asked in a recent interview what structures I'd like to see, I answered 'the means of attainting happiness', but without the time to explain what I meant by that remark. What I failed to say in my answer is how Scotland should be restructured to face the modern world.

Where to begin? We need few things in life to be happy, a home, food, warmth and friends we can depend upon, the pack instinct. Some want children too, but all the materialistic paraphernalia we acquire is superfluous, things a capitalist consumer society sells to us that we do not need.

We should be living in ideal times, history tells us how to do it, but we live in a confluence of crises, our chances of creating a truly democratic society are slim faced by the tyranny of our colonial neighbour, and the onset of disastrous climate change and pandemics.

Climate Change: The impending destruction of life on Earth is *the* most urgent task for nations to tackle as a matter of profound urgency. We have the solutions to alter things now, if we have a mind to do it. If we do nothing, quite frankly, we are history, except there will be nobody around to read it.

Humankind is well on its way to extinguishing itself and the flora and fauna on the planet, living things that have had nothing to do with nuclear war, mass pollution or habitat desecration. There will always be those among us who hate their fellow humans. I do not, though I am wary of a few specimens.

I cannot bear to contemplate the destruction of the wonderful things humans produce, great art that lifts the human spirit, in my homeland the creativity of R.L. Stevenson or Frederic Lindsay, the poetry of Robert Burns or Sorley MacLean. art of Allan Ramsay or my wife, Barbara Rae. Hope for Scotland to be a better place lies in our hands, or at least in the hands of the young, if you don't feel up to helping out.

Restrict Bank Freedoms: The removal of bank regulation was the worst thing to happen to western economies, the result of deeply flawed neo-liberal, half-baked ideology that grew out of capitalist's alarm at seeing the rise of unionism and socialism, creeds enthusiastic to redistribute wealth. Businessmen of America cobbled together a quasi-religion to justify their plan to take back wealth and suppress the masses. A mad woman called Ayn Rand wrote some nonsense about greed being good for humanity, and bits of her lunacy was woven into the story of false gods we should worship. So far, it has worked well.

The religion was created in Europe, mainly by Friedrich Hayek, an Austrian-British economist, refined and led by the likes of American economist Milton Friedman and his free market economy, a faith based superstition claiming, no matter what crises arise, an unregulated Market will always be a safety net for a health economy. We know this to be bunkum, the law of the jungle. It takes no account of the venality of men.

In 1981 Friedman published a paper, a very influential document, in which he stated that 'the sole purpose of corporations was to enrich them', not the population. Unfortunately Friedman's wobbly theory was given credence by a Nobel Prize for his "achievements in the fields of consumption analysis, monetary history and theory and for his demonstration of the complexity of stabilization policy". The prize gave his hypothesis acceptability. Contrary to his argument, his brutal theories depend on very little competition between corporations. They do free trade deals that are mutually beneficial. Monopolies rule.

When there is competition, big companies gobble up small companies until they become giant conglomerates more powerful than democracies. Overnight they can shift money out of people's hands and banks to places where it cannot be taxed or subject to socialist principles. In essence, Freidman's theory is little more than feeding a large horse the best oats, and the rest of us live off what comes out the other end.

Though it will most assuredly put off a few financial houses from migrating here, Scotland must reintroduce restrictions on banks, separating people's savings from investment funds. Banks of a certain size and wealth should belong to the nation, smaller private banks subject to the same rules.

Moreover, the bonus culture is corrosion incarnate. It encourages greed where those who get paid the most, gain the greatest status in the community. My guardian would have been shocked to learn you can sell anything in a contemporary economy, from your place in a queue for tickets to an event, to your own child for sexual exploitation. Everything has been given a monetary value. The enemy of extreme capitalism is socialism. Those who dismiss socialism have never seen it operate successfully because there have only been half-hearted attempts to try it in full.

The bank crisis of 2008 took decades of taxpayer money because they were 'too big to fail', their employees pocketing massive amounts of cash even as their companies rushed toward Death Canyon. We bailed out corrupt and inefficient banks, allowed them to carry on as before. There is every sign they have not altered their ways, another economic crash inevitable, propelled by the cost of pandemics.

Tax Havens: If you want to bleed a country of its capital, create a few legal tax havens and deny society money to build hospitals, schools, pay for a sound health service, and get rid of food banks.

Welfare ought to be a right, not selective judgement by bureaucratic officials following political instruction. While mega-corporations and Internet companies exploit tax loopholes, the burden of taxes fall on the population, increasing yearly.

Money secreted to a tax haven should see the miscreant, individual or institution, fined the same amount, and if in business, banned from holding directorships. If the money is lost, secreted into a maze of offshore accounts, the person or persons involved should be charged with theft from the nation, and given a suitable jail sentence. Scotland has to outlaw tax havens if it is ever to shake off a corrupt UK where people create wealth and the few who employ them remove it, permanently. The myth that entrepreneurs create wealth is exactly that, a myth. They do not do it by themselves.

Secondly, money granted to a company for start-up investment, or to bolster its existence, ought to put the company in the nation's hands until it pays back the loan. We simply cannot let it fall into administration hands, sold for a £1, taxpayers the losers.

Elections and Referenda: Democracy is the best system we have for the individual not considered a cog in a wheel. Ignore the system and it will grind to a halt and rust, or be stolen and sold by those who prefer a laissez-faire system.

For about the last fifty years we have seen a constructive, illiberal assault on our very existence, an attempt to take away our rights and reduce us to that cog in a wheel. I like the mandatory Australian voting system, you *must* vote, you must participate, voting is compulsory, by-elections too. Only ill-health hospitalised precludes voting or death! (At the last count twenty other countries have compulsory voting.) From age 18, all citizens must vote. This avoids embarrassing outcomes where, in England, for example, less than half a population vote on a major referendum issue and get Brexit.

Naturally, the same should apply to referenda. I have no problem with referenda or multiple plebiscites. The Swiss Cantons – districts – utilise referenda sometimes more than once a year. It need not be a national plebiscite. It can be one pertaining to a local area, votes placed only by those affected.

In addition, a politician can be elevated to lead a party on the basis of a few hundred votes, and an inhuman policy proposed by that leader supported by a few thousand members of that party and adopted. If the party wins an election, even a small majority, it has the authority to put that policy into operation though it might be highly controversial and people suffer from its effects. In Scotland, we saw this with the Poll Tax, and lately, a Hate Crime Bill.

Referenda allow an issue to be judged by the people either before it is implemented, or after, if it proves bad or unpopular. The anti-democratic argue people are not fit to judge. They will say 'the issue is complicated'. Icelanders knew what to do. They voted to tell Gordon Brown and his threats to go to Hell; Iceland was not going to pay for bank losses the people didn't cause yet were asked to shoulder for years to come, money owed to the United Kingdom in dodgy investments.

Ownership of Land: Like many before me, I believe abolition of the private ownership of land is a necessary step toward a world in which we are expected to live in peace with our neighbour. I think of how the clan system cleaved land into segments, and clan fought with clan to take possession. On a bigger scale, I think of the Union. Scotland does not want a part of England, but successive English governments assume they own Scotland. (Wales has the same problem.) Labour and Tory think they own Scotland completely and automatically after a General Election even when they lose in those nations. This is an intolerable situation.

Land includes the sea bed. If the people of Scotland had owned the North Sea, Tony Blair would not have had the right to steal the oil under it for the sole exploitation of England's economic agenda.

Despite an SNP government dedicated to radical land reform, Scotland still lives with the majority of land owned by very few people. In times of crisis, as now, it becomes almost impossible to wrestle land off landowners to use in emergency, unless one day climate change is deemed a war, and war laws apply.

Some method has to be found to place land in the hands of the nation. Perhaps not allowing it to be sold to anybody other than the government, held on behalf of the people, is one route to take.

Taxation can help too. Land is what we have to pass to the next generation. The land is our history. The few with so much land is why so many are piled high in cities.

Scottish Names: I admire Iceland having an approved list of traditional names Icelanders can use. The first thing colonial invaders do when taking possession of another's country is eradicate the local language. You must learn to speak as the colonial speaks. With that history goes indigenous stories, writing, poetry, and song. I recall the outrage when the then First Minister Alex Salmond got a Bill passed to add Gaelic names to all signposts and maps. Some people were shocked. They saw it as a waste of money.

People will protest an official list of names is an attack on personal freedom, when in reality it protects their culture and traditions from dilution and eradication. You know a Scotsman or woman because so many of us have a surname beginning with 'Mac' or 'Mc'.

It follows that I am addressing first and middle names. I am all for a child given *two* first names. They can choose which to use when older. Those first names should have a linear, identifiable heritage. It does not matter if the name originated in Ireland, Italy, Norway, Denmark, France or Timbuktu. If a name can be proven to be extant in Scotland for, say, 100 years or more, they should be permissible as a Scottish name. A national register can be augmented year by year, if people wish new names added to the list that are discovered in past records, and that includes their spelling.

I expect this attitude to protecting our heritage the most challenged, such is the belief in the cult of the individual together with deeply ingrained feelings of 'Britishness'. A national register of Scottish names avoids the schizophrenic disaster of the 'Amber McClutchie' sort, or 'Wayne Clint MacGlinchy', rapper and basketball cheerleader.

Caring for the Vulnerable: We know our nation is a wealthy one, always was, hence England holds tight to our taxes and resources. Some of that wealth ought to be put aside for a minimum wage as good as any in Europe, and a pension just as equitable.

Four-day Working Week: The few experiments carried out in countries such as Finland prove to have great benefits for the population's health and happiness. Not only did their work effort rise knowing they worked only four days a week, but they had more energy. People had more leisure time to spend with their family and in leisure activities. The latter presupposes some trades will not see a shorter working week unless they can afford to rotate staff, pubs, restaurants, coffee houses, shops and entertainment establishments.

Happiness means finding a balance between your work and your home life. A survey showed 63% of salaried staff would back a four-day work week. In another study, conducted by the Chartered Institute of Personnel and Development (CIPD), it revealed that 60% of UK employees work longer hours than they want, with 24% overworking by 10 hours a week. On the flip side, 78% of employees who work flexible hours believe it's had a positive impact on their lives. Longer hours don't necessarily lead to heightened productivity.

In Scotland with our limited summer weather and dark winters, I think a shorter week a boon to better mental health. In Denmark, where workers put in four hours less per week on average than those in the UK, productivity is 23.5% higher. More leisure time does not necessarily lead to boredom.

There are many more changes I'd like to see: planting millions of more trees, evergreen mixed with deciduous trees, millions of tress, as Japan did in a ten year span, and the reuse of good land left fallow, enriching the soil with the likes of seaweed fertiliser to grow food, and include the rebuilding and regeneration of lost villages that can be made self-reliant.

In time the battle between socialism and capitalism will fade away with the old men who argue about it endlessly. Right-wing cranks and capitalist crooks grow old and acquire the distresses of old men, bald heads, fat bellies and enlarged prostates.

Candide said, "cela est bien dit, mais il faut cultivar notre jardin" – we must cultivate our garden. Who would disagree, especially given the garden that is Scotland?

12

ICELAND'S CRIMEFINDER GENERAL

When the Royal Bank of Scotland got caught out in its race to be the biggest bank known to the galaxy, too cocky to undertake due diligence on acquisitions stuffed with toxic sub-prime debt, I joined others in calling for heads to roll. Back came angry bank staff and die-hard capitalists to tell me honest bankers had done nothing wrong. Gambling with our savings was 'strictly legal'. I asked how they knew the motivational detail of *individual* cases and departments. They repeated their facile claim, bankers were blameless, their behaviour might be immoral, but not illegal.

Apologists for the banksters demanded to know what I would have done to save banks. My answer was, I thought, common sense: let the bankrupt departments fail, retain the profitable sections, reintroduce rigid regulation, close down on the venal bonus system, separate savings from risk investment, and reimburse ordinary folk from the public purse adversely affected by the corporate scam. Risk takers should get no help. Not an economist, I was duly jeered out of court, but in Iceland they had a champion.

On a recent visit to Iceland I wanted to find out first-hand how Icelanders managed to indict their bankers. The banks had been privatised in 2000 making excessive expansion without regulation high risk. It transpired that at base it was the Elliot Ness Sting; if you can't get the villain on the dead bodies, check his account books.

Iceland is a vast land mass, population few, currently no more than 340,000 living in an area over 40,000 square miles in size, land getting bigger by the year as its glaciers melt. And yet by 2001 Icelandic banking expansion had reached a zenith of frenetic activity, so fierce it was given the nickname 'Viking capitalism."

Like Scotland's RBS, the three Icelandic banks Glitnir, Kaupthing and Landsbanki embarked on a spree of acquisition. I was surprised to learn they owned the football club West Ham United and Hamleys the London toy shop, among other prize assets. The frenzy didn't end there. Across the nation's population, hotel porters, waiters and fishermen became full-time financial traders. Mortgages were dished out like confetti. Tourism took off as never before with the pound sterling and dollar great value against the Icelandic Kröna.

Almost overnight Icelanders got materialistic. Car and jeep sales soared, house construction quadrupled, a grand concert and opera house was approved for construction, exotic clothes shops and restaurants opened in the capital and main towns, and McDonalds moved in with a vengeance. In his book *Frozen Assets*, Armann Thorvaldsson claims that, in 2006, Iceland was one big boom town, and Bang and Olufsen sold more televisions in Reykjavik in a year than anywhere else.

When the Great Crash came Iceland was hit like a car stalled on a railway level crossing. Unlike the UK where the population got punished for the bank's greed, helped by prime minister Gordon Brown, bag man to the banks, Iceland was smarter than us. They let their banks fail. People congregated in thousands outside their parliament demanding justice. Robbed, trust abused, advice given to them seriously flaky, they refused to accept the dictum 'too big to fail'.

In panic, the national parliament, 'The Alþingi', responded by creating the post of 'special prosecutor' and gave it the authority to investigate as little as a rumour of financial impropriety. Nobody wanted the job. A year later one man picked up the gauntlet.

A small-town, burly policeman took it, a man you might assume from his ample girth more interested in pork pies with chips than detective work. His parliamentary employers were happy. Until he got fired up by patriotic justice his biggest investigations were "assault or a drug case". He looked a suitable patsy. They were wrong.

With masterly sleuthing, his calling arrived, Olafur Hauksson accomplished impressive feats of criminal detection and arrest unknown in our corrupt United Kingdom. Hauksson, 52, is now Iceland's district prosecutor in charge of investigating all major crimes on the island. He is the only person I can think off to have jailed a big bank's chief executive. Executives of the lower order have been jailed in various European countries, not a top executive.

Hauksson did not just jail one. He nailed Larus Welding, former chief executive of Glitnir, guilty of fraud. This was followed by two more chief executives, Hreidar Mar Sigurdsson of Kaupthing and Sigurjon Arnason of Landsbanki, who were each handed two separate convictions and jail terms.

Of his financial cases, fifteen reached the Supreme Court for judgment, bringing eleven convictions, two acquittals and a retrial. So far he has indicted forty bankers, a number surely fit for inclusion in the *Guinness Book of Records*.

Hauksson began with nothing more than an office, desk, two chairs, one telephone, no computer, just a set of empty file covers. And that's pretty much what he has now except he has a computer and his files are bulging. He also pursues politicians who took back pocket money. How did he succeed where our representatives failed us?

In Hauksson's own words, "The lawyers in other countries go for the keyboard person, the underling who performed the trade, rather than someone up the food chain who instructed the trade. I made it my job to concentrate on the top man, the one who sent the memos." He might as well have said harass the top man till he got a confession, so determined was his nature to get his man.

Hauksson concentrated on the big fish – a good Icelandic tradition. Many of the cases were highly complex, involving market manipulation or breach of fiduciary duty through the use of shell companies to prop up the banks' share prices or loans where the lenders bore all the risk. So how did he go about pursuing the people at the very top?

He says it's about following the document trail very carefully, particularly in times of stress and crisis, emails can be especially revealing. "Keep to the logical conclusion rather than stopping; find out who is responsible. It is important to make employees aware that if they cannot point to someone else, they will be the one to blame."

He discovered employees opened accounts *without* customers' authorisation. Hauksson traced back the memos and emails to the person at the top who made his specific order turn into daily natural business.

The banks themselves accounted for up to eighty percent of the trade in their own shares on some days. Executives kept reports showing how much the bank itself was actually buying up its own shares, so they couldn't deny what had actually been happening.

The bank collapse caused Iceland's currency to plummet, which in turn led to inflation and loan repayments soaring. Icelanders who had taken out loans in yen or Swiss francs at a lower rate of interest found they were now facing penury. Almost everyone was affected by the crisis one way or another.

The Great Bank Scam is Iceland's biggest crime. As for political, economic, and social reactions to the crisis, the Icelandic government was motivated by an acute need to explain to the public what had happened, to determine accountability, and to preserve a measure of social cohesion. But there's a negative side to hunting down wily villains – they have friends in high places, including iffy judges. The price of integrity is personal and family sacrifices.

"During some prosecutions we are more at work than home. It is bad, working late hours and weekends, and it wears people out. We have had incidents at work where we have actually had our employees very badly ill. I have four times seen one of my employees going into an ambulance. That's not an easy thing, so you actually feel a little bit the pressure that comes with the job."

In his early investigation Hauksson proved to be one stubborn son-of-a-bitch, aided by the Icelandic parliament's special investigation commission, a kind of truth and reconciliation group of the type I suggest instigated for the day after Scotland's formal independence.

What I read about Hauksson is refreshing. He dispensed with the 'not immoral' bullcrap of British bank staff, and the financial jargon they use to obfuscate plain unadulterated theft. He calls a spade a spade. Banksters committed embezzlement. They were not inept or naive.

As the months went by the then prime minister of the UK Gordon Brown discovered many local councils had invested in Icelandic banks and lost the lot. Brown demanded their money back and if not forthcoming, threatened all sorts of reprisals. (There was Dutch liability too.) Two 'Icesave' bills to pay liabilities were rejected in parliament. In a masterstroke, Brown's Icelandic counterpart Gier Haarde called a referendum to gauge the people's opinion. In a landslide they voted to tell the UK to get a life. The rupture with the UK has yet to heal. The Icelandic folk remember the Cod War, and how they won that skirmish.

Iceland's prime minister, Sigmundur Davíð Gunnlaugsson, once thought of whiter than a filleted haddock, was forced to resign after appearing in the 'Panama Papers' revelations concerned with illegal offshore companies. The anti-establishment Pirate Party is gaining adherents. Tourism continues to flourish. If newspaper articles and letters in the press are anything to go by, trust in Iceland's parliament at an all-time low, though it cannot be lower than the disrespect for the UK parliament by the people of its four nations.

Iceland's criminal bankers are held in an open prison – there's barely a murder every decade to justify a concrete citadel of solitary incarceration – nevertheless, Iceland has shown its people have more regard for honesty and openness than the Brits. Here in Scotland, not a single executive banker has seen the inside of a court room. After taking billions of public money to remain in the style they are accustomed, we watch as local banks are closed and wall tellers removed to protect those hallowed bonuses. We are paying doubly for the crimes of bankers. And the banks are on their way to another crash, unless they are nailed down once and for all.

Iceland is a resilient country, an example of the fortitude manifest by small nations reliant on their own solution to problems, but like the fish it traditionally trawled from the seas around its coastline, the people know there are good times and there are bad times; you make the best of what you have. Warnings of doom tomorrow are dismissed. Small country, big confidence, but then it is an independent country.

13

THE WEALTH OF SCOTLAND

When researching aspects of the Highland Clearances it dawned on me that those dark episodes in our history were the beginnings of capitalism in Scotland. Over ninety percent of Scots lived off the land. The landowners discovered they could get a lot more profit out of wool than from renting property, and so the evictions began in the same way a company today would lay off workers, but in Sutherland's case, without redundancy payments. Those who had lived off the land found themselves with nothing.

From that moment on the dispossessed sold their labour in order to survive. Employers soon understood they could acquire great profit by keeping wages low, and workers dependent on their employment. The adage all folks are born equal is a bare faced lie from the moment the midwife cuts the umbilical cord.

The gibe commonly thrown at Scotland by the pillars of the British State to the point of chronic boredom, is how poor we are and how poor Scotland will be if we restore independence. To make a falsehood stick, repeat it endlessly.

Scotland is rich. Independent we would be one of the richest nations in the world. One of the positives to appear out of the referendum debate was bright economists sympathetic to Scotland's plight. They illuminated the *real* deficit – a lack of economists working in Scotland supporting independence, the few who popped up to give evidence self-appointed charlatans ready with figures skewed to Unionist purpose. When those paid economists of the British State – often lecturers in our universities – talked of 'the wealth of our nation' it was always in terms of our culture, the arts, and what a fantastically inventive country we are. They avoid translating our output into what we earn and are not allowed to keep.

Irish economist David McWilliams is well respected because he also correctly predicted the global financial crash of 2008. Now of course, this was not reported in UK media, but it was on Irish news. Interestingly, he also predicted that the Scottish independence vote would change Scotland's relationship with the UK Government forever. Here is McWilliams showing how much stronger is Scotland's economy to Ireland's:

> *"Look, it's clear to me that Scotland could be an independent economy. There's no doubt of it. The Scottish economy is bigger than the Irish economy, the rate of unemployment is half of our unemployment, it has oil, lots of it, it's population structure is quite young in comparison to other parts of the UK. So this is an economy that could survive on its own without any real problems – it could even thrive on its own. We're not talking about a bit of the UK, we're talking about an economy that has [2014] one hundred and ninety billion Euros, GDP – so its big by any standard. There's no reason to think Scotland can't survive and thrive. The fib lies in telling Scotland it gets more out of the Barnett Formula than it puts in. If you judge an economy on a projected deficit you're putting the cart before the horse. The question is, how do you get there, and can the Scottish economy be dynamic enough to generate revenue over – let's say – the next ten years to reduce its expenditure and narrow that deficit.*
>
> *In actual fact, a deficit does not matter as long as they can finance themselves, and I've no doubt that they can. People need to stand back and see what's there. You've an economy in a wealthy country that says going independent now is probably the best time they could do so. Because for the next forty years they have oil revenues, substantial revenues, and they can deploy an investment strategy to attract multinationals – like our own – their wages*

are much lower than Ireland's, one of their main competitors. So, there's every evidence to prove Scotland can and will survive and thrive.

What we're getting is a policy of a lot of scaremongering on the part of the establishment of Westminster, by that I mean the political parties, and the corporate block for the simple reason they don't want change. Now, there's no doubt there will be complications but that's the negotiation period. However, this notion – what currency? – it somehow changes the dynamic that Scotland could not manage the transition and be a normal country with wealth generated by a normal society, is to me just not credible.

The [world] will see there are two English speaking countries, Scotland and Ireland, and Scotland will see inward investment coming to them because Ireland has had the pitch to itself. And as long as Scotland was part of the UK corporation tax was never going to be touched because London didn't want it touched, denying the Scots the game we're playing, but whether its a Yes or a No [14 September 2014] all that will change.

My grandparents were Scots. If I was there I'd vote 'Yes' because there's something very exciting about the right to govern your own affairs. This is something that is deep inside all of us. Even if the vote goes No this is going to change the relationship between Ireland and England and Scotland in ways people would never have contemplated a few months ago."

Other economists followed suit, such as Richard Murphy, and Yanis Varoufakis. An article in the *Independent* newspaper a couple of years ago did the same as McWilliams, it explained exactly why Scotland has all of the ingredients to become the world's richest country on a per capita basis. Is there a problem why some think otherwise? Yes, we are loaded down with debt accrued by the UK. We are obliged to help pay it back under Westminster rule, but not if independent. They then call that Scotland's 'deficit'. And there is oil. Oil is good for at least the next fifty years, not forty as McWilliams states based on the information he had in 2014. McWilliams' reasoning does not rely entirely on oil. He echoes a widely held belief voiced by outsiders which opines that Scotland could easily implement the Irish model of reducing corporation tax slightly in order to attract huge American multinational corporations to set up home in Scotland. The policy can attract tens of billions of pounds into the Scottish economy, and would also provide excellent jobs with excellent pensions and benefits to thousands of workers who are currently undervalued in the UK's low wage economy.

The former Canadian governor of the Bank of England, Mark Carney, got in on the act. He told a press conference that "the broad brush assets of the Scottish financial sector" is worth at least "ten times GDP", and admits that to be "north of a trillion pounds sterling." Currently, that equates to over £1.8 trillion. Scotland already has a higher GDP Per Capita than France, Spain, New Zealand and Japan. So if one argues Scotland isn't rich enough to be independent again, then one is claiming the same about those nations, which is preposterous. I've already written about New Zealand, a country similar in many ways to Scotland but without the string of pearls that is Scotland's natural resources. It survives well, and with no submarines!

No wonder Scots are paranoid. Absent from the British mainstream media was any mention of that healthy economy. They will bring themselves to mention success achieved by Scots companies but as a one-off fluke. They won't join up the dots for us.

What is the secret to being the wealthiest country on earth on a per capita basis? Well that's easy to answer – have lots of wealth and *share it with a relatively small population*. The argument that a country might be too small to survive is so much nonsense. Moreover, a small country means you can see your elected representative going to work each day, or shirking their duties. That closeness generates accountability and less opportunity for state corruption. Being smaller also makes it easier for a nation to remain competitive and attractive to foreign investment and corporations.

Forbes magazine, a periodical no one can call left-wing, made the same observation, "the British Government has lied to Scotland to keep it under control." Nothing new about that, Mr Forbes, but nice of you to tell us conspiracies actually exist. One man who discovered the financial shenanigans from the inside was John Jappy, 'the man who knew too much'.

John Jappy is one of Scotland's unsung heroes, or he would be had we an honours system of our own and the shared belief in our country as an homogenous society. He ought to be up there among Scotland's ten best champions of open democracy. There is no Wikipedia page on Jappy and you will be hard pressed to find a decent obituary. And here we are in 2021 still answering the same inane questions thrown at us by defenders of a crooked, failed Union. For all the truth he spoke of, Jappy might as well have been a sandwich board man walking up and down the High Street, his message reading, 'Destiny is at hand'.

Jappy was among the first to scotch the myth that Scotland was subsidised by London. In truth it was, and is the reverse, Scotland pays more to England's coffers than it receives in annual allowance. If one also takes into account the profits from North Sea Oil the sum adds up to trillions. I know of no nation that would accept this grand larceny without mass revolt, yet the person in the street thinks it is not a criminal conspiracy.

Back in 2014, I and others drew attention to Jappy's work for the Cause when he published his exposé prior to the referendum vote. What he had to say then is as relevant now as it was when he published it. Jappy had a Road to Damascus moment. He discovered his London masters were liars and crooks, the Labour party a gang of thieves, Tories, House Jocks urinating on people's hopes, crawlers, coattail hangers-on and cap doffers siding with the power elite so they were offered preferential elevation.

Jappy made a telling contribution to the Yes. He was an insider who knew the UK Government's accounts. He achieved high office in the General Accounting Division, with links to the Treasury. His tale is worth retelling to students and to our children. No one wants them duped as we have been.

Here is Jappy's story in his own words:

"As a civil servant in London, and being part of the establishment, I always accepted the general view that an independent Scotland would not be able to survive on its own without financial help from the London Exchequer.

In fact it took another 30 years before the first chink in their armour started to appear. This came unexpectedly on 13 January 1997 when, in reply to a series of questions put by SNP Leader in the Commons, Alex Salmond MP to the then Tory government, Treasury Minister William Waldegrave admitted that Scotland had paid a massive £27 billion more to the London Exchequer than it had received since the Tories came to power in 1979 (ref: Hansard). Statistically this works out at £5,400 for every Scot. There were no attempts to refute these figures, which caused much embarrassment to the Tory Government of the day. The facts were quickly covered up by the Unionist controlled media.

When the Labour government came to power it announced a 1p cut in the standard rate of income tax. From my detailed knowledge of income tax, I felt that this was the worst possible thing that they could do, as extra monies would be needed following on from the Thatcher era, if they were to fulfil even a fraction of their promises to the electorate. I came to the conclusion, and I still feel that I was right, that this was done by Labour to prove to the voters of Middle England that they could match the Tories in tax cuts.

After the debate it took the Labour Party a whole week to admit that they were wrong. There was in fact a whole chain of errors which the Labour Party tried to blame on "printing mistakes". However Labour could not deny the fact that in their calculations the UK average figure, which included the high wage earners in the city of London and the booming economy in the South East corner of England (which if I may say so were the result of the selfish policies of Mrs Margaret Thatcher), the figure used was almost double those of the average Scottish wage which at that time stood at £17,000 per year. Looking closely at the figures and taking the year 2006 as a benchmark, I found that Scotland had an annual relative surplus of £2.8 billion, which works out at £560 for every man, woman and child. In contrast the UK had a deficit of £34.8 billion. In November 2006, the UN published its annual "Human Development Index".

For the sixth year running, oil rich Norway topped the list, and won on such factors as generous welfare payments, education, high income and a long life expectancy. Norway wisely created an "oil fund" in 1995 which in 5 years reached a total of £250 billion, so that Norway sailed through the Credit Crunch.

Any doubt that Scotland more than pays its way, or survives on subsidies, was dispelled by a report published in the Daily Mail on October 12, 2007. The Daily Mail, which by no stretch of the imagination could be described as a supporter of Scottish nationalism, devoted a whole page to the analysis of the report which was based on tax paid per capita as against spending; Northern Ireland received £4,212 more than it paid in tax, North East England £3,133, Wales £2,990, North West England £1732, South West England £978, West Midlands £931, East Midlands £185 and lastly Scotland £38. Only the South East corner produced a small surplus due to tax paid on the high wages within the city of London at this time (pre-Credit Crunch). It is no longer refuted that Scotland exports more per capita than the rest of the UK. In 1968 when I first discovered that Scotland was in surplus in relation to the rest of the UK, its exports could be broken down into whisky, meat, timber, fish, and of course tourism which is a huge hidden income.

Those exports are supported by a population of only 5,000,000 as against 45,000,000 for the rest of the UK, quite a substantial advantage. With the oil boom, Scotland's economy was transformed. Scottish oil has to date funded the Treasury with £300 billion, which has pushed Scotland up from 7th place in World Wealth rankings, had it been in control of its own resources, to 3rd place.

On 29 May 2008, Labour Chancellor Alistair Darling admitted in a back-handed way, that Scotland's oil revenue had been underwriting the UK's failure to balance its books for decades. There is still 30 years of oil supply left in the North Sea (some 150 million barrels) valued at 2008 prices at 1 trillion dollars. This excludes the new fields being brought into production in deeper waters west of Shetland. Meantime whisky exports, which I listed in 1968 as one of Scotland's top assets, have risen at a phenomenal rate. For example, whisky exports to China amounted to £1 million in 2000/2001, by 2012 they had risen to £71.5 million and have continued to rise.

On the economies of Independence, in North Sea Gas Scotland has 18 times its requirements, which on current trading is more expensive than oil. The country exports 24% of its surplus electricity south of the Border, with much of the back-up by Hydro Electric unused.

Even if nuclear is excluded, the future looks bright; the new Glen Doe hydro station on Loch Ness which was opened by Scotland's First Minister last year can produce enough electricity for 240,000 homes. Further projects down the Loch which have now reached the planning stage will increase this to over 1,000,000 homes. Wind and wave energy will also contribute significantly in the future.

Having worked on the preparation of UK National Budgets for most of my working life, it irks me when I hear Tory stooges spouting forth figures condemning Scotland to financial disaster if it votes for Independence. They are simply reading from a script given them by Tory chums. They pull the strings. In fact I once met a Chancellor of the Exchequer who could not even work out the PAYE tax for his domestic employees. The only reason why he didn't get someone else to do it was that he was ashamed of how little he was paying them!"

As John Jappy proved all those years ago losing Scotland means England-rUK takes a massive hit to its GDP. The UK would lose oil reserves, gas reserves, hydro power, arable farmland, forestry, sea area, reservoirs, fishing waters, gaming lands, rock and granite quarries, slate reserves, tourism income, export income, and a staging post to train half-baked comedians trying to make it in politics. Just watch some of England's indigenous companies and financial institutions move to Scotland in double quick time.

We can expect a very long caravan of sensible but anxious settlers arriving in Scotland for a 'better life', in which case we'd damn well should ensure we are in charge of all we earn and keep it in a very large, safe metal box to distribute as we think fit.

The only reason to let wealth go south is because we are giving England a loan!

14

DEFOE THE UNION SPY

Daniel Defoe left his mark on the world in two ways. Among what amounts to an entire recycling plant of political pamphlets, mostly forgotten, and a batch of novels of which only two are remembered by the public, *Moll Flanders*, and the much adapted *Robinson Crusoe*, Defoe perfected the craft of black propaganda that inspired generations of flaky journalists. Almost single highhandedly he designed the architecture of Unionist falsehoods still exploited to this day.

One strand of Defoe's thinking chimes with England's current feverish search for cricket and warm beer purity. Defoe considered Englishness – heterogeneity – eradicated. This is a good place to start before analysing his influence on current politics. In *General History*, a book in which Defoe expounds his theory that a union will see Scotland 'regulated according to plan', he compares Scottish hegemony with England's.

> *"Tis true, England is more mixed in blood. The reason for this is plain, in that being a nation powerful in wealth, fruitful in soil, and above all, increasing in commerce, more nations have sought to settle among them, more people have flowed in upon them, from all parts of the world, blending their blood with the most ancient families, and have destroyed all that can be called National…."* (General History p2)

A regular riposte from British Unionists today in arguments over immigration is the one about Scotland not suffering as England has from "uncontrolled immigration". (No matter where they settle, colonial English tend not to see *themselves* as incomers.)

In the same treatise Defoe points out how Scots have somehow managed to preserve their "ancient families". Paradoxically he goes on to argue both Scotland and England are infiltrated by foreigners "by virtue of frequent invasions made upon them". This gives Defoe the excuse to suggest Scotland and England are better as *one* nation – Britain. Think about that; what Defoe is saying is what is said now; Scotland is safer from attack only if part of Britain. He says nothing of physical and material attack from England, a reality threatened in 1706 if Scotland did not come to the negotiation table, and now by Westminster withdrawing Scotland's powers to weaken the movement to full self-governance. In contradiction, Defoe is facing both ways simultaneously, protect Scotland's character by merging it with another until indistinguishable one from the other, which exemplifies the Unionist mind-set of contemporary British power.

Daniel Defoe (1659–1731) was born Foe, adding the 'De' to imply he had posh foreign ancestors, another contradiction in his quest for an English Britain. Born in London, son of a butcher, his family were strict Puritans. Rebellion against a claustrophobic home life might be one reason he took a dislike to religions of the day except Presbyterianism, a rejection that in turn led to his politics. He was certainly argumentative. His writing is not known for its humour but well skilled in contrariness. He was a trader of tobacco, ale and wine – after the Act of Union, shipping them to Scotland, and was in and out of debtor's courts so much that in time he turned to writing novels as a secondary income. He was sharp, smart, his style acerbic and polemical. It was just as well that he had talent for the pen because having eight children by his only wife couldn't have helped his finances. He was driven to become prosperous, a sure reason he took the English gold sovereign to be their spy in times of penury.

Defoe was a racist, nothing odd in his day, or now in the English psyche, considering the endless wars England with Dutch, Spanish and

French. He especially disliked the French. Troubled by the pro-French, Jacobite ethos that persisted north of the border, he gravitated to Scotland where his fellow Presbyterians were members of an established kirk. He set up shop as a trader. No sooner ensconced in Edinburgh, he began to write leaflets against Roman Catholics and Jacobites in particular. In time he came to feel that a union would not just help Scotland economically, but would be good for Protestant England facing threats from the continent. Here lies the beginnings of modern Scotland exploited in England's interests.

When Defoe went to Edinburgh in 1706, it was as a secret agent working for the Crown. Given the unpopularity of the proposed Union in Scotland, this was a risky move and an even riskier commission. A contemporary reported Defoe was "*a Spy amongst us, but not known to be such, otherways the Mob of Edinburgh had pulled him to pieces*". Defoe denied in print that he was a spy, but in private company he dropped his concealment and boasted of it. Showing off was typical of the man. There's no doubting Defoe revelled in his role as spy. Defoe was very good at it. Moreover, a salaried spy gave Defoe status, a degree of executive authority, superiors listened to him, and he got well remunerated. Today, such people are categorised as placemen or women, some plain unadorned carpetbaggers.

Defoe told his spymaster, the government minister Robert Harley, that he spoke to everybody "in their own way", chameleon fashion. He managed to appear the inquisitive journalist to lords, an expert in law to lawyers, the informed businessman to businessmen, and the honest broker to traders. He was adept at learning their jargon and using it to prise information from them. If speaking to an independence sympathiser he became one; if talking to a ditherer unsure of keeping Scotland separate from England's rule he expressed similar doubts to theirs. His tactic was to *tease* people towards a union.

Defoe churned out hundreds of pages of pro-union propaganda, arguments familiar to students of modern Scottish history. They ranged from England being Scotland's biggest trader, England being Scotland's gateway to world trade – no need of another Darien-type adventure, and Scots should not be foreigners in Britain. (Yes, *that* old chestnut.) Until then, Scotland had been a wealthier country per capita than England but Defoe helped promote the 'too wee, too poor' mantra that we hear to this day. Behind the scenes he ghost-wrote speeches for the slow-witted and the inarticulate. That way he ensured conformity of opinion. He testified to a parliamentary committee, and made himself so indispensable that (as he later boasted), his proposals on taxing beer "stand in the Treaty of Union in my very words." Defoe was a wizard with weasel words.

Just as Union propagandists today burnish their lies by omitting salient facts in order to spread doubt or spurious 'alternative choices', so did Defoe. Take the moment in 1706 when protesters, frustrated by their impotence to hold fast to their own country's future, attacked the Edinburgh home of Sir Patrick Johnston, one of the Treaty negotiators. This is Crusoe's description of the event:

> "*His Lady, in the utmost Despair with this Fright, comes to the Window, with two Candles in her Hand, that she might be known; and cryed out, for Gods Sake, to call the Guards: One Captain Richardson who Commanded, taking about thirty Men with him March'd bravely up to them; and making his way with great Resolution thro' the Croud, they Flying, but Throwing Stones, and Hallowing at him, and his Men, he seized the Foot of the Stair Case; and then boldly went up, clear'd the Stair, and took six of the Rabble in the very Act; and so delivered the Gentleman and his Family.*"

Read the paragraph carefully and you see the dishonest journalist setting the precedent for today's press hacks. Defoe was *not* there to witness the event but he makes it *seem* that he was. By adding small significant detail, Defoe implies he saw the attack happen: "two candles in the lady's hands", an approximation of "about thirty men", and "six of the rabble in the very act". Later in his report Defoe goes further by adding one person in the crowd threw a stone at him for watching the fracas.

Defoe charges the rabble were "all Jacobites". How did he know? Like an absent BBC Scotland head of news announcing independence supporters and Unionist supporters clashed in George Square, Defoe embellishes and in so doing purveys a lie. The event *did* happen, just not as he describes it. We are subjected to those sly omissions and exaggerations daily by unionist journalists and the thick end of councillors in their rush to kill democracy. A *Daily Record* headline to that story would be "SNP Mob Stone Journo".

His propaganda literature is designed to convince a weak Scotland that it is under attack, and union is the only way to peace and stability. Pamphlet after pamphlet is written in this manner – the author at the centre of events, the expert warning of doom. No wonder he took to writing fiction novels late in life.

Defoe had on eloquent opponent. Indeed, people repeated key parts of his speech for years into the future, a speech made in 1706 to the Scottish Parliament supporting a free Scotland – John Hamilton (Lord Belhaven and Stenton), a fiery advocate of Scotland's sovereignty. His oration to the Parliament in Edinburgh became legendary. The speech is too long for my purpose here, so I limit it to three excerpts.

> *"I see a free and independent Kingdom delivering up that, which all the World hath been fighting for since the Days of Nimrod; ..... a Power to manage their own Affairs by themselves, without the Assistance and Counsel of any other."*

> *"I speak this, my Lord, that I may encourage every individual Member of this House, to speak their Mind freely. There are many wise and prudent Men amongst us, who think it not worth their while to open their Mouths; there are others, who can speak very well, and to good Purpose, who shelter themselves under the shameful Cloak of Silence, from a Fear of the Frowns of great Men and Parties. To say, you'll agree to the Union of the two Kingdoms, before you agree in the Terms upon which they are to be united, seems like driving the Plough before the Oxen. The delivering up of our Sovereignty, gives back with one Hand, what we receive with the other. There can be no Security without the Guarantee of a distinct Independency betwixt the Parties."*

"Good God! Is this an entire Surrender! My Lord, I find my Heart so full of Grief and Indignation, that I must beg Pardon not to finish the last Part of my Discourse, that I may drop a Tear, as the Prelude to so sad a Story."

Defoe was too clever to scorn Belhaven. He didn't ask smugly, "Do you have a Plan B?" Just as Nicola Sturgeon's speeches are admired by the undiscerning, Belhaven's was immensely popular. Street smart Defoe showed gracious respect for Belhaven's statesmanship while planning to weaken it step by step, like a star fish cracking open a whelk to suck out the innards. It took him almost a year to create an alternative opinion that argued as follows: far from a powerful cri de cœur on behalf of sovereignty of the Scots, Belhaven resorted to a romantic, clans and broadsword, ancestral infused argument, a backward vision wholly unsuited to the new, thrusting age that a union promised. That must sound familiar to supporters of autonomy tired of being described as *Braveheart* fans.

Defoe wanted a union united in speaking English and reading English. He wanted no trace of Scottish culture to remain. And he knew enough to state that ethos should be consistent and for all time. Reading his pamphlets one gets a whiff of the arrogant Englishman telling Scots how to live their lives better.

The intellectual tension between Defoe and Belhaven continued until Belhaven's death in 1708. Belhaven was certain, as were other of his mind, that a colonial doctrine spelled the end of Scotland. Moreover, he also argued it would not just unite the nations but also eliminate 'England' as a distinct nation – and in many respects he was correct.

Had there been one person, one vote, union with England would never have seen the light of day. The mass of the populace were violently, passionately opposed to it. Petitions mounted in their hundreds. Looking objectively, petitions were irrelevant; power was in the hands of the few... just as it is to this day. Defoe was the forerunner of the conformist opinionated pundit. His malicious influence continues to stalk the independence debate. With the removal of Scotland's regiments, English votes for English laws, forced withdrawal from Europe, endless imposed austerity, *there is **no** union left* but you'd never believe that to listen to Unionist politicians. Defoe would be proud of them.

Sadly for Defoe, the future of the Britain he loved is just as ambiguous now as it was when presented as a 'union of equals' by Defoe and his confederacy of paper lies. The Union was always a fraudulent deal. England wants its parliament for its self and Scotland to pay for it.

15

DECOLONISE YOUR MIND

In my opinion the seminal document of the first Independence debate was Alasdair Gray's essay *"Settlers and Colonialists"*, a document equal in power to the government's *White Paper*. It took careful aim at the Scottish arts establishment. His thesis was icicle cold and sharp, straight to the jugular: settlers enrich us, colonials suppress us. The colonial is not an inspirer, he is a pacifier. His rules are repressive, his instincts self-serving.

Gray's elegy to Scotland's perpetually relegated drama and literature was never matched by what came afterwards. No one rose to his challenge. The British press attacked him, and to their shame the SNP shunned him. Isolated, disillusioned by the hostile reaction, he returned to voting Labour.

There was not an anti-English sentiment in the essay, but to close it down that's how it was depicted, attacked savagely by unionists and their media machine despite Gray welcoming English who live and work here. He and we were made to feel guilt for using the term *colonial*. Overnight *colonial* became a taboo word, not be uttered in polite media circles. People advised each other not to make the Great Debate one of ethnicity. After days of media generated controversy '*settler*' and '*colonial*' were dropped from debates, a small but highly significant victory for the oppressors of linguistic freedom.

By *colonialism* I mean a society **stunted** by a deeply implanted sense of degradation and inferiority. It is governed by an alien administration or state that dominates and imposes. What is the moronically repeated slogan, "Too small, too weak, and too poor" if not the manifestation of a colonial mentality that sees its satellite territories as inferior to itself?

Brexit tells us neo-colonialism is alive and thriving – described by the Scottish National Party (SNP) as a power grab by Westminster. In the outcome of negotiations to leave the European Union, Scotland is told it must take what it's offered, which is a contraction of its economy, loss of immigration, and trading routes. This is classic colonial power. I understood the regressive process better when researching facts and material for a screenplay on the massacre of Glencoe, (1692) a dramatisation where the action switches back and forth between King William of Orange's court, the Scottish Secretary of State's office in Edinburgh, and the slopes of Glen Coe itself.

Clan chiefs and elders (*clann* means children) were educated in European universities. They were proficient in English, Latin, French and Italian, as well as their own native Gaelic, yet a mixed language filmed production was judged too problematic to communicate to a predominately English audience. We are taught that to embrace foreign languages is a positive thing; to embrace our own is backward. The main objection to *Glencoe* was one of language. I have no evidence of the reverse having taken place, that a Scottish broadcaster rejected an English production because it did not take account of Scottish cultural idioms and traditions. In most countries spoken and written language are the same. Not so in Scotland. To communicate beyond our border we must use the Queen's English. We are happy to comply for we speak a version of it within our border. You could argue we speak lots of languages in Scotland, not only Gaelic, Lowland Scots and old Scots, but many dialects in the Islands and Highlands, across Aberdeenshire, through Glaswegian to Dumfries and Galloway and the Borders.

I became aware of the chasms of communication and values that separate English from Scots. In the words of the Nigerian novelist

Chinua Achebe, for the first time I could see how the "materialist, the romantic, and the phenomenological were irreconcilable". For Scots, the problem lies with our educational system, once the envy of the world, but now an offshoot of English culture and job opportunities. Edinburgh has the greatest proliferation of fee paying (private) schools in Scotland; no wonder it shamed the nation by voting against self-governance. But that's the corrosive club that one joins for advancement. I did not attend a privileged school. I soon discovered it left me at a disadvantage. By attention to bourgeois good manners and flattening my accent I learned how to gain access to polite society. By borrowing superficial bits of another's culture I felt I had gained some self-esteem. That, of course, is exactly how colonialism works. You feel better emulating your masters ways.

I don't see much difference today. I could weep; my home city, crucible of the Scottish Enlightenment is tragically, avowedly, repressively colonial in outlook. Well-heeled bourgeois Edinburgh votes against autonomy, but working class, deprived Glasgow votes universally for control over its nation's destiny.

Our culture, our language, our resolve is everything. It conveys all our codes of ethics and values. And that's what I want to concentrate on in this essay. To deride, demean or remove our culture is to obliterate an entire people's humanity. English colonialism is born out of its imperialist past, one it is determined to reignite. It was an imperialism some Scots took part in enthusiastically, but always as subalterns, that is, we were not part of the hegemonic English power structure. A few of us made great profits but the core of the British Empire was the Monarchy. The Crown owned the wealth.

We were employed to do a job, from policeman to ambassador, from captain of a slave ship to boss of a Ceylonese tea plantation, often did it better than our colonial masters. Those who became rich from their efforts naturally felt to be seen as English was a good thing, even if the English would never regard them as that, but more a good loyal Jock. Never achieving real equality, strutting around in plus fours and brogue shoes is not freedom. It is quite a few levels below that.

In time we came to believe our inferiority was reality, to accept it as a natural state of being. We accepted the demotion or exclusion of our poetry and literature, our heritage, as a small price to pay for belonging to a Union we thought benign and all powerful, and for those lucky enough to exploit the class system, a way to wealth. For the rest it was poverty and sub-standard tenement living to service the industrial might of England, or farm work, or even harsher living in the North West islands of Scotland.

After two world wars in which thousands of Scots died for the freedom of others, we started to question our relationship with England. Power and progress appeared all one way. No matter how we looked at it, something was wrong.

The ultimate effect of governance by another country is evaporation of a belief in our names, our language, and our culture. You can see it taking place now. Confidence shaken by the defeat of the 2014 Referendum, some question the goal of self-reliance believing it remote, an infantile dream. We invite contempt, castigated because we are allegedly irreconcilable, 'divided'; squabbling among ourselves, 'tribal' is the commonest expression.

Merely talking about self-determination is categorised as 'divisive'. This is the propaganda of the bourgeois colonial. The notion that changing minds over power structures is only a chat in a Morningside coffee shop – don't frighten the diners – is ludicrous. Somebody is sure to have their sensibilities outraged. No one said the struggle would be over by tea time. Scorn and contempt are the tools of a corpus of state capitalists, faux academics, craven journalists, students keen on preferment, working class who happy to function under authoritarian rule, weak-witted politicians thinking they are cleaning up the Internet.

Colonialism exists to control a nation's wealth and redistribute it to the victor. We protest at the closure of our heavy industry but can do nothing to stop it. To attain those ends the dominant nation embarks on a sustained campaign to undervalue the subservient nation's culture, its history, its wealth, it's very language.

The ultimate sanction is warned we will be treated as foreigners should we ever exercise free will. Autonomous, we cannot be one of them. And yet, we never are, even when desperately impersonating 'one of them'. (Lord Darling and Michael Gove please be advised.) Believing in a nebulous 'Britishness' as the be-all and end-all of a good life, we become disassociated from our own environment.

That alienation is reinforced in the teaching of our history, (Braveheart *is bunkum, the Duke of Wellington is a hero*) geography, (*Scotland is a wet, mountainous, infertile region, England is the fruit and bread basket of the UK*). On the economy, (*Scotland is a banana republic, England is the great creator of wealth*), and finally our music, (*it's all bagpipes and sword dancing, Morris dancing is sublime*). I call that oppression.

One antidote is the Scottish Government asking for a degree of Scots literature and history to be taught in our schools. We can afford to dump any of JK Rowling's derivative Harry Potter door stoppers for any of RL Stevenson's novels or for anything by Frederic Lindsay, or Margaret Oliphant, Irvine Welsh, or Ali Smith. The obvious contradiction in this thesis is I write in English, the only way I can communicate to the widest audience. I recognise a large slice of my heritage is lost to me. Then again, if I had not recognised the omission, I would not have penned this essay. It follows; I am not thinking like an Englishman, I am halfway to decolonising my mind. But that's no reason to subject Lallands Scots, the Doric, or Gaelic, or any of our dialects to extirpation by colonial decree or dismissal.

The poet and co-founder of the nationalist movement, Hugh MacDiarmid, understood how the rot starts from the top. He saw that process at work. He encapsulated his ideas in his epic masterpiece, "*A Drunk Man Looks at the Thistle*". "I'll hae nae haufway hoose, but aye be whaur Extremes meet." Had the poem been published on the Internet, a colonial nonentity would pop up to claim "No one speaks like that today!" MacDiarmid's analysis of the Scots psyche is an intellectually challenging work, a work designed to draw attention to our neglected literary history.

In the same way a Cornishman is proud of his native language and traditions, so should a Scot be proud of his heritage. It is the language of a specific community with a specific history, a history based on specific values and ethics. It is the way we perceive ourselves and our place in the world.

The first step to decolonising our minds, throwing off 'the cringe', is to take pride in our heritage and culture. The second step is to *demand* that it is given the respect and the promotion internationally that other cultures are given. Let no one argue otherwise: the movement to reinstate self-governance is a ***unifying*** force. It is the language of honesty and equality. That's what unnerves the colonial mind. It sees the subversive; it sees a challenge to conventional orthodoxy, the core of its power. The colonial offers pretence that he frees us from poverty and ignorance. In reality he imposes both.

Scots have retained their identity over 300 years of alien rule, against all odds, it has to be said. But we are in the midst of a determined assault to wipe out differences once and for all time, and if we lose a second referendum or plebiscite, or find an alternative to restoring self-governance, disillusionment in our worth is sure to follow.

We must keep a tight hold of the regenerative connection with our roots and reject the primacy of English culture. Suffocation lies in accepting England's political agenda and its class system. Suspicious of liberation, the colonial mind will be just as cynical when it sees freedom expressed in a novel, a play, a film, an essay, or as minor a thing as a tweet. We can see how brutal and cruel they can be. The colonial mentality will always want to control.

Colonials are not unifiers. They are pacifiers. They narrow the debate, they constrain urgency, they generalise a sense of fairness. They defuse civil and constitutional rights to a vacuous pleasantry, 'we all share humanity'. They want us to feel eternally guilty for daring to question their power. They want our obedience. Colonials keep telling us we must learn caution and responsibility. They tell us welfare must be cut; the NHS must contract or be privatised to survive, pension age rise. But those changes never apply to them. They squander millions, secrete millions in tax havens, and avoid bankruptcy rescued by government subsidy paid from our taxes, call it high class welfare, if you like. Colonialism is a crime. Colonialism is racist.

Freedom to choose is a right enshrined in international law with its inclusion in the United Nations Charter in 1945. Article 1 of the Charter states that one of the purposes of the United Nations is: "*To develop friendly relations among nations based on respect for the principle of equal rights and self-determination of peoples.*"

In the International Covenant on Civil and Political Rights and the International Covenant on Economic, Social and Cultural Rights, this is made even more explicit: "*All peoples have the right of self-determination. By virtue of that right they freely determine their political status and freely pursue their economic, social and cultural development.*"

Reinstatement of Scotland's self-governance is the basis of internationalism recognised by all nations as a human struggle for equality, justice, peace and progress. We seek full civil rights and ownership of the entire productive resources of our nation. Argue over the detail all you will, but never lose sight of the essential goal: an independent nation is a confident nation, its people motivated to solve problems and support each other. Decolonise your mind and free yourself.

16

ALISTAIR IS NOT MY DARLING

He began his political career tramping streets in marches of left-wing radicals and ended it on the right-wing having helped to cheat Scotland out of its birthright in return for a shoulder or ermine and a red velvet robe. Then again he was born in England, Hendon in London, to be exact, no surprise he preferred his motherland to inferior places. Alistair Maclean Darling, Baron Darling of Roulanish, a very British Labour Party politician who served as Chancellor of the Exchequer in the Labour Government from 2007 to 2010.

For leading a campaign demeaning and demoting Scotland, Alistair Darling was made a peer of the Realm. To retain your sanity you can only view the honour as a cruel jest, his allegiance to corrupt rule made an obscenity by the elite, and all to teach Scotland its place in the scheme of things.

As chancellor following the accident prone Hapless Gordon, the dour Scot Gordon Brown, Darling threw himself – in the slug-like way he has of self-contained composure – into saving crooked banksters from jail, and condemning the Scottish Government's White Paper on life after 300 years of union limbo in a ludicrously brief thirty minutes *after* its publication, all 650 pages. As a speed reader he's faster than the disappearance of fake goods on a Customs market raid. As a person to trust, his credibility never surmounted his characteristic of remaining eerily unruffled in a force 10 gale.

Buttoned up is an understatement. Zipped top to bottom and padlocked is more accurate. His slight Scottish burr was acquired from an education at Loretto's, a private school in Musselburgh, outside Edinburgh, and at Aberdeen University. He became a solicitor and then a councillor in Lothian Regional Council supporter high rates rises, the first sign of a socialist soon to fulfil the cynical maxim, all socialists end their days voting Tory. His political career is full of contradictions, a veil best pulled over it.

He did utter one truth: in a political career distinguished by nothing much, he admitted Scotland can survive governing its own affairs and by its economy, but somehow thought it 'undesirable.' The colonial mind cannot fathom why any nation would not want to be British, like a stick of Blackpool rock, have it written all the way through. He's a geographically challenged Moses leading Scots to the same place they left behind.

It comes as a surprise he enjoys being detested. The impression he gave me when I met him was of cardboard, a non-person, without personality, ever so slightly pompous, the sort of guy who picks his teeth behind a covering hand. We were alone in his constituency office for thirty minutes. He was MP for central Edinburgh. I was a constituent seeking his help to improve health and safety issues in my street where the council had failed to do anything about errant drivers, pedal to the metal boy racers. He failed miserably to be of help. Shortly afterwards he took over from Gordon Brown as chancellor of the UK Treasury. I found him evasive, remote, without the slightest hint of humour.

Witty banter is wasted on him. Darling laughs only when he decides to laugh, never voluntarily. A crumpled face that needs a beard – he sported one later – he had an unnerving way of not looking at me as we talked, then turning to me slowly to shoot a disapproving glare above his glasses. For my teenager years my mother only ever ventured one single piece of advice on assessing character: "Never trust a man who cannot look you straight in the face, and never trust a woman who can." That seemed pretty good advice at the time and has stood the test of time. Darling failed on both counts.

He wore a fluorescent white jacket, standard issue hair shirt and black silk tie, framing those dancing hairy caterpillar eyebrows in expensive bend-them-to-buggery-and-back, titanium-nickel spectacles. When checking a man's integrity there is a lot of detail to take in.

Disconcertingly, rudely, he kept turning his back on me as we talked for reasons I cannot explain – I don't suffer from bad breath or sweaty feet. As I enumerated the problems of residents in my beleaguered mews lane, he attended to superficial matters, his focus undisciplined: shifting a pen from desk top to desk drawer, rearranging papers, hunting in his briefcase for something or other, perhaps the last of a bacon sandwich. When he spoke his mean mouth always returned to a tight pout, an instinctive reaction to swallow his words. Was he listening to me? Maybe I was last in a long day's queue and he wanted to get home. I found him heavy going. Mean; a man moving up in the world with no time for those below. And he took a sly look at his wristwatch while I was speaking. Since he left the fray of daily punchbag politics, his wife has taken to the Internet, tweeting risible attacks on honest supporters of self-governance. One is left with the feeling she publishes what she and hubby discussed over waffles and honey for breakfast. (New para.) As for the socialist agitator now wholly absorbed body and soul into colonial life, he is the only man I know who can light up a room by leaving it.

17

A CONSTITUTION FOR SCOTLAND

A constitution guarantees liberty and citizen rights under the law. It is the foundation of civil liberties. It tells other nations of our values and standards. It sets out the principles by which we hope to live. It bedevils elected authority that dares to become a tyranny. Yes, it is taken for granted that in time, much of a constitution is forgotten or overridden by subsidiary laws, but I believe firmly a set of ideals is critical for the start of a country's rebirth.

The writing of this constitution was an intellectual exercise, a way of looking at what makes a better Scotland, a basis for discussion, or a template, if you like. This draft challenges existing conventions and shibboleths. I readily admit it expresses my prejudices as they relate to creating a civilised society, plain common sense.

ERRORS AND OMISSIONS

Alert readers will find key omissions. The absence of the Union of the Crowns is one. The issue is contentious. I am a republican at heart, but I have to face the reality a great deal of the populace warm to the shenanigans of the Royal family and their ill-gotten gains.

I prefer our aristocracy was like Norway's; the Monarchy has a day job and a bicycle to get to it, their presence retained for cere-monial occasions. Who wants a society in which a Monarchy free to refuse assent to a parliamentary Act instigated by the people, or give

Royal Assent to a bill that traduces Scotland's sovereignty, or stymie Scotland's laws for their protection? On that score and others, I take for granted the Supreme Court of Scotland will usurp the UK's court on day one of independence.

Constitutions ought to use plain language as much as possible, without being patronising or complicated linguistically. I hope this one meets that self-imposed standard

Article 1: Scotland is a constitutional State of civil rights and justice, social, democratic, sovereign, independent, unitary, intercultural, multinational and secular. Sovereignty lies with the people, *whose will is the basis of all authority*, and it is exercised through public bodies using direct participatory forms of government as provided for by the Constitution. All authority incorporates the tenets of the Declaration of Arbroath.

Article 2: The flag of the nation is the Saltire, known as the St Andrews Cross. There shall be a coat of arms, a national anthem, and a national animal, as chosen by the people, and as provided for by law, each symbols of the nation. St Andrews Day shall be substituted by Independence Day as an annual holiday.

Article 3: Scotland's official languages are Scots-English, Old Scots, and Gaelic as the people wish to practice them. They shall be used to enhance intercultural ties. The State shall respect and encourage their preservation and use.

Article 4: There shall be no State religion. Religion shall remain separate from State in all things. Religion shall not be taught in schools other than the history of its variety, nor shall it be imposed as part of an educational curriculum. The young are encouraged to have an open, questioning mind. Secular ethics are the basis for public service. The people are free to worship whomsoever or whatever they please, be it deity or philosophy, however, the State shall not encourage religions as worship.

Article 5: All land ownership shall be registered in Scotland, any registered outside the State shall be forfeited immediately and expeditiously by law to the State and returned to public ownership. Land is a finite and crucial resource to be owned and used in the public good.

Article 6: The law of the land is Scots Law which is supreme in all regards, and exists to uphold the Constitution. Any citizen coming before the Law charged with a crime shall be presumed innocent until proven guilty.

Article 7: The capital of Scotland is the city of Edinburgh.

Article 8: The State's primary duties are:
1. Furtherance of the well-being and happiness of inhabitants by guaranteeing *without discrimination* rights to housing, education, free health care, food, old age pensions, and in times of personal hardship, social security provided by the State.
2. Guaranteeing and defending national sovereignty.
3. Eliminating poverty, and promoting sustainable development.
4. The equitable redistribution of resources and wealth to the majority of inhabitants.
5. Promoting equitable democratic mechanisms by a process of participation.
6. Protecting the country's natural and cultural assets.
7. Nurturing a democratic society free of corruption.
8. Guaranteeing inhabitants the right to a culture of peace.
9. Protect the right to opt out of society and its structures if an individual so desires.
10. The prevention of crime.
11. Protection of Nature, indigenous mammals, birds, and areas of scientific interest.

12. Protect the populace from the propaganda of consent in all its forms.

Article 9: The territory of Scotland is a single geographical and historical whole, passed on to us by our ancestors. This territory includes the mainland and all the adjacent Islands, including special island groups such as Orkney and Shetland, maritime space, the undersea continental shelf of the North Sea, the Atlantic, and the Irish Sea, the ground under the land and the space over our mainland, islands, and maritime territory. Boundaries are those determined by treaties with neighbour States.

Article 10: A citizen of Scotland is anybody born in Scotland of parents living in Scotland who are also Scottish. Citizenship shall be granted by right, automatically. A child of Scottish parents born outside Scotland but not residing permanently in another country shall be given citizenship as a matter of right. Citizens of other nations can apply for Scottish citizenship and a passport on the basis they provide evidence they intend to live and work in Scotland, either employed or self-employed, for a period of no less than five years. Individuals already residing in Scotland shall be eligible to apply for citizenship by naturalisation. Citizenship shall not be refused on grounds of sex, gender, race, colour, religion, personal beliefs, status, or sexual orientation.

Article 11: Elections to national government, a single-chamber Parliament, shall be held every five years, no later. In times of war the Parliament has the right to extend its term by one year. Voting is compulsory in General Elections, and referenda. In elections a candidate attaining the greatest number of votes is duly elected to office. If there is a tie or a near tie within 100 votes in a constituency vote, both candidates are eligible to take their seat in government. A candidate rejected three times by the electorate will be ineligible to stand for office for ten years.

Article 12: Political parties shall be financed by their individual members *only* to a maximum of £5,000 each person annually. That sum can be increased or reduced by parliament every 10 years. No corporate entity, company, union affiliation, or foreign state shall finance a political party for any reason. Political parties accepting covert donations shall be punished by law, the sum in question forfeited to the State.

Article 13: Entry to Scotland either for the purpose of a single short visit, or on a work permit, shall only be refused in cases of a threat to the physical safety of citizens.

Article 14: The exercise of rights shall be governed by the following principles:

1. All persons are equal and shall enjoy the same rights, duties and opportunities.
2. No one shall be discriminated against for reasons of ethnic belonging, place of birth, age, sex, gender identity, cultural identity, civil status, language, religion, ideology, political affiliation, legal record, socio-economic condition, migratory status, sexual orientation, health status or disability.
3. All forms of discrimination are punishable by law.
4. Everyone has a right if eligible to a free defence in courts of law.
5. The rights and guarantees set forth in the Constitution and in international human rights instruments shall be directly and immediately enforced by Scots Law.
6. No legal regulation can restrict the contents of rights or constitutional guarantees.
7. All principles and rights are unalienable, obligatory and of equal importance.
8. Recognition of the rights and guarantees set forth in the Constitution and in the United Nations declaration of human rights shall not exclude the other rights issuing from the European Union.

9. Any deed or omission of a regressive nature that diminishes or undermines or annuls without justification the exercise of rights shall be deemed unconstitutional.
10. These rights shall be exercised in accordance with this Constitution which shall be the supreme law of the land.

Article 15. Newspapers and media shall be encouraged to be independent, that is, free of proprietorial influence, and without external ownership.

1. The State shall foster plurality and diversity in communication, guaranteeing the allocation of radio spectrum frequencies for the management of public, private and community radio and television stations, as well as the access to free bands for the use of wireless networks for the benefit of the community prevails.
2. Facilitate the creation and strengthening of public, private and community media, as well as universal access to information and communication technologies.
3. Not permit the oligopolistic or monopolistic ownership, whether direct or indirect, of the media and use of frequencies.
4. All persons have the right to look for, receive and exchange, produce and disseminate information *that is truthful*, accurate, timely, taken in context, plural, without prior censorship about the facts or events.
5. Gain access freely to information generated in public institutions or in private institutions that handle State funds or perform public duties.
6. There shall be no confidentiality of information except in those cases expressly provided for by the law. In the event of a violation of human rights, no public institution shall refuse to provide the information demanded of it relative to the case in question.

Article 16: Freedom of speech is every person's right, sacrosanct and immutable, whether in written word or spoken, made in peaceable group assembly and association, or in digital communication, so long as not deliberately malicious. The burden of proof of malicious intent shall be placed upon the litigant to establish. Commercial free speech shall be governed by the laws of consumer protection.

Article 17: It is forbidden to broadcast advertisements in any form by individuals or political parties that foment violence, discrimination, racism, drug addiction, sexism, religious or political intolerance and all that undermines rights.

Article 18: In matters of individual conscience the State shall guarantee the professional secrecy and confidentiality of the sources of those who inform, issue their concerns through the media, or other forms of communication. No whistle-blower shall be punished in any way by State or employer for making public their concerns.

Article 19: Work is a right and a social duty, as well as an economic right, source of personal fulfilment and the basis for the economy. The State shall guarantee full respect for the dignity of working persons, a decent life, fair pay and a healthy job that is freely chosen and accepted.

Article 20: The right to social security is a right of all persons. It cannot be waived. The State must bear the prime duty and responsibility for this right. Social security shall be governed by the principles of solidarity, obligation, universality, equity, efficiency, subsidiary, adequacy, transparency and participation, to meet individual and collective needs.

Article 21: The right of persons to migrate is recognized. No person shall be identified or considered as illegal because of their migratory status.

Well, there it is for what it's worth, months of thought and revision. I'm sorely tempted to add a few highly personal clauses, such as banning Christmas advertising until the 1st December, and implementing a four-day working week! I'd like lots of public holidays but I name only one, *Independence Day*, an affirmation of free thought and free will. After the fiasco of the robber bankers, who wants to celebrate *bank* holidays? I would want to see a clause stating alterations or augmentation to the Constitution must have 90% support of the populace eligible to vote. In Scotland, the people are sovereign.

Whatever happens to delay Scotland's ambition to become a free nation state once more, remember, no nation ever rose up to demand its abolition.

18

CROWD POWER

I still see people suggesting protest marches are a waste of time. Do they protest about it? Marches and rallies have an affect on the onlooker. The statement they make is, there is a large consensus who wants to make a difference in society.

Protest marches express an ideal. Marching is the difference between a keyboard warrior and an activist. Marches confirm we are not helpless against corrupt authority. Marches can convince the indolent to be active. People feel comfortable belonging to a large group, especially if it is good natured, affable, the camaraderie genuine and heartfelt. Marches gather together people from all walks of life. All for one, and one for all.

To know the power of congregations of like-minded protestors you need only think of the Romanian crowd videoed outside President's Ceausescu's palace that turned volatile. They had good reason. Their anger began a revolution. They realised Ceausescu and his wife intended to maintain a brutal, corrupt, dictatorial hold over the lives. They toppled the regime in a week that some thought invincible.

Marches are an indispensible civil liberty. Marches confront the power of the state. Ask Podemos in Spain. Ask any number of mass movements for democracy. Marches are the energetic outcome of a restlessness to be heard. And Scotland, one of the last British colonies, damn well needs to be heard.

The British establishment knows the worth of crowds and marches only they call them patriotic parades. They organise an anniversary parade or a solemn commemoration, get the faithful lined up to waft Union Jacks, and hey presto, blind, unthinking patriotism is restored, the wrong kind of patriotism supporting the status quo not democracy.

There is an irresistible dynamic to physical protest. Supporters of restoring Scotland's self-esteem know crowd power has a health benefit – it fills people with hope, it signifies the best in human nature, it raises spirits. Happy people are positive people. You learn from participating. You learn from others.

Solidarity demonstrates strength of support, political cohesion and resolve of purpose. Why else does the state determined to retain authority engineer police and mainstream media to downgrade numbers as a way of undermining that unity?

Marches have spectacular historical precedence: Martin Luther King discovered their potency early in his campaign for equal rights; Gandhi's Salt March some historians believe was a watershed in India's move to independence; The Long March (October 1934 – October 1935) of Mao Tse Tung was a march of a different sort, a military retreat undertaken by the Red Army of the Communist Party of China, the forerunner of the People's Liberation Army, to evade the pursuit of the Kuomintang (KMT or Chinese Nationalist Party) army. It altered the destiny of China. For the participants, joining a march became a demonstration that symbolised the transition from passive dissent to protest.

To those holding power over us above and beyond that which they were given, there is nothing more certain to concentrate the mind than a phalange of marchers approaching you demanding civil rights. Marches are an antidote to bad governance, and a colonial government's tyranny.

If under threat, how do we protest our civil rights? We meet. We congregate. We march. We rally. We agitate. We cry liberty, equality, fraternity. Resistance is persuasion. Marches are a manifestation of optimism to make things better. Solidarity is a good thing.

19

CHURCHILL IN DUNDEE

Whenever a journalist writes a piece on Churchill's stint as Liberal MP for Dundee – research unearths a skip-full of identikit articles, shallow and derivative – one aspect is mentioned without fail. They begin or end with the loaded statement "The *only* evidence of Churchill's presence in Dundee is a *single small* plaque on a street wall". A cursory study tells us Churchill cared little for Dundee folk; the plaque is an embarrassment.

Let's begin with the man. Sir Winston Leonard Spencer-Churchill (1874–1965), was a British politician, army officer, and writer. He painted a bit as a hobby and not very well. For all his waving of the Union Jack, Churchill was of mixed English and American parentage.

Churchill was born in Oxfordshire to a wealthy, aristocratic family which probably accounts for his arrogance. He was a direct descendant of the Dukes of Marlborough, born into the governing elite. His paternal grandfather, John Spencer-Churchill, 7th Duke of Marlborough, had been a Member of Parliament (MP) for ten years, and a member of the Conservative Party who served in the government of Prime Minister Benjamin Disraeli. His own father, Lord Randolph Churchill, who died of advanced syphilis or a brain tumour, whichever fits your prejudices, was elected Conservative MP for Woodstock in 1873. His mother, Jennie Churchill (née

Jerome), was from an American family whose substantial wealth derived from finance. To say Churchill was born into privilege is an understatement. He arrived with a silver spoon sticking out of every orifice. He came into being when the British Empire was at its zenith and the elite ruled without mercy.

In appearance he was unprepossessing, or as Scots say, nae oil paintin'. Below average height (5'6"), with a large head, small chest, he tended to wear high hats to increase his stature. Photographs show him podgy, prematurely bald, with small hands and feet and skinny legs.

His speech defect, a splashy sibilant 'S', later to become his trademark together with a fat Havana cigar, did not help him. His over-weaning self-confidence compensated to an extent attracting a succession of sexual liaisons, but by all accounts women left him as quick as attracted, finding him egocentric and a misogynist, finding it difficult to subordinate themselves to him completely. Churchill was thirty-four by the time the twenty-two year-old Clementine Hozier accepted his offer of marriage, "He talked entirely of himself." He had already been rejected on four known occasions by women of good judgement and taste. Clementine was the daughter of Sir Henry Hozier and Lady Blanche Hozier, although that is in doubt because her mother was infamous for her infidelities.

Clementine was not purblind. She kept a wary eye on his gambling and a close watch on his wandering eye for shapely women with money. She disliked his Tory friends in whom Churchill found convivial political views and told him as much. Disputes were problematic, "He shouts me down!" That aside, they were a good match, she disciplined his bad habits, he brought people of political status home. And they shared a penchant for spending money lavishly they did not have.

For a member of the Liberal Party recently defected from the Tory Party, Churchill tested fate. He disliked Liberal leader David Lloyd George, continually opposing Lloyd George's policies as weak or woeful. The feeling was mutual. In fact, Churchill's Liberal peers neither liked him nor trusted him, and the same prevailed when he crossed the House again to rejoin the Tory party years later. MPs from all sides of the House thought him a serial failure, racist, bombastic, and a bully. Their charges were water off a duck's back. As he said himself, "Any fool can rat, but it takes a certain amount of ingenuity to re-rat."

Trailing those lead weights behind him, how did he manage to win a seat in Dundee? On his appointment as President of the Board of Trade, Churchill had to fight a by-election in Manchester North. He lost by 400 votes to the Tories. A day later he received a telegram from Liberals in Dundee inviting him to stand there, a safe Liberal seat, a shoe-in. As is Scotland's fate, we Scots are infamous for inviting the enemy to our door.

The sitting MP was handed a peerage and his suitcase packed, Churchill given the red carpet treatment as replacement. His Dundee opponent was a devout Christian and socialist prohibitionist, Edwin Scrymgeour, not much of a rival at that time.

To win, Churchill adopted a hyper-critical style, describing the Tory Party as "filled with old doddering peers, cute financial magnates, clever wire-pullers and big brewers with bulbous noses." The enemies of progress were "weaklings, sleek, slug, comfortable, self-important individuals." He could almost have been describing himself.

By the time he reached Dundee his talents were coming to the fore. Outside self-serving expediency he had a fine oratory style; he could think of a biting retort to a political opponent in an instant. He won with a 7,000 majority, but all was not sweetness and light. In a letter to Clementine he wrote:

"This city will kill me. Halfway through my kipper this morning an enormous maggot crawled out and flashed his teeth at me. Such are the penalties which great men pay in the service of their country."

Privately, he had formed a dislike of Dundonians. "It is an awful hindrance to anyone in my position forced to fight for his life and always having to make his opinions on national politics conform to local exigencies." As far as Churchill was concerned, Dundee was a small provincial town of no great importance other than for saving his political skin. Like so many Englishmen who followed him to Scotland, it is difficult not to see him as just another ligger and a carpetbagger. In return, Dundonians learned to loathe his expensive lifestyle, his long absences, especially his active social life amid the aristocratic elite.

At first, Churchill was at well-received in the city. The Liberal Party was popular among the city's working class communities. Dundee had never been a Tory city; the Liberal Party had values people admired. One policy was the National Insurance Act of 1911, another the establishment of Labour Exchanges – now called 'Job Centres' – a successful idea copied from Germany. Churchill was not known for paying attention to detail. His impetus was to avoid waste. For him, that meant an organised labour market to benefit the state, the interests of the individual to be subordinate to those of the nation.

To the man in the street, a policy of putting men back to work appeared progressive, men out of work were better in work. To Churchill, the policy was "a remorselessly unsentimental government attitude to the people's sacrifices for the future of the race", a maxim more Tory than liberal. By siding with Liberal policies Dundonians initially misinterpreted Churchill's allegiances. For almost a decade they held to Churchill's representation and he retained the seat until 1922.

Nevertheless, as was his character, Churchill could alienate as fast as he could impress. He set up his headquarters in the city's Queen's Hotel and spent much of his time in the Dundee Advertiser's Bank Street offices, poring over proofs of his speeches as they were typeset within minutes of his meetings. (The job of writing history to his own image began early in his career.) During his tenure he made himself unpopular by deploying troops during the both the miners' strike in Tonypandy, Wales, in 1910, and the transport strike a year later that concluded with two people dead and 400 injured. Also, some Dundonians were not slow in blaming Churchill for the First

World War Dardanelles failure and the slaughter of so many men at Gallipoli during 1915.

At the beginning he found himself popular with the Irish in Dundee but that soon waned when he sent troops to Ireland after the war. Churchill's attitude to every nation England had conquered, and ultimately to his own, was one of colonial master to lowly native.

Churchill was adept at advocating one policy one year and reversing it the next. For example, in June 1908 the Liberals created a Budget League, a convenient mechanism to head meetings around the United Kingdom to debate budget proposals. A meeting in Edinburgh in July saw an angry Churchill announce that if the Lords rejected the budget the government would dissolve Parliament and fight an immediate General Election. Liberals were outraged that he had announced a non-existent policy. He found himself formerly rebuked, apologising a day later. In 1907, he had described the Lords as an anachronism, a "one-sided, hereditary, unpurged, unrepresentative, irresponsible and absentee". In September he talked of a representative assembly and a "miserable minority of titled persons who represent nobody", a decade later Churchill was spouting the opposite sentiment. The hereditary House secured, "the vital breathing space for consideration and for more stable forces in the community to assert themselves".

Churchill's misogyny was self-evident. He refused to back women's suffrage, an obsessive opposition that dogged his Dundee tenure from start to finish; having previously made public his belief women had rights "through your husband". He varied the goading with "through your father, brother and son." To Winston, women only had uses in the kitchen and the bedroom, or if pretty enough, on formal social occasions hanging on your arm.

One Irish suffragette, Mary Maloney, a leading member of the Women's Freedom League, followed him to every speaking event to ring a loud school bell as soon as he stood up to speak. Her most famous interruption was during his campaign speech at a Blackness factory in May, 1908. The meeting had to be aborted. Churchill struggled good-humoured against the incessant clanking, but gave up in despair, saying, "If that woman thinks that is a reasonable argument she may use it. I don't care. I bid you all good afternoon."

From then on Maloney was known as the "La Belle Maloney".

She was not the only female warrior to torment him. The suffragette Ethel Muirhead pelted Churchill with an egg during a political meeting in 1910, while another suffragette jumped into his carriage at the Tay Bridge Station and harangued him. Like so many in the city, they were women working in the mills and factories, the breadwinners.

Throughout his representation Churchill was a minister in the cabinet in one post or another, but as the years went by high office failed to impress voters. By the time elections rolled round in 1922, Churchill just had an operation to remove his appendix, an operation that probably saved his life.

Hospitalisation and recuperation delayed his campaigning in Dundee allowing opponents a free hand. Arriving late he threw himself into the fray with gusto – Churchill was never a slacker. He was renowned for working hard whatever the task before him. Near the end of his tenure, where the opening speaker was drunk, Churchill tried to make a speech but was shouted down by the audience.

Churchill was thoroughly beaten by Edwin Scrymgeour, a native of Dundee who became the only person ever elected to the House of Commons on a prohibitionist ticket. He lost by a landslide 12,000 votes to Scrymgeour who first stood against him in 1908. Scrymgeour held the seat for nine lonely years. And so, Churchill's Dundee "seat for life" was anything but. The campaign coincided with Churchill losing his cabinet post. Dundonians had had enough of him and Clementine, who had paraded her wealth ostentatiously.

Churchill's open views on education also contributed to his flight from Dundee. He believed in a two-tier system, one for the elite and one for the masses. His idea of state-backed gambling was also rejected but came to fruition under Margaret Thatcher. In that he considered horse racing was for the rich and should be given state support, and greyhound racing was for the "new degeneracy" – working class gamblers.

He went on to stand as a totemic symbol of the power elite's fear of social and political revolution, helping to crush the General Strike of 1926, protect land reform from taxation, giving tax breaks to wealthy Americans to live in the United Kingdom in "sporting counties", and cutting the level of benefit for the unemployed. But, by a quirk of fate, a Second World War was to resurrect his career, and he grabbed the opportunity with both hands. As for Dundonians, they went on to vote overwhelmingly for Scotland's independence – must be something in the water.

20

THE ENGLISH ON ENGLISH

Depending on how you use it, the internet is a force for good or an evil invention. For my part, I've made good friends out of it, tested my political arguments to destruction, and got maligned by the malicious. You take the good with the bad and learn how to give a tongue lashing to trolls and sloganeers. The wise avoid social sites like the Tory party avoids reason; it just isn't good for one's reputation. I calculate ninety-five percent of Twitter and chat site chat is dross. Addicts like me wade in, restoring Scotland's independence the ultimate goal, permanently wound up for a brutal, bloody boxing match.

Some years back, writing on a fast disintegrating and degenerate website concerned with cars and car enthusiasts, the site infected by the new wave of UKip lovers who hate foreigners and think being English is a gift from God, I got frustrated by the constant, unwarranted attacks on the integrity of patriotic Scots.

In time the vitriol and infantile arguments from budding sociopaths became so repellent I was compelled to write to the site moderators to demand all my contributions be deleted. By then the 'dedicated' founder-owner had sold the site to Michael Heseltine's car magazine empire for a bag of retirement cash and he disappeared.

I had had enough of fools and farts tearing into Scotland's life and traditions, in particular beginning ungrammatical sentences with the pompous, arcane 'methinks'. The moderators duly agreed to wipe all my work, a sheet cleaned and ironed flat included a 28-hour session without sleep calming readers after one of the well liked contributors committed suicide.

For that sacrifice I lost some of my best prose on the pursuit of happiness but content the neo-fascists appearing on social media wouldn't benefit by it. I didn't want my work left to rot like meat crawling with maggots on what had become a repository of naked bigotry. A few psychopaths tried to follow me to my new site but in time they got bored.

What scunnered me was the car site had made the serious error of adding politics to its chat room categories. Naive about internet social sites back in the day, what I didn't realise was the then owner of the site was increasing traffic so he could make more money out of advertisers.

Opening pages on British politics was a joy for the child-like UKippers and odious British National Party thugs. Soon, the worst of Unionist Rangers football fans joined in spewing hate at anything SNP or Scots independence. They waded in with all the fervour of bankers desperately trying to justify their fat bonuses.

I don't think I wasted the time there, though I wasted too many hours answering pig ignorant assertion from brain dead amoral right-wingers keen to emulate Papa Doc Duval, or Joseph Goebbels. It was a good training ground for the Grouse Beater site.

For one thing it taught me that a lot of males with expensive cars are polishing queens. They don't know how to drive them, and never take them near a race track. The cars are there to feed their narcissism. The worst of them were automotive illiterate in the same way the enemies of Scotland are proud of their ignorance. Ian Stewart, racing driver of *Ecurie Ecosse* fame, was the first to notice the hideously stupid comments appearing that proliferated what was once a friendly chat site for car enthusiasts exchanging tips on car maintenance and car bargains.

At the point I decided to call it a day. I penned a final article, one to wreak revenge on my persistent, inane antagonists. It was not a site to post essays, so I posted the article in short paragraphs. Just as well, with few exceptions those on the site never read past a tabloid headline without getting a headache.

To provoke outrage I posted a number of attacks on English mores and attitudes, one after the other, in the form of phrases and epigrams. Soon as I received a neo-fascist expressing outrage, usually from an odious party called UKip, I posted another negative epigram or aphorism of the English. I cannot remember them all; here are a few.

1. The English share an unconscious patriotism and an inability to think logically.
2. English patriotism is thick-headed and proudly insular – the bulldog is an animal noted for its obstinacy, ugliness and stupidity: Englishman of working-class origin considers it effeminate to pronounce a foreign word correctly.
3. English takes pride in celebrating defeats and retreats, like Corunna, Gallipoli and Dunkirk. The most stirring battle-poem in English is about a brigade of cavalry which charged in the wrong direction.
4. England's homicidal lunatics are well employed in killing each other, but sensible Englishmen keep out of their way while they are doing it.
5. Englishmen know good port when they taste it but have not the breeding to put it in the right glass.
6. An Englishman that overvalues himself will undervalue others. If he undervalues others he will oppress them.
7. *Paradise Lost* is a book that once put down, is very hard to lift up again.
8. England is the most class ridden country. It is a land of snobbery and privilege.
9. The English have always been wary of foreigners and intellectuals.
10. English moral indignation is jealousy with a halo.
11. There are people who believe their opportunities to live a fulfilled life are hampered by the number of

Asians in England, by the existence of a royal family, by the volume of traffic that passed by their house, by the malice of trade unions, by the power of callous employers, by the refusal of the health service to take their condition seriously, by communism, by capitalism, by atheism, by anything, in fact, but their own futile, weak-minded failure to get a fucking grip.

12. English do not expect happiness. I had the impression, all the time that I lived there, that they do not want to be happy; they want to be right.

13. The British nation is unique in this respect: they are the only people who like to be told how bad things are, who like to be told the worst.

14. It is sometimes said that butlers only truly exist in England. Other countries, whatever title is actually used, have only menservants. It is for this reason that when you think of a butler, he is bound, almost by definition, to be an Englishman.

15. Statistics show that the nature of English crime is reverting to its oldest habits. In a country where so many desire status and wealth, petty annoyances can spark disproportionately violent behaviour. Envy and bitterness drive a new breed of lawbreakers, replacing the old motives of poverty and the need for escape.

16. The Great Potato Famine came to an end. Thousands of Irish died because of it, but it ended. And how was this wonderful thing accomplished? Why, in the simplest way imaginable. The famine was legislated out of existence. It had to be. England's Whigs were facing a General Election.

17. English people living in the USA should keep a low profile on Independence Day.

18. The English have always been madly overambitious, and from one angle it can seem like bravery, but from another it looks suspiciously like a lack of foresight.

Readers can imagine the tsunami of vituperation flung in my direction, the outrage those remarks triggered. Bile flowed onto my computer screen like wasps falling upon a rancid Apple. How dare I insult English sensibility so wilfully and so vilely? I was deemed a racist incarnate, a foul chauvinist, a sweaty Jock. It was exactly the reaction I planned. I let the righteous, riotous mob bray and scream for almost a day enjoying every minute of their discomfort.

In truth the statements published were *not* mine, not mine at all. To trick my assailants I had omitted quotation marks on all I had written. They were written by Englishmen of Englishmen. With glee I admitted my sleight of hand *pro tem*, and announced: "Every statement I posted was coined by Englishmen of the English. Here is the list to check for your selves. Goodbye and bad luck, suckers."

1: George Orwell. 2: George Orwell. 3: George Orwell. 4: Bertrand Russell. 5: Prime Minister Gladstone. 6: Samuel Johnson. 7: Samuel Johnson. 8: George Orwell. 9: George Orwell. 10: H.G.Wells. 11. Stephen Fry. 12: Quentin Crisp. 13: Winston Churchill. 14: Kazuo Ishiguru. 15: Christopher Fowler. 16: Edward Rutherfurd. 17: Stephen Magee. 18: Ben Aaronovitch.

Revenge is sweet when provided free of charge by your dumbass tormentors.

21

SPELIN, GRAMMUR
AND SPEEKIN' RIGHT

Flicking through a glossy magazine in the dentist's waiting room, I spotted a photograph of a woman at a football match holding aloft a banner she had composed. Alluding to the opponent team's winning prospect, the banner's large letters read: "TREBLE MY ARSE!" For the want of an apostrophe between *treble* and *arse* the poor woman was communicating her derriere could do with a degree of enlargement.

As a writer I get asked to spell words by as many adults as children, *en passant*. I don't claim to be a walking dictionary and often experiment to create new words that the ill-educated consider 'wrong'. It's called creative writing. Writers and journalists are expected to be highly proficient in the job of putting letters, words and punctuation in the right order. No surprise then that, like any other flawed human, I make errors. Typos belong to the speed I use a keyboard and a schedule that allows little time to check drafts. My new-ish keyboard has already lost the 'a' and 's' owing to being thrashed by a hunter pecker.

There is wonderful scene in the Woody Allen comedy mockumentary *Take the Money and Run* (1967), where his inexpert bumbling character Virgil Starkwell tries to hold up a bank by passing a note to the bank teller to hand over cash because he is 'Holding a gun'. The gun is fashioned out of soap, painted black.

Unfortunately, he has written the note so badly it reads 'This is a gub'. The bank teller turns the note over in his hand. "The note says 'This is a *gub*', sir," says the perplexed teller. There follows a comical scene of would-be robber and bemused teller arguing over the letter 'n' looking like a 'b'. "It says 'gun'," answers an annoyed Virgil. The teller consults his colleague.

> **Bank Teller One:** Does this look like "gub" or "gun"?
> **Bank Teller Two:** "Gun." See? But what does "abt" mean?
> **Virgil Starkwell:** It's "act". "A.C.T."
> **Bank Teller Two:** I still don't get it.
> **Virgil Starkwell:** Act natural. Please put fifty thousand dollars into this bag and act natural.
> **Bank Teller One:** Oh, I see. This is a holdup?

The confusion sparks an argument throughout the entire bank over whether Virgil wrote "gun" or "gub", "act natural" or "abt natural." Virgil the robber is foiled. Virgil's surname sounds like a typo error, Starkwell instead of Stockwell. Life is full of those unplanned howlers that so easily throw us off course. Hurdles and traps lie everywhere. The Two Ronnies classic sketch asking for "Fork Handles" in the hardware store and the shop assistant thinking he has heard "Four candles", is a prime example. Wars are known to have started over words and meaning misunderstood. This same holds true for everyday conversations, a slip of the tongue, a poor pronunciation, and anything posted on social sites. I think there should be a law making it is impossible to practice as a teacher if they suggest written speech has strict unbending rules.

Spelling howlers litter the history of literature. Back in the day it didn't matter, but once dictionaries were published the pressure was on to conform. First printers and then publishers wanted their job made easier.

"You're a writer," said a plumber. "Spell 'containerised'," he asked, trying to fill in an order form. No matter how often I use *renaissance* I hesitate, is it two *s's*, or millionaire, is it two *n's*? It took a while to accept that *judgement* can be used without the 'e'. Spelling is a nightmare, especially if, in my case, you have been susceptible to American spelling. I worked in Los Angeles for many years. I like some US spelling, dropping the *'u'* from *honor* is very helpful. Americans have a different word for almost everything.

Who doesn't feel cheated taught by primary school teachers the strict rule of 'i' before 'e' except after 'c', only to discover later in life any number of exceptions: neighbour, weigh, weight, freight, sheikh, deign, vein, caffeine, and so on, and so forth. Confidence is knocked and dented. Life was simple, now complicated. Exceptions abound. ('Exceptions abound' is not a proper sentence. There is no verb in it!)

Here's another thing: how to write the plural of a single letter, such as the letter 'e' without it looking distinctly odd. Write it as 'es' and it's singular. You have to stick an apostrophe in the middle – 'e's', normally done to indicate the possessive. However, it's not necessary when a capital letter, as in 'Ls', but it looks better with the apostrophe: 'L's'. Or does it?

Memory fail is most often active when trying to think of synonyms. I can spend ages going around a word in my head that isn't quite the one I want. Take 'block', for example. The word I really want is *halt*. "We must halt the spread of colonialism" is better in meaning and scansion than "We must block colonialism". There are personal foibles: I remind myself one gets *irritated* by something or someone if *already* annoyed. Irritated is universally used the wrong way. People talk of being *irritated* by this or that when they mean *annoyed*.

I console myself knowing the very worst grammarians are automobile journalists and property agents and lawyers. They have a jargon all of their own. One copies the other blindly. Car interiors are described as 'flexible' as if the seats bend when you sit on them. (The seats in my British built Mini did actually bend!) Property agents misuse the same adjective to describe the layout of homes when they mean 'versatile'. Scotland's First Minister, Nicola Sturgeon, tweeted "*back peddling*" to an opponent when she meant *back pedalling*. I assume it was her not a speech writer. Malapropisms are spoken everywhere. The first malapropism I coined was during my final year dance at primary school. It took some time to screw up enough courage to ask my favourite teacher if she was free for the next dance, but when I approached her nervously it came out as, "Miss… are you *vacant* for the next dance?" The howls of laughter echo inside my skull to this day.

"When should I use a comma?" is another popular question. There's no single answer to that. Read over the paragraph you've written and drop in commas where you feel they help to make the sense communicate. Personally, I play safe. I sprinkle commas like rain, liberally, wherever possible, in my prose, to stay on the safe side.

In everyday speech we omit grammatical accuracy for immediacy of meaning. We break up sentences, fracture them, recast, hesitate, and repeat words. No matter our education, we pay little or no attention to grammar when communicating verbally. Yes, despite (should that be in spite of?) what teacher told us, in written language you *can* begin a sentence with a conjunction such as *and* or *but*, as we do in everyday speech. But in speech we often adopt the rules of written language when it isn't necessary. We have chanced upon a pundit or politician answer a question by saying 'eg' rather than *for example*. "That is" is spoken as 'ie'. We talk of 'a' we can do this, and 'b' we can do that" when recounting a list of things.

How do you avoid the infamous split infinitive? The answer is you don't have to if you don't want to. The problem of the split infinitive only arises when the infinitive appears with the preposition *to*, and an accompanying adverb, or adverbial phrase. If you put adverbial words between the '*to*' and the verb, you split the infinitive. Pedants think those who employ split infinitives are uneducated. The glitch is in the relationship between English and Latin. In Latin the infinitive appears as one word. You cannot split the infinitive in Latin. We dropped Latin grammar when men wore tights and cod pieces. I avoid the split infinitive only because it makes a sentence sound clunky. The rule is, there is no rule. Treat the split infinitive as a preference.

My primary education was severely wanting in anything remotely connected to cultural education. I was chastised for saying 'aye' instead of '*yes*'. I was told to lose dialect words, such as 'siver', the Edinburgh word for the drain in a road gutter, 'stank' in Glasgow. The colonial's first attack is on the native language. And when I entered drama tuition I was warned sternly to lose my Scottish accent or expect to lose my career in theatre. My tutors were English and sadly Scottish too. Colonised habits die hard.

Older readers will remember the furore over the Glaswegian speaking journalist Cliff Hanley's entry to BBC Scotland's morning radio news programme. Outrage poured from all quarters of society, thousands of furious listeners, from Glaswegians to posh Jocks, all railing against a non-BBC Southern voice. What was the BBC thinking? Snobbery and pomposity flowed as thick as molasses. Today, after years of allowing local voices to broadcast, Scotland is hearing more and more English accents. Language colonisation is rampant when a nation seems likely to revert to self-governance. Gaelic and Old Scots is in short supply.

When I worked a short time with the Royal Shakespeare Company, I was surprised to hear English actors speaking Shakespearian lines and sonnets in their local tongues, Somerset, Devon and Suffolk. The artistic director Trevor Nunn explained that local accents enrich characterisation. "That is the reality those actors bring to the role. Why should I demand a BBC accent and have everybody sound like a blueprint of voice tuition?" English accents and dialect words make Shakespearian verse rhyme, otherwise the verse doesn't scan. Today, fashionable actors speak with plummy voices once more, Eton educated. Presumably they're no longer expected to make Shakespeare's verse rhyme.

We are left with Scottish politicians who want people to think they had an upper crust English public school education. When it comes to affecting an English accent the former MP, Malcolm Rifkind, is among the worst offenders. Next is the *Spectator* magazine's editor Fraser Nelson who can torture a vowel to death. He graduated from Dollar Academy with a 'Scots' accent that pronounces '*parliament*' like a seventeenth century fop sucking a lemon – "*power-lay-a-mint*". Did he see the word written and invent how to say it, or is he trying to sound terribly English by emulating the late art critic, Brian Sewell?

As for pronunciation of words, that's a craft that holds all sorts of traps, impediments and local idiosyncrasies. The English language is full of fault lines. Stumbles include *Cholmondely*, pronounced 'Chumley', and *Mainwaring* pronounced, Mannering. People spell them as they hear them. To my credit I can spell *Balquhidder* without a slip, and speak it as it should be spoken. Ask an Englishman to do the same and he will stutter. Depending who you are talking to and where they were born, the painter Van Gogh can be pronounced with infinite variation: Van Gogh with a guttural 'gh', Van Gock, Van Hock, Van Go, Van Whoa. Take your choice. The Oxford book of *Modern English Usage* has the great grammarian Henry Watson Fowler (1858–1933), actually argue that we should pronounce the silent Greek 'p' when it appears as the first letter of a word, psychologist, psalm, pseudo, psyche. Gulp! Such wild eccentricity is enough to cause Scots to revert to their own language and not try to emulate the Monarch's English. I like the old cartoon showing a psychiatrist standing in a stream up to his waist in water. The caption reads simply, "Psychiatrist has a silent 'p'".

I hold to the advice rules of grammar should be observed, but I counsel if meaning is clear, so what? Grammar is more elastic that teachers think. A child who wrote: "And damned be him that first cries hold, enough" might find their teacher chastising them for beginning a sentence with 'and'.

As I said, writing and speaking English is a trial of one's heritage, an indication of one's social standing. I now 'boldly' hand this essay over to the grammar pedants, or is it pendants? Malapropisms rule – okay?

22

THE LONG ALLIANCE

The rotten-to-the-bone right-wing UK Government has never treated Scotland as a valued "equal partner", surely the cruellest joke of the century heaped on a subservient Anglophone territory. Scotland was dragged out of Europe screaming and kicking by England's far-right Etonians, an entire nation isolated in trade and travel, in direct contradiction to the relationship enjoyed by Scotland with its European neighbours over a thousand years. Scots were educated in European universities, clan chiefs and their sons too. Good ol' England. One day you take for granted you are European and the next forced to buy a visa and stand in the Alien line at airports.

The average Englishman's view of Europeans is repugnant: the worst see the continent a place full of potential immigrants and refugees from God knows where, desperate to steal British jobs. Moreover, they think the European Union (EU) squanders Britain's money. Neither curse stands up to the slightest scrutiny. The UK received millions in annual EU grants, many more millions than it gave the EU, and enjoyed freedom of movement. England's odious right-wing has left European countries to the rise of fascism in their borders, the same British right-wing keen to meet and exchange ideas with fascists. France's General Charles de DeGaulle knew the mind of Englishmen inside out. He never trusted them.

Unperturbed by the scorn of the better informed, an Englishman will tell you there is no democracy in the EU; it has grown from a shared common market into an undemocratic, power hungry, monolithic, centralised state. This comic book lie took hold among the lumpenproletariat of Middle England, to the absurd height that tens of thousands of workers in the car industry voted themselves out of Europe though the materials for their jobs were supplied by European companies.

When it comes to empires, only England is eligible to have one. There is always one more 'decisive battle' to win and the enemy will be vanquished forever. English politicians hate the Germans still, depressed at how well their economic miracle absorbed the former East Germany and Syrian refugees, envious at their "*Vorsprung durch Technik*", no matter that England's Monarch and the Mountbattens are descended from the House of Hanover.

There is, however, a key aspect of the EU can do with democratisation – Europe's Central Bank. The way it dealt with the near-bankruptcy of Greece is reprehensible. Money was poured into Greek banks on usury conditions that sent the interest charges straight back to the Central Bank. The Greek people, jobs and infra-structure saw no investment.

Kicking Greece in the groin goes back a long way, to 1945, in fact. Greece was one of the few countries denied a grant under the USA's post-war Marshall Plan, (1948) a mechanism by which the US government constructed to widen its sphere of influence by keeping nations in hock to the United States of Amnesia. Greece was a socialist country, under commie-hatin' American generals, not eligible for support, though it fought Nazi Germany as fiercely as any other European country. Italy was similarly treated. The US financed Italy's right-wing groups to eradicate socialists and communists. From these murky handouts the CIA was born to keep tabs on America's burgeoning number of clients.

The UK took until 2006 to pay back the largest share of the Marshall Plan, having defaulted three times. Scotland has never been bankrupt in its entire history and was once a wealthier country than braggadocio England.

England's xenophobic decision to dump Europe and 'Johnny Foreigner', the name English give anyone who speaks with a foreign accent, is the equivalent of self-harm short of suicide. Calling Scots foreigners who seek to restore self-governance, or too stupid and too weak to govern their own country again – they rarely add *again* because it is an admission of past success – is a racist comment. Anything that belittles Scots and their traditions is racist, if not a specific criticism of a characteristic. Colonialism is racist.

During the run-up to the 2014 Referendum, some truly bright English political personalities took to calling Scots foreigners, as they had in 1705 if Scotland refused to sign a treaty. It reappears in the monotonous taunt: "Why return to a union with Europe and leave one with England?" The colonial never sees himself as a tyrant. In 2019, Scotland had no one to appeal to who could ensure we remained in the European Union, at least continuing as a trading partner in the Free Market if nothing else.

In one swift slash of a halberd, Brexit removed the power of Scotland to trade with Ireland in the west, and Europe in the east. Our reliance on encouraging immigration to augment a falling population is hampered, as is the exchange of students and scientific research.

England embarks on a policy of impoverishing its neighbour to keep it docile. It engineered constitutional jurisdiction over Scotland's economy and progress because it cannot survive without Scotland's oil fields, taxes, or goods. Parched by scorching summer heat, it will need our water. The English Treasury is like the Roman, caught in a never-ending search for greater revenues and food. In the 12th century we *could* appeal to a supreme European power, the Pope. And we did exactly that.

Once again, it was English arrogance that drove Scotland to reach out to Europe. The story is a simple tale of colonialism. The Archbishop of York claimed authority over the Scottish Church. This was not received well among the Scottish clergy, always of an independent mind, John Knox a tiny tickle in their loins. Snorting, steam coming out their Ears, Scotland's angry clergy wrote to the Papacy in Rome.

The Pope, Celestine III, mindful of winning hearts and minds, issued a Papal Bull, known as a '*cum universi*'. The year was 1192. The Pope waxed melodious in Latin: Scotland was a 'special daughter' of the apostolic see. An Episcopal see is derived from Latin *sedes*, and here means the area of a bishop's ecclesiastical jurisdiction.

This event was a miracle. Scotland was not a Catholic country. The Pope reassured us, Scotland had nothing to fear. There was no middleman, no interpreter, and no English churchman with a degree in Ecclesiastical Intervention, to appropriate Scottish pulpits. The Scottish Church was deemed an *independent entity*, part of the warm embrace of the European community and subject *only* to the Pope. Scotland was welcomed into the premier league of worship.

There you have it; the polar opposite differences between Scotland and England, there from our earliest history. England went on to wage endless wars with Spain and France, frantically removing our ancient forests to build their man-o-war ships, and desperate to dragoon Scottish sailors to sail the things against the Spanish Armada, or wee Netherlands fishing boats working too close to the south coast of England. We, on the other hand, kept trading with our friendly European nations, recycling the Spanish and Italian red roof tiles for our houses, used as ballast for ships sailing up the west coast laden with goods from warm countries. (Today we are replacing some homes with turf in lieu of climate change!)

My point is, Scotland invested a lot of time seeing its best minds educated in European universities, and they in ours. A jealous England looked on and sighed. As in this century, medieval and renaissance Scotland was heavily invested in European culture. And yet, here we are, casualty of English exceptionalism, trying to find an exit from Brexit while pining for the Pyrenees.

Men who possess real power in our world rarely have the intention of stopping wars, hot or cold. In the 21st century we hear again the old refrain, our safety is threatened by any number of evil enemies, Russia, China, Syria, North Korea, *ad nauseam*. Europe is the latest.

Having failed to convince Scots we not European in any way, our English tormentors decided they should try instead to convince us we are united in a common Anglo-Saxon way. Well, we are not. That is the shared humanity line, which has nothing to do with civil rights, politics, or topography. We are part-Irish, part-Nordic and part Danish.

Our colonisers try another tack: there is no such thing as a 'pure' Scot; no mention of those pesky Normans, of course, the one's that beat King Harold, nor Romans who left us so much of their civilisation. This was a clever wheeze to get Scots confused and bewildered over who we are. Told Alba was not a real country leaves Scots susceptible to be ersatz English.

England has tried and tried again to exert authority over Scotland by claiming its creation as a homogenous country is older, more notable than Scotland's. The most incompetent historian will admit this is nonsense and irrelevant, a convenient myth, but that is what lies at the root of England's feelings of superiority over its neighbour.

The myth was widely held in the Middle Ages. Much of the blame for the fallacy can be laid at the door of the Welsh cleric Geoffrey of Monmouth, a key figure in creating an unreliable history of Britain, famous for his tales of Merlin and King Arthur. (For 'unreliable, read 'uncertain' or more likely, 'fiction'.)

There is confusion as to his ancestry, Welsh, Cambro-Norman, Breton or plain French, and very little evidence he could speak Welsh. Hence, studying his writing requires a great deal of salt kept handy. If Geoffrey was alive today he would be writing adventure stories for children. As it was, he was most likely imbibing too much mead.

Old Geoffrey was the man to quote to prove England had its roots in antiquity. In his '*History of the Kings of Britain*' ('*De gestis Britonum*' or '*Historia Regum Britanniae*'), he argued that Brutus, grandson of Aeneas, the Greco-Roman hero, was the eponymous founder of Britain following the battle of Troy. He embellished the fantasy: when inheritance time came, Brutus' sons divided the land among themselves, or so Monmouth's Latin narrative relates. The largest portion, the section we know as the breadbasket of England, East Anglia to Kent, was given to Brutus's eldest child, Locrinus, the land that became England. Brutus's second son, Albanactus – note the first syllable – inherited 'Albany' or Scotland as we know it, whilst the youngest son, Camber, got the short straw and inherited Wales.

This literary forgery was an attempt to finalise where the centre of power originated. Edward I was a devoted follower, the folklore a convenient falsehood. For all his prodigious output, poor Geoffrey would have been better sticking to the tales of Merlin the Wizard. Science fiction mixed with magic is the route to riches these days.

Scotland was not slow conjuring – excuse the pun – its own myths and magic to prove its antecedents held a greater, verifiable link with Europe. Brutus of Troy could go eat neeps. Scotland's name, according to legend, came from a woman, Scota. She was an Egyptian princess, a Pharaoh's daughter. (How remarkable people identify with aristocracy not plebeian slaves.) She belonged not to Greek mythology but to Biblical scriptures. Scota's antiquity trumped Brutus'.

Anyhow, we chose a woman as a Mother Earth figurehead who married a Greek prince, and all this was three hundred years before England's Brutus was conceived. Apparently this is the origin of Scottish spirituality, a quality attributed to the Scottish affiliation with mountain, flood and glen. I hazard a guess it has more to do with the mood we encounter walking in rugged topography that echoes with the ghosts of long lost clan communities.

George Orwell dismissed our sense of the mystic. "In the end, Scottish independence is really about power", he said. This is an obvious truth. Orwell's Etonian pals have stolen a large chunk of Scotland's influence in their quest to see Scotland's potency eviscerated. It should be noted; Orwell finished his days on the Scottish island of Jura, completing his last novel, *1984*, a depressingly bleak dystopian world view of authoritarian governments, the very thing Scotland suffers at the hand of a brutal Westminster run by a bunch of Etonians.

How did we get the name of Scotland? Well, the myth relates how Scota and her husband Gathelos (from whom my Celtic name derives, Gareth, also Garth), took a sailing trip from Egypt, stopping as any tourist would, first at Spain – Gibraltar's and its tourist kitsch streets was not a choice in those days – and then Ireland, before braving the chill winds of Scotland's verdant shores. Somehow Scota and Gathelos made a home on the west coast and did not miss sun stunned days living beside the nourishing Nile. When archaeologists find blackened postcards made from tree bark, buried along Scotland's Roman Antonine Wall, microscope enlargement discovers handwriting in Italian saying, "Mama, eeza so cold here. I wanna come home."

As if an Egyptian princess making her home on damp and dreich Skye does not stretch credulity past breaking point, the story goes that she brought with her a large stone we call the Stone of Scone. Most Egyptians would have brought a hand-painted folding stool, but we are told it was a large stone later used for the coronations of Scotland's kings.

This last element fits the Scottish psyche; we are a practical minded people, a stone to sit on something tangible and useful. Edward I thought there was enough substance to the myth that he nicked the stone himself and stuck it in Westminster Abbey, until it was 'taken' back again by a clandestine group of Glasgow University students.

My point in recounting these Scottish-English myths is to show how Scotland's roots are held hard into the soil of European culture. The more England exerted aggressive authority over Scotland, the more Scotland increased ties with Europe. We are in the same position today, desperately emphasising Scotland's association with Europeans. The 'Auld Alliance' with France resurrected in conversations. By insisting on a continuous line of kings, originating with Gathelos, Scotland hoped to lay the ground work of its genealogy;

at the same time asserting we had no identification or affinity with English culture or politics, ever.

What else is the *Declaration of Arbroath* of 1320 but a reassertion of Scotland's intellectual independence? As part of the Declaration's justification of autonomy, it states clearly how 113 kings had ruled in Scotland since its foundation as a single nation: "the line unbroken by a single foreigner'. Well, we had to call non-Scots foreigners sooner or later, tit-for-tat.

Myths of ancient European identities are Scotland's attempt to thwart English claims on Scottish land and throne, to prohibit potential English colonialism. That tension has always been in existence between the two untrusting lands. The Union has not lessened that one bit, if anything, a dislike of England's political agenda has grown exponentially as England's power increased over Scottish affairs.

I made mentioned earlier of Scotland's long association with great European universities. Here again, Scotland can lay claim to European roots but in a more verifiable and concrete way than mustering myths and fairy tales.

When it came to learning for learning's sake, Scotland was ahead of the world, bar China. China was ahead of the universe. (Scotland chases China in the store of its inventions, an amazing achievement for a small country.) By 1500, Scotland had three universities, or more accurately, *foundations*, each immersed in European intellectual culture. The University of St Andrews, for example, owes its foundation to Henry Wardlaw, (a variation of my surname, my own a variation of Wardle) around 1410, I think. He was bishop of St Andrews, royal tutor to James I of Scotland, a graduate of Paris. Another bishop of scholarly mind, William Turnbull, founded Glasgow University in 1451. He was a graduate at St Andrews, in addition to studying at Leuven in Belgium and Pavia in Italy. Scotland's other notable university, Aberdeen, was the result of hard endeavour lobbying over years by William Elphinstone, King's College, his vision, made real in 1495. He was Aberdeen's bishop, a graduate of Paris and Orleans universities. Records show there were two Aberdeen Universities called colleges back in the day at the end of the 16th century, the Protestant Marischal College merged with Kings in 1860. Medicine and Law were taught at Marischal, and Arts and Divinity at King's College.

Yes, some Scots chose one of England's two universities, Oxford or Cambridge, but the mass of Scots chose European education over English. Outward looking Scots who spent time in Europe enriched our own educational system. Another essay is required to list all the notable Scots who took to a scholarly life in Europe. To name two: the rector of St Andrews, George Lockert, an Ayrshire man, taught at Paris University, and John Mair from the east coast town of Haddington, taught theology and philosophy at the Sorbonne before lecturing across Europe, and then becoming principal of Glasgow University and provost of St Salvator's College in St Andrews.

It was not all one way. European scholars came to Scotland to teach and some stayed to make a life here. In the 1530s, the Abbot of Kinloss in the far north of Scotland recruited the Italian humanist Giovanni Ferrerio to overhaul the curriculum for pupils at Kinloss and nearby Beauly. By all accounts he was much liked by his students. And some Scots who went to Europe to create a future did well, and brought home their skills. Androw Myllar lived in Rouen, capital of the northern French region of Normandy, a port city on the river Seine. Records tell us he learned the printing trade while there.

Somewhere in the early 1500s Myllar settled in Edinburgh because in 1508 he established Scotland's first printing press in the capital with Walter Chepman. The two partners operated under a charter granted by King James IV issued in 1507 which gave them a nice monopoly in printed books within Scotland. Androw Myllar, learned his printing trade on the continent and then introduced it to Scotland.

Move to modern times and we find Chambers Dictionary published in Edinburgh, updated every year, not every five years like the Oxford dictionary quoted by England press as the lexicography bible. And there is the phenomenal success of Collins books, once the world's biggest publisher, bought over by the odious Aussie Rupert Murdoch for his own aims.

English claims to be non-European are for English to live with. Scotland shaped European thinking and Europe shaped Scottish thinking. Scotland's European links are historic, rich, powerful and abiding and sacrosanct, not to be dismissed or airbrushed out of our history. We are Europeans, and we will remain so.

23

THE PITCH

To an outsider, a fan of cinema, life as a filmmaker must appear glamorous, filled with event, travel, and parties. I have attended a few premiers and each time, what should have been a fun event was filled with stress, nervous smiles, and social faux pas.

A filmmaker, whether a producer or an auteur, spends a great deal of their lives looking for money, cap in hand. Just as you think you have secured a budget, you discover a handshake on Friday is worth nothing on Monday. The deal is off. No reason given. As Michael Caine once warned film students, "Don't go out and buy that fast car. You aint seen a contract!"

Meetings to discuss investment are always stressful, whether grants or charged with high interest rates and conditions. The man who cuts the cheque holds the power. Meetings can be humiliating. Only one I encountered was a pleasant experience. Seated before Australian Film Fund executives, I opened my portfolio to begin pitching the film's plot when I was stopped. "You can have half the money," said the main man, chuckling. My jaw must have dropped open. "Surprised, Gareth? But that's what we do here, make movies."

What a difference from my own BBC Scotland in Glasgow. On leaving the head of BBC Scotland's office after a lengthy discussion on potential projects I had to offer set in Scotland, a strong feeling of being patronised washed over me, this despite the man on the other side of the table a former colleague. When I reached his office door to leave I heard him say, "Gareth, if you do not get any commissions, I hope I don't read about them in the press tomorrow. I know your polemic can be cutting." I hesitated momentarily. "Are you telling me," I answered, "that the head of BBC has no veto over staff decisions?" And so it transpired. Here is the meeting that followed with the commissioning editor.

The head of BBC Scotland Drama Unit kept me waiting over twenty minutes, an open area in the deathly mausoleum they call Pacific Quay headquarters. I'd come a long way for the meeting, from Los Angeles, my second home and place of work, my first still in Edinburgh. I called the meeting to sell BBC Scotland some Scottish talent.

Looking around me in that high, wide, empty interior space, office levels stacked around its four walls, I couldn't help but think how bereft it was of anything that gave a clue to the creativity that is supposed to happen inside. Not a pot plant, sculptural bust, or artwork in sight, nothing but generality, cold steel, concrete and glass, and an echo. The architect, David Chipperfield, could do with a dose of humanity. The place needs a woman's touch!

Entrance to the atrium, the inner sanctum, is by security gates, reminiscent of an airport. You are given a tag, expected to wear it until you leave. Whoever goes in must come out. It's a wonder I wasn't asked to take my belt and shoes off.

What secrets do they keep there that demands such tight security? They hardly make a thing in-house bar some low grade comedy shows and local news. Everything, but everything is sent to London… if an independent producer is lucky. There it stops, hits the buffers – London Central.

I wait. As time passes I know from experience it is not a good sign.

Out she comes. Preoccupied? A bad phone conversation?

Blast, she's younger than me; won't see me her generation, neither cool nor topical. Doesn't matter I have international awards; I'm an unknown to her. She might listen, unless, that is, she has my name in a wee black book. Paranoia, why does it rise to the surface? Wait, she was told to meet me by my old colleague now Controller of BBC Scotland. Be confident. You arrive recommended, a VIP.

Maybe, maybe some other advice was given. "Placate this guy but offer no commissions."

Stay positive. Freelancer's livelihoods depend on achieving. People like me are continually pushed into a corner where we are left arguing for indigenous talent, but against faceless money men in London. Calm down. Smile.

She sits in front of me, no apology for the lateness. The silence between us has me expect a lump of tumbleweed to blow by. She waits. Does she expect me to break into song, to entertain her? Okay. Deep breath – me first.

I open with the usual small talk, see her glance this way and that, (bored?) listen to her harden up her answers to let me know she carries limited authority, for she senses I am not convinced by her. I notice she was not educated in Scotland nor born here.

One by one she dismisses well researched proposals, all Scottish sourced material, some with funding attached, all with serious actors. Whatever way I pitch, with enthusiasm, prepared to fine tune, alter main character, offer compromise, back comes the negative. "No, London is doing something similar. No we have a project about women. No, I wouldn't get that passed HQ London." She hesitates on one novel for which I have the rights. "I'll read this over the weekend and let you know."

She then goes into a long spiel about how she has no power; all decisions are taken by BBC London. She exists merely to bring London's attention to a project that has topicality or commercial worth. "I'm afraid I'm just a conduit", she explains, with an apologetic flick of the head and shrug of her shoulders. She gives me a look that says she's resigned to her fate. That one gesture renders the whole BBC Scotland a phony front. It's like a fake stall set up to attract suckers. No doubt the place will have a few favourites, the meek, and the compliant that will toe the line for the sake of a commission. The system is an elimination process, not a creative cooperation.

This, remember, is the same place that stole independent's best ideas when told the BBC had to accept a percentage of their output from freelancers. The BBC sent a rejection note, passed the idea upstairs, gave it a different title, and then made it as an in-house originally conceived production. "They'll just humiliate you," said my wife as I set out that morning to be thoroughly humbled. She was right, in every respect.

Christ! What am doing here? I'm here trying to get work for others.

I try one more time. I boost my pitch. I lift a hardback novel from my satchel and hold it up, a detective thriller. "I have one of his Glasgow-set novels filmed to good acclaim, "Best Screenplay" from the American Film Critics. Please give him sound consideration."

"I will, but nothing else you offer is of interest."

Six mature projects, all contemporary material, all full scripts, and only a book held back. Is she patronising me?

As a last-ditch at solid Scottish material I blurt, "I have a project on the Highland Clearances, *female* led—" I stress 'female'.

She cuts me short. "I'm not interested in historical costume drama."

Jeezus. The Scots invented the bloody historical novel. There's an entire national library of fine novelists specialising in the genre. Has she not seen "*Braveheart*", "*Rob Roy*"? Where was she when Hollywood dramatised the novels of R. L. Stevenson?

Now what? Will she tell me BBC has committed its entire drama budget to another obscure Anthony Trollope novel, "*Barchester Chronicles*"? Is that the excuse? Maybe it's another version of "*Pride and Prejudice*", the fifteenth. I've lost count.

I pause. "If I offered you an action man, *fantasy* series, how about that, you know, like a Scots Batman?" Her eyes light up. "Yes, I'd like that." She moves into a description how that sort of series is all the rage in the USA. I pause again, timing my riposte to hold her gaze. "Batman is a costume drama."

Damn! That bit of impudence will alienate her.

What is a non-Scot doing running a major cultural department for BBC Scotland? Does she have any knowledge of Scottish literature? Did she study at a Scottish university, decided Scotland was the place to live and work? What are her criteria for selecting work? What are her standards?

I decide to test her.

"Tell me, what's *your* favourite Scottish drama?

I knew her answer before she spoke it. She hardly hesitates. "*Monarch of the Glen.*"

"Ah," says I, "I can see why, light comedy, prat falls, stereotypes, very popular." I take a deep sigh and throw caution to the wind. "I'd call that series sub-Compton Mackenzie."

Back comes the shock reply confirming my worst fears. "Who is Compton Mackenzie?"

We never met again.

Epilogue: The novel, a series of short comedic stories set in World War II army days, was rejected, but a BBC comedy series about the army was produced later by BBC London, though set in modern times. And a USA-made Scottish costume fantasy series, '*Outlander*', a big success State-side, soon followed.

24

THE REPUBLIC OF BARBADOS

Barbados is going to become a republic! How about that? And the United Kingdom is going to let them, or it seems they cannot stop it. This is much more of a surprise. Why a surprise? Those idyllic, soporific sandscapes and palm trees, the Caribbean islands where you can see right to the bottom of the warm sea bed, were once a cesspit of unhappiness and despair. Forget all that postcard kitsch. Barbados was the birthplace of slavery.

Those British elites spared no one in their hunt for bigger and better profits from sugar cane. Tate and Lyle have some explaining to do. There is doubt over whether the company was involved directly in slave trading, but it certainly exploited slaves to cut sugar cane. Delving into the history of sugar and you wonder if the Tate Gallery should change its name, or the august All Souls College in Oxford should repent "paid for by the profits generated by the slaves who toiled and died at the Codrington estate in Barbados", according to the historian of the book *Sugar in the Blood*, written by Andrea Stuart.

Once the Portuguese and Spanish vacated the place – having given it the name of bearded fig trees – 'Barbados', the island was seized by the English, a British colony from 1625 until 1966. (Barbados was claimed from 1625 in the name of King James I of England.) Since 1966, it has been a constitutional monarchy and parliamentary democracy modelled on the Westminster system, but with a lot more dignity. Elizabeth II, Queen of Barbados, is head of state, though not for long.

Barbados shaped by the trade winds of the tropics, is carved from the historical sting of immigration, exploitation, and colonisation. The country got its independence in 1966. Longer than Scotland's struggle, 361 years have passed since the English walked in and imperiously instructed someone to help tighten their girdle. Now Barbados is to be a republic. They are taking their freedom. No fuss, no bother, no marches, no civil war, and definitely no referendum. When I write *take*, I mean grab.

Barbados, where every second person is called Clarke or Braithwaite, or it seems so, the home of natty chatter and writers who know their history, one of the finest actually called Brathwaite, Kamau Brathwaite, who died in 2020. One poet won the 1960 Nobel Prize for Literature, Saint-John Perse. Their writers do not run around in circles debating which currency Barbados will use – they have their own dollar and also use the US dollar – instead, they consider the challenges of rebuilding their societies following decolonization, the mature thing to do.

How did Barbados secure its independence? It used a poll. Scotland has not considered a poll. It should, if only to answer the defeatist asking, "What alternatives do you suggest to the SNP's plan of infinite delay?" The Barbados poll asked the simple question, 'Should Barbados be independent. 'Why not?' came the sub-Arnold Brown reply.

Barbados has been at the beckon call of the Dutch, Portuguese, Spanish, passing pirates, tropical storms and of course, the British Crown, it's a wonder it still exists. During the English civil war, when Oliver Cromwell was chopping off heads everywhere from Cornwall to Dundee, the islanders got very upset when Charles I was executed by order of Cromwell, another to lose his head, not that that put an end to aristocracy presiding over the masses.

The island's government went all wobbly for the Royalists so the Commonwealth Parliament opted to bring the recalcitrant colony to heel. The Commonwealth Parliament passed an act on 3 October 1650 prohibiting trade between England and Barbados. They blocked the Dutch too. This caused the First Anglo-Dutch War. (At some time or another, England has been at war with almost every nation, large and small, on the planet.)

Narked by Barbados supporting Charles II, the English parliament sent an invasion force under the command of Sir George Ayscue, which arrived in October 1651 using Scottish prisoners as a small army to beat the Barbadian Royalists. To cut a long story short, on January 11, 1652, the Royalists surrendered. The Scots were too much for them. They fought as if they hated royalist supporters. The conditions of the surrender were incorporated into the Charter of Barbados (Treaty of Oistins), signed on 17 January 1652.

The Irish found themselves in Barbados. Starting with Cromwell who tried to 'pacify' Ireland – a euphemism for bloody genocide – a large percentage of the white labourer population in Barbados were indentured Irish servants transported from Ireland, treated very poorly. Barbadian planters had an evil reputation for cruelty. The word soon got back to Ireland, and once freely known, Irish refused to look for work in the plantations. That led to kidnappings and involuntary transportation as a punishment for crimes. Political dissenters were sent to the plantations as were vagrant labourers. It is estimated over 10,000 Irish were cutting sugar cane together with the poor indigenous slave population, the Irish all but slaves themselves.

There were any number of slave and worker rebellions, all put down by force by English troops. Even after the abolition of slavery, the plantocracy class retained control of almost everything political and economic, with workers living in relative poverty. If hurricanes did not kill them, 4,000 on one occasion, disease did its best. Soon, workers were emigrating in large numbers.

By the start of the 1900s life on the sun soaked, tooth rotting (from chewing raw sugar cane) Barbados was pretty awful. By the 1930s resentment at living conditions and lack of democratic controls saw Barbadians begin demanding better conditions for workers, the legalisation of trade unions and a widening of wealth, which at that point was limited to male property owners.

Unlike Scotland, geographically linked to England, Barbados was too far away and costly to threaten with another trade blockade. In any event, Britain was recovering from the bloody First World War only to see Adolf Hitler threaten all sorts of new hell. Those 'black fellas' and the plantations were of secondary concern. The British sent a commission in 1938 which recommended enacting many of the requested reforms on the islands. As a result, Afro-Barbadians took a prominent role in the colony's politics.

Once a majority of Barbadians held sway in their Assembly it was a simple matter of voting for independence. The Barbadian Labour party facilitated the conditions, unlike in the UK, where the Labour party is entirely set against an independent Scotland. It took Barbadians a mere ten years to achieve independence.

In time a champion of the people arose, Errol Walton Barrow, a trained lawyer, a QC and as it transpired, a first-class statesman. He evolved the theory of 'liberation theology". Removal from the pulpit for his beliefs did not dent his theology or his concern for poor black workers.

In 1938, Barbados still an exploited backwater British colony, seven black progressive activists established the Barbados Labour Party (BLP). From the beginning, lawyers were prominent in the BLP. As a result, close attention was paid to constitutional forms within the party and also on the wider political scene. The political culture of Barbados was irreversibly transformed. Grantley Herbert Adams (later Sir Grantley Adams), was chosen as political leader. The movement was left of centre, challenging the conservatism of the white planter-merchant oligarchy. The BLP was an "historic necessity."

In 1937 only 3.3 percent of the people had the right to vote – 6,299 out of a population of 190,000. The BLP was a voice for the voiceless. The party launched a sustained campaign of education in order to raise the political consciousness of the people and mobilize support. It took until 1951 for all adults to secure the right to vote.

With the BLP at his back, Barrow began a concerted campaign with a well-worked out strategy for independence. His family were political activists. He lifted their tactics and used them to cause as much inconvenience to the British authorities as possible: non-co-op-eration, delaying or blocking disliked laws, organising civil disobedi-ence, one protest after another. With so many unemployed, thousands turned up to rallies. Britain with local problems to think about, keen on jettisoning small territories, independence was achieved on the 30th November 1966. Westminster looked for a quiet life.

Barbados ended 361 years of British rule and became an inde-pendent sovereign state.

After independence, and a tussle over the constitution, Barrow became the first prime minister. The declaration of independence saw a few compromises, the British ever guaranteed to extract a pound of flesh from a nation daring to walk tall: Barbados would throw off its colony status but stay a Commonwealth country, the Queen as its head.

Throughout the Seventies and Eighties Barrow was an indomitable advocate of Caribbean sovereignty, ferociously opposed to interference in Caribbean affairs, particularly by the USA. He spoke out forcefully against the United States invasion of Grenada and he was scathing in his criticism of other Caribbean leaders who kow-towed to Washington in the hope of getting economic handouts:

"Mr. Seaga thinks that the solution to Jamaica's problems is to get President Reagan to play Santa Claus. I do not believe in Santa Claus." [Prime Minister of Jamaica, Edward Seaga]

Like our own Alex Salmond, Barrow was smeared by accusations of infidelity, none proven. Later, the singer Nina Simone claimed in her autobiography to have had an affair with him, and the British press used that to belittle his popularity.

Prime Minister Errol Barrow died at his home on 1 June 1987. By an act of Parliament in 1998, Barrow was posthumously named as one of the ten National Heroes of Barbados.

[This biography is greatly attenuated for his achievements were considerable. Readers are recommended to study his work. GB]

And here we are in 2021 watching Barbados sever all British control as we in Scotland struggle to think of any way to achieve liberty other than by delayed referenda.

Barbados Governor General Sandra Mason, Queen Elizabeth II's official representative in the country, announced that she would soon be out of a job. "The time has come to leave our colonial past behind." (A representative of the Queen using the 'c' word?! Whoa!) Mason added that by Nov. 30, 2021, on the 55th anniversary of the country's independence, Barbados will break up with dear old Lizzie and instead swear in a local Barbadian president as head of state. In doing so, Barbados is going to become a republic. The announcement was not a surprise for Barbadians:

The debate on republicanism has been alive and well for around 40 years. So, where is Barbados in the modern world? 280,000 people depend heavily on the tourism industry pretty well holed under the waterline by the Covid-19 pandemic. Like Scotland, Barbadians are harangued by the enemies of democracy told beating the disease is more important that becoming a republic. Mia Mottley, the country's popular and charismatic prime minister, just laughs and gets on with the task.

The criticism of Mottley is based on a fear that with radical changes looming in the British Royal family, Barbados could give other Commonwealth nations the cue to leave the fold. It needs only an *amicable* settlement to see how easily full freedoms can be restored. Advocates of a republic point to Brexit and a self-weakened Britain. They want a republic now, now is the time to strike. The opposition leader, Guy Hewitt, reiterates the same things Scotland's parties say, a republic is all very well, but "now is not the time".

Mottley campaigned on republicanism, winning a landslide victory in the 2018 elections on that platform, her party winning all 30 seats in the House of Assembly. She shows her confidence openly. In her own words, she has "a mandate from the people".

Under Barbados rules, she needs a two-thirds majority vote in both houses. Since parting with the United Kingdom has long been popular – old wounds never healed – she is likely to get all the support she needs. One suspects a sex smear may be in the offing.

Inequality is rising on the island, in part due to remnants of colonialism and "post-colonial oligarchy." And Barbadians, including the prime minister, are still fighting to get reparations from Britain and Europe after a commission established by Caribbean heads of government called for the implementation of a ten-point reparation plan. Moreover,

Mottley has decided to go ahead *without* a referendum. "We were elected to achieve a republic, why should I ask the people a second time?" In this ambition she is opposed by right-wing newspapers. Recently, the *Nation*, (there's another coincidence with Scotland), Barbados's largest newspaper, opined in an editorial, writing: "a referendum should *not* be off the table."

Unlike the SNP, Mottley's party is *preparing* for the nation's liberty. It gave no warning to the British government of becoming a republic, assuming Westminster would spot that the Barbados Labour Party had been canvassing and got elected on a platform of installing republicanism. Barbados did not warn the British Foreign and Commonwealth Office the separation was coming officially before the throne speech, though it told Buckingham Palace. There's cheeky for you!

The Barbados government announced the creation of a *Republican Status Transition Advisory Committee*, a 10-member committee with the mandate of thinking through what the republic should look like, how to say ta-ta to Lizzie, and what the role of the president should be. The committee will "examine previous work done on the topic, such as a 1998 report on republicanism. They are charged with proposing 2004 constitutional amendments; will hold discussions with the public and influential examinations"; and will come up with recommendations.

In October 2021, Barbados elected its first president as it prepares to be a republic, removing Queen Elizabeth as head of state. Dame Sandra Mason, will be sworn in on the 30 November, 2021, marking Barbados's 55th anniversary of independence from Britain. Yes, dear readers, it's as easy as that.

Mottley is known for having the last word, which I am happy to give her:

> *"Barbados' desire to become a republic is a matter for the Barbados Government and its people, no one else. The UK enjoys a warm, long-standing relationship with Barbados and will continue to do so, but it is time to say goodbye to our colonial past. Republicanism will not change everything. We will still drive on the left."*

The reader will appreciate a few biographical notes on the main protagonists in this essay: Born in 1920, Errol Walton Barrow, PC, QC was a Caribbean statesman and the first Prime Minister of Barbados. Born into a family of political and civic activists in the parish of Saint Lucy, he became a WWII aviator, combat veteran, lawyer, politician, gourmet cook, publishing a book on his recipes, and author. Mia Amor Mottley QC, MP, EGH, OR is a Barbadian politician and attorney born in 1965. She is the eighth person to hold the position of Prime Minister in Barbados and first woman to hold either position.

25

THE ART OF PERSECUTION

Facing the destruction of our planet from humankind's folly and our untrammelled greed intent on mass suicide of our species, my mind wanders to what could have been my country's place in the world on the morning after Scotland's independence referendum.

Anyone with a sliver of intelligence knows the British state takes revenge on rebellious colonies. The referendum saw 53% of indigenous Scots vote to restore self-governance, and of those that voted no to full civil and constitutional rights, over a third wanted greater powers short of absolute autonomy. What other reason was there for the eleventh hour panic offer of a fraudulent Vow from the agents of the British state, vaguely suggesting Scotland would be given unspecified extra powers, an offer made well after canvassing is legally allowed?

A soon as the Referendum was over a commission was set up, the Smith Commission, named after Lord Smith of Kelvin its appointed chairman, a safe pair of hands and mind. (One cannot get anything blander than a body of enquiry called 'Smith'.) The powers needed to progress democracy were laid before the committee by the SNP, the membership consisting of Labour, Tory and Liberal-Democrats, all of whom promptly vetoed anything that moved Scotland closer to an autonomous state. What was left was hollow, a token gesture. The animus exhibited by parties of the British state towards anything that looks remotely like a free Scotland was taken a step further by the appointment – I almost wrote *anointment* – of Nicola Sturgeon as First Minister, successor to Alex Salmond, who made the noble gesture of resigning, having served Scots magnificently by giving us the opportunity of deciding the future of our country. We had not failed him. We had been outwitted by the demographics and the inculcated fears inherent in a colonised nation.

"Scotland will be the most powerful devolved parliament in the world", claimed Hapless Gordon Brown, one-time UK prime minister and bag man to the crooked banks, a son of the manse. He is a Scot who refuses to visit the Scottish Parliament. In his Edinburgh student days he gathered a group of radical intellectuals around him and published their essays in what he entitled, *The Red Paper*. The people he chose to publish read like pillars of Scotland's socialism in the seventies: playwright John McGrath, author David Craig, future MP and "ethical" Foreign Secretary, Robin Cook, academic Owen Dudley Edwards, John McEwan, who went on to write a searing expose of the greed of Highland landlords.

A pedantic Jim Sillars is there too, espousing the kind of template socialism that makes pub socialists comfortable. When rejected by Scotland, Sillars tossed a Malvolian rebuke at voters as he left the political stage: "Ninety-minute patriots" he shouted at them in disgust. What he had then to undergo was his wife, Margo MacDonald, a star and stalwart of the SNP, being persecuted by elements in the SNP. Eventually she left the party and became an independent MP.

Brown's Red Paper was full of woolly thinking; meritorious proposals for Nirvana north of Gretna Green. The assembled scrievers could not bring themselves to allow the phrase 'independence is natural' pass their lips; each treatise attacking the centralisation of power in London increased Westminster control. Hapless Gordon was all for maintaining the integrity of the United Kingdom, that is, England's dominance, and yet without an iota of contradiction he was able to write: "Nationalism should not be regarded as a disease". Ever since that ironic remark the British state has taken every opportunity it could to persecute intelligent thinking.

Brown's mantra is super-devolution, big imperial nationalism of England greatly preferred to the small country pride of place of Scottish nationalism. Denying his kith and kin full constitutional rights is a form of repression. A gauche individual, poor in social skills, he spends the autumn of his political career selling his tincture to the Blue Rinse Brigade of fans, invariably locked in a room while he strode manfully back and forth on a dais lecturing them, drunk on his ideal vision of civilised oppression, a pawn of the British state.

On the night Alex Salmond led his troops inside Holyrood Parliament to glorious victory, on a voting system designed to stop his party gaining power, Gordon Brown is reputed to have made a series of frantic telephone calls to leaders of other political parties, in the hope they might help organise a coup destabilising Scotland's new government. One can imagine a comparable attempt to overthrow an elected government in some tinpot South American country, but Scotland? The warning signs were all there, not enough of Scots heeded them.

Losing the 2014 Referendum depressed an entire nation for weeks, the ghosts of past fighters for the Great Cause insulted, their graves desecrated. But the people regrouped and handed Salmond's chosen successor a landslide victory, Nicola Sturgeon, a buttoned up individual more suited to the role of governess of a girl's boarding school than first minister of Scotland. She did nothing with the vote, and nothing with subsequent mandates.

The orchestral conductor, Sir Thomas Beecham, was asked what he owed to his long success on the concert podium. "When on holiday", he answered without a moment's hesitation, "I always deputise a second-rater." The off-hand remark sunk his regular deputy Sir Malcolm Sargent, who maintained a stoical dignity for the rest of his career. Alex Salmond probably felt handing the future of Scotland to Nicola Sturgeon was an astute move, a fine politician in the making, but alas, she never matured, never learned statecraft.

What she did learn was ways to assassinate political colleagues and somehow never be seen holding the knife.

Hardly had our Acting First Minister slipped her feet under her architect over-designed desk at Holyrood than she began demoting Salmond's achievements and those of his former colleagues. Her set of proposals on the economy of a revitalised Scotland were weak and unadventurous, looking more like a demotion of Salmond's historic *White Paper*. Colonials are well versed in the craft of driving a wedge between people who are united in a cause the state dislikes. They are able to create a section of the most influential who are eager and able to do the dirty work of the coloniser. Our first minister was first in line.

The list of articulate, dissenting Scots persecuted to various degrees by the SNP on trumped up charges, or initiated by Sturgeon's civil servant advisers, both aided by the Crown Office of the Procurator Fiscal (COPFS) and Police Scotland, reads like the burial basement of a serial killer. Alex Salmond MP, former First Minister; Alasdair Gray, novelist and illustrator; Craig Murray, Human rights activist; Mark Hirst, independence campaigner; Marion Miller, independence campaigner; Clive Thomson, independence supporter; Manny Singh, independence marches organiser; Dave Llewellyn, independence campaigner; Tommy Sheridan, ex MSP and independence campaigner; Stuart Campbell, blogger for independence; Julie McAnulty, SNP councillor; Ron MacWilliam, Highland SNP councillor; Brian Wilson, Will Mylet, Kenny MacLaren and Mags MacLaren, SNP councillors; former SNP politicians Natalie McGarry, Mark McDonald, Neale Hanvey, Michelle Thomson and Kenny MacAskill, former Justice Minister; Gary Kelly, independence campaigner; Joanna Cherry, SNP MP; Margaret Ferrier, SNP MP; myself, (found *not* guilty of anything with the exception of a brief sentence in a 2,000 word essay that "might be construed" as a thought crime), and a dozen councillors and other supporters smeared or damned.

The list is not exhaustive by any means. All that carnage of the great, the good and the loyal, has to be added to a pile of Nicola

Sturgeon's deeply flawed blunderbuss bills causing widespread public conflict and disunity. This is the outcome of a person who is unable to find the proper balance of things.

Scotland's joyous revolution betrayed by the "Queen of Selfies", her critics' name for a habit of taking endless photographs of herself amid crowds of admirers. She was sold as a *president* of Scotland. Psychologist and psychiatrist could make a living dissecting how well she carried out the work of the British state. By engineering an atmosphere where it would not be beneficial to write or say the wrong thing counter to received wisdom, under her incumbency, Nicola Sturgeon inducted an era of calculated repression in all its forms, from smear to imprisonment, via banishment from her party.

Scotland's colonial overlords relaxed until they saw the disenfranchised and the disaffected join a new party called ALBA. When a revolution is betrayed new parties always appear. Near the end of *The Seagull* by Anton Checkov, he has the aging protagonist Boris Alexeyevich Trigorin, seen earlier in his youth, push a pram on stage and say with a heart heavy of lost opportunity, "Where has it all gone?" I hear people say the same of Scotland's independence hopes As demoralising as it is, we are consoled by seeing successive waves over a beach, movements for greater freedoms are unstoppable.

26

'BRAVEHEART' REVISITED

The American movie *Braveheart*, with Mel Gibson as star and director, is an essential weapon in the arsenal of unionist derision aimed at Scotland's history. Massively popular worldwide, the movie won five Academy Awards and is shown on late night television regularly. The film arrived in time to coincide with a growing confidence in Scotland's political ambitions. That made it a prime target for the antagonistic colonial. Opponents of Scotland's right to exist are determined to see Sir William Wallace's legacy diced – a second death sentence – hung, drawn, quartered, his memory and achievements defiled.

To reject the film outright one might as well claim all art is phony, call Théodore Géricault's *The Raft of the Madusa* a load of utter tosh, or 'pish', as Scots say. Outrage perversely misses the point of art's existence. It ignores allegory and symbolism. Shaking his head, did Stone-Age man deride the magnificent drawings of a deer hunt, signed by a palm print on the cave wall saying, "This isn't how we hunt; this isn't true to life"? The horses and hunters depicted were the reproduced spirit of their fight for survival. The energy in the cave paintings imbued them with fire and intensity. It invigorated them. They placed their palm prints on the wall to tell others they exist.

Too busy spitting gobs of blood over the film's success, the only thing the ignorant miss is Wallace clean shaven and not sporting a full beard. Mel Gibson plays Wallace as the only man in Scotland who owns a razor. For the record, I have two caveats; the French love interest is pure Hollywood, and the opening sequence of Wallace as a youth, filmed at the plodding level of a BBC education programme.

A common, utterly spurious criticism is, *Braveheart* contains factual errors. Everybody is a movie critic. A few unwary Scottish historians, flattered by media attention, confirm there are inaccuracies. Drama is *not* documentary. Who condemns William Shakespeare's version of *Macbeth*, historically insane though it is. Historians recount Macbeth was one of Scotland's most popular kings. In the hands of the satirical or the malicious, written today, Henrik Ibsen's *The Master Builder* could be claimed a facsimile of any number of high statement world architects, more ego friendly than environment friendly.

For drama to be good drama and not mere soap there must be conflict, metaphor and symbolism. Drama is a reinterpretation of events. Filmmaker Werner Herzog argues effective storytelling is not about representing facts accurately. He points out the obvious, stories focused on factual accuracy get at "superficial truth, the truth of accountants." On the other hand, "There are deeper strata of truth in cinema, and there is such a thing as poetic, ecstatic truth. The mysterious and elusive can be reached only through fabrication and imagination and stylisation."

Peter Watkins directed *Culloden* on a shoe-string budget using only amateur actors. It has immense power though the plot is restricted to events concerning a few soldiers in close up. *Culloden* proves you do not need massive physical sets to understand the motivations and madness of warfare. You need only inventiveness to fire the cinema-goer's imagination. *Braveheart*'s battles are as accurate as we need for the mechanics of bloodletting to feel real, our disbelief suspended. Wallace's speeches were never recorded so those have to be re-imagined, but the film is true to Wallace's political ideals. This irks the hell out of Scotland's detractors. They are happier if watching a load of fiction about Winston Churchill.

Moreover, no Unionist denies Wallace was *not* hung drawn and quartered. They avoid the barbaric bit, including those who knew Wallace carried a letter of protection from arrest.

And on the subject of mythologizing national heroes, did Sir Frances Drake actually play a game of bowls as the Spanish gunboats hove in sight toward the English Channel? We are taught that he faced down and sunk Spain's old, heavy ships, too low in the water to turn quickly. In reality they got caught in a severe storm, the survivors beetling up the west coast to Scotland for safety, a country with whom they traded. The myth relates how Drake refused to stop his game of bowls to captain the fleet, the English phlegmatic character on show. How many know a year later, in 1589, in a disastrous attack on Spain, Drake's fleet lost 40 ships and 10,000 to 15,000 lives? That is not part of the story of England as a great maritime nation.

Robert Falcon Scott, "Scott of the Antarctic", is celebrated as an iconic "British" hero. There has been any number of filmed dramas made of his life and exploits. Unlike his Norwegian counterparts led by Roald Amundsen, skilled at polar exploration, Scott's plans and arrangements to reach the South Pole first were lethally incompetent: the wrong date to start his trek to the South Pole, the wrong provisions, the wrong clothing, using horses instead of dogs, man-hauling the preferred way to lug heavy tents and provisions on sledges, and using tractors whose engine froze solid in an instant. Only one companion had medical skills. The expedition was a monumental failure. Scott was the architect of it. In fact, he was heavily criticised in his day for his inexpert planning and for the death of his companions. That was then. In time, Scott and his doomed team became heroic treasures of the British state and John Mills starred in a British film about his last journey.

The English adore failures, the bigger the better. Did the film's producers shoot it at the South Pole for historical accuracy? It was mostly Ealing Studio mock ups and lots of salt. We didn't notice no one had frozen breath when they spoke. At least the writers had the benefit of Scott's last words lifted from his diary, all the more tragic knowing he knew his expedition was doomed.

Scott is celebrated a hero in the English mould, not an all-time casualty of his own hubris. What of his competitors, Roald Amundsen and his team? Well, Amundsen wasn't English; therefore we have nothing to learn from his undoubted superior skills, prowess, leadership qualities or tenacity. Scientific cooperation was not countenanced in the British Empire.

No Scottish historian draws attention to the risible myth of Lord Horatio Nelson's final words, the apocryphal, "Kiss me, Hardy." Oil paintings depicting his death are given a beatific treatment, part and parcel of a nation's embellishment of great achievement in *extremis*. Of course, not much is said of how badly Nelson treated his wife while having that affair with Emma, Lady Hamilton. Some things should not be spoken of. There is plenty of scepticism suggesting one man alone could not have generated naval exactness to the extent that it disciplined England's navy so precisely it won the battle of Trafalgar without setback or difficulty. Many other brave officers and sailors played their part, plus a few ill-chosen French vessels and Villeneuve's tactical decisions. (Pierre-Charles Villeneuve, the French Admiral.) Five of the ships under Nelson's command were captained by Scots but it's depicted as an English victory, not a Scottish-English one. The flags that exhorted every man to do his duty did not spell out "for the United Kingdom", or for Great Britain. They said, "England expects." As ever, we Scots were employees.

Again, *Braveheart* gets lambasted by English colonials for casting an Australian in the main role. This is a difficult gibe to take lying down. Cate Blanchett, a skilled actress and an Australian, played Elizabeth I not once but twice. Both films are so devoid of historical accuracy and crammed with banal dialogue as to be risible, but the costumes are pretty. An Australian, Russell Crowe, played an English sea-captain in the excellent *Master and Commander*. The film has him running down a dastardly French warship. In reality and in the novel on which the film is based, it was an American ship. England was at war with America at that period in its history, but being a film financed by Hollywood, the poor French are depicted as the fall guys. It's called commercial necessity.

There's no one to beat Crowe's brooding intensity when it comes to swashbuckling epics. He went on to play Robin Hood Prince of Thieves with an iffy north of England accent. In fact, a previous Australian played Robin Hood to success many years earlier, Errol Flynn. In one scene he rides in a hurry passed 20th century pine forestation. And in another all-American financed epic, Kevin Costner took on the role, the film mustering a great flub when he sits astride Hadrian's Wall that, according to the film's plotting, passes close to and alongside the white cliffs of Dover.

Now and then, the English get uppity when their productions take creative licence. A good example of the genre is David Lean's film of *Bridge Over the River Kwai*. On being sent the script, Major A G Close, wrote from the War Office's PR department to the producer Sam Spiegel: "I do not think much of this story. In the first instance it is quite untrue and only very occasionally resembles the facts as they were at the time. I am perhaps biased as I worked for three and a half years on this particular railway." He had sent the script to others "and they agree with me that it would not go down well with the British public". The deputy director of PR at the War Office agreed, saying it was difficult to believe that any British commanding officers would act in the way that the character Nicholson did.

The scriptwriter Carl Foreman, who was blacklisted in Hollywood after admitting to being a member of the Communist party and was *not* credited in the final film, tried to reassure the War Office, highlighting script changes, and the fact the film did portray acts of sabotage. Eventually the War Office grudgingly stood back, but stressed it was "not entirely happy about this film story". Carl Foreman was writing a story of unilateral moral dilemma, how not to co-operate or appease the enemies of democracy.

The War Office sought a long disclaimer at the beginning and end of the film, rejected by the producer Sam Spiegel. He favoured a short denial. In the end, Spiegel's wording was used, but only at London screenings, and not in other parts of the country. This incensed former prisoners of war in the Japanese camps. The unhappy including Lt General Arthur Ernest Percival, general officer commanding Malaya, who surrendered on 15 February 1942 at the fall of Singapore, described by empire loyalist Winston Churchill as "the worst disaster and largest capitulation in British history".

English movie history is littered with wild creative licence. The fine military epic, *Zulu*, written by historian John Prebble, chose to depict the regiment stationed at Rorke's Drift as Welsh infantry, a rather neat way of concentrating attention on Welsh military culture and giving its producer and star, Stanley Baker, the excuse to cast his Welsh pals. A spirited interpretation, it distorted historical fact. The Warwickshire Regiment defended the encampment, a company with more English than Welsh, not a Welsh regiment, although they did recruit from the Welsh border. They did not sing "Men of Harlech". They sang "A Warwickshire Lad".

The Zulu "hoards" are shown as noble savages, ooggy-boogy black fellas, as if blood thirsty American Indians of the kind seen in silent films, or the dumb natives in King Kong movies, without individual character. Those creative flaws did not stop *Zulu* becoming a milestone in British-American film co-operation, but the film is riddled with historical and ethnic liberties.

Does it matter if Arthur Wellesley, the Duke of Wellington (a native of Ireland, but let's gloss over that uncomfortable fact), did not invent the Wellington boot at all. He merely instructed Hoby's, his shoemaker in London, to make his hessian boots watertight? It was Hoby who dubbed them the Wellington, a smart selling ploy.

Remember, no British critic objected to Gibson the Aussie playing Hamlet in a filmed version, scenes set in a castle outside Edinburgh. This was Shakespeare, after all. Of *Braveheart*: "I cannot bring myself to think of that awful film," uttered a half-dead earl in the House of Lords. Unlike William Wallace, no one can recall the earl's name. And if that isn't enough to have colonial fools choke on their cream teas, two films Hollywood financed were released in 2019, one on King Robert the Bruce, *Outlaw King*, and one on Scotland's Monarch, *Mary Queen of Scots*, another piece of revisionist history feminist driven. At least the belittlers could not complain about Aussie actors taking chief roles. Betrayed Mary was portrayed by a Celt, the Irish-born Saoirse Ronan.

England has a right to its heroes and their elevation to mythical status, but not at the cost of Scotland's achievers. England is not entitled to demote Scotland. If only the enemies of democracy were honest. It is not what *Braveheart* gets historically wrong or omits that is objectionable. It is what it stands for that is the real threat.

27

THE DESPAIR OF UNEMPLOYMENT

Like many another I am a confident person when I have a pound in my pocket but a miserable wreck when my pockets are empty, such is life in a capitalist system where the rich get richer and the rest are reduced to passive consumers or welfare 'scroungers'. For freelance 'creatives', as bureaucrats are wont to categorise those of an artistic bent, unemployment is a constant stalker. Having the American Embassy stamp my passport 'VIP Creative' made no difference to my career prospects in Scotland, but it did get me swift entry through Los Angeles's LAX airport; jet-lagged, that is a pleasure.

You can tell how caring a country is of its citizens by the cleanliness of its public toilets and how well it looks after the unemployed and the homeless. Scotland is generally good at both. The mega-successful children's writer J.K. Rowling will attest to that from her unemployed days in Edinburgh as a single mother.

Doing nothing does not come easily to my nature. You won't find me hugging a pint in a boozer's pub or sunbathing on a Spanish beach. If a quiet hour arrives, read a book. A natural-born freelancer, I am used to hearing the prowler's footsteps behind me, though I should add that when not working on a paid project, *I am not without work.* Unemployed but inventive presupposes having the ability to create tasks that keep mind and body together, and by imagination and industry achieve income no matter how meagre. And so when push came to shove one makes good: designing a garden for a friend, an Edo period Japanese garden replete with thatched Tea House, moon window and red footbridge over a stream. That got me free meals and a double hernia. I emptied gardens of unwanted weeds and concrete into skips in monsoon rain, carrying bags of gunge carefully through well kept house halls that had no back gate, and enjoyed the physical activity. Now and then I noticed women who engaged me to 'clear out the overgrown backyard' had husbands not pleased to see a rather too healthy Mediterranean type around their wives when they came home from work. Perhaps my gardener's green one-piece overall unbuttoned to the belly button and nothing underneath unhinged them.

I had writing skills. I wrote formal letters for those in need of a wordsmith, legal letters, pleading letters to court officials, applications for social security, letters complaining to the Gas Board of excessive charges, helped the dyslexic fill in complicated forms, tasks undertaken in return for a few pounds sterling, invariably traded last minute for a bottle of wine because the client was broke, on the dole, like me. Most had very little money. Charging fees was out of the question. Hard to believe that in this day and age there exist adults who can barely write. "You were a teacher, an' tha', you ken better how tae do this," they would say. Some were in the throes of terminal poverty.

A love of well-designed cars – a hobby interest – and the ability to write about them with some degree of sardonic humour secured regular fees as an automobile journalist writing for franchised columns in UK and USA magazines. For Tomáš Sträussler hailing from Zlin in the Moravia district of Czechoslovakia, later famous as playwright Tom Stoppard, testing cars was problematic. He found writing car reviews a handy stop-gap when unemployed but knew nothing of cars. "I just sat in the car and described what I saw." My Sicilian father had been an Alfa Romeo mechanic before caught up in Mussolini's ill-fated army, his genes gifting me an easy understanding of how a car and its engine work. Stoppard's father was a doctor, a mechanic of the body.

Being a factotum kept the wolf from the door and self-esteem reasonably intact. When people ask for your help, you are somebody again, not a non-person, a statistic. But on reaching middle-age, the time we should be comfortable enough to become expansive in interests and in community spirit, I was hit by a two-year spell of no work offered at all. Magazines wanted young, trendy, celebrity writers. Life ground to a halt. It was an extremely low time. I lost my home and everything in it.

In one desperate evening a long, distraught call to the Samaritans at 4am resulted in a £40 telephone bill. And I was stony broke at the time. Double jeopardy. You feel events are conspiring to ensure you don't rise again. The elderly voice at the other end was very sympathetic. No matter what I said that was negative, despairing, he commiserated; he understood my predicament and plight. "Oh, I can see how that must have felt hopeless."

There are two anecdotes to relate emblematic of how survival hangs by a thread. After some weeks collecting my fortnightly unemployment cheque I was offered an interview for a lowly temporary job, the kind that requires no mental ability, just stacking supermarket shelves. I had £1.50 to my name, just enough to cover the bus fare to reach the interview. As I tied my shoelaces one lace snapped. It was too short to knot. New laces cost £2.10. I was 60p short of a pair of new laces, a tiny amount between hope and disaster.

I remember sitting on the outside doorstep immobilised, humbled. How could such a trivial, insignificant incident take on the mantle of a full-blown crisis so easily? Gripping the loose shoe with my toes I reached the interview, lace-less shoe hidden as best as I could manage. I didn't get the job, considered 'overqualified'. The store interviewer looked perplexed when he read my *curriculum vitae*. "You should be store manager," he said. No, I thought, store owner is nearer the truth. If I was dictator of Scotland I would bring in a law making mandatory all long-term employees become profit shareholders for the company they worked.

The second incident involved a visit to the Job Centre, (a misnomer of a title if ever there was one), to sign and collect that life-sustaining unemployment cheque. On that occasion I did not have the bus fare at all. My pockets were empty, not as much as a dead moth. I walked seven miles to the office and unsurprisingly arrived late for interview. You are sanctioned for lateness like a recalcitrant schoolboy. Regular interviews were a new thing back in the day, implemented to determine you had evidence of looking for work, still breathing, still alive, not lying in bed or working abroad. Job Centre staff often half your age scolded you for being a bad person. I doubt that has changed.

My time in the wilderness coincided with Westminster's sea change of attitude to the unemployed. One day we were people made footloose by the decisions of others, citizens receiving state aid from funds we had paid for in our taxes. Overnight we became a burden on the state, malingering work shy subsidy junkies.

As I stood looking for the booth I should sit at in the centre, the official spotted me, checked his watched, and bellowed across the space between us, "You're late! What's your excuse?!" By a combination of theatrical speech training in voice projection and an inbred Sicilian reaction to indignities, I roared back, "Lower your voice! I am not a child!" The official was startled, an articulate brat. He shuffled the papers on his desk nervously, face scarlet with embarrassment, locally known as 'a big riddy' or a 'beamer', and asked me politely to take a seat. Then, as if to apologise, he looked up from his notes. "Hey! Aren't you the guy who made that film that was in the papers? You shouldn't be here." And as an apology for his error of character judgment added, "What are *you* doing signing on?" What is worse, getting bollocked in public or thoroughly patronised?

A few weeks later I stopped signing on. It was too painful. I have my pride. We all have. You stand in the line of shame wondering if the elderly guy in front will ever recover from redundancy. You take a sly glance at the young woman behind, and wonder if her role in life will be a perpetual shop assistant not her dream of an animal lover in a vet's practice. Perhaps she will succumb to the advances of an opportunistic scumbag, his affection a con. I decided those living on the streets could do with the money more than me.

Eventually, by chance, I stumbled into fee paid work after twenty-four months of despair, but not after an education in how the poor cannot write and how the middle class don't care. Karl Marx did not care either. His theories are almost all connected with the sea of struggling poor he saw in his day. Few could solve contemporary society's problems. He had no answers for the middle-classes. Vladimir Ilyich Ulyanov, better known by his alias Lenin, felt the same way only with a dash of barbarity. Asked by philosopher Bertrand Russell how the Bolsheviks would handle Russia's middle class Lenin laughed. "The poor will hang the middle class from the nearest tree!" Unsurprisingly, Russell did not like him for saying that.

Standing in a job centre queue, one surveys the line of damp clothed, bedraggled humanity and see dead people walking. Angry, one considers seeking out the minister for the unemployed and punching his lights out, but you give in, certain you will find another line of angry people waiting to see him.

One is powerless, caught between life's vitality and life's lottery. You feel a failure, worthless. You are prone to prolonged bouts of depression. You can't think straight. Small problems become major handicaps. Luckily, my health was good, constitution strong. The only drugs I took were coffee and happiness. In any event, a friend offered a room till times improved. I took it eagerly and with good grace.

The Tory administration in London had no plans to lift the stigma of being jobless. The writing was on the wall; the unemployed, the ill, the vulnerable, the poor, were dubbed pariahs. The traditional ladder of individual improvement has been pulled up and away from the masses. The new generation of youth are made to pay for a basic education, to be in hock for half their lives – a classic method of keeping them docile, afraid of expressing dissent. They live with their parents. Who wants to live in a nation bereft of empathy?

All this despair happened when the European Commission released a report on expectations for a new year. It forecast low growth and increasing unemployment. Unemployment is destroying a generation, no trivial matter. Prolonged unemployment kills hope. Unattended, it stores up trouble. In a meretricious society feeling no one cares, you are tempted to return the gesture in physical ways.

The House of Gothic Horrors called Westminster has plans to unravel the Welfare state. Our elected representatives turn a blind eye to the consequences, the impoverishment of Scotland, the rise of fascism, neo-Nazi groups and sentiments arising across Europe and in their own backyard. Jews and refugees denounced part of the problem. The seeds of fascism lie dormant awaiting only nourishment. Now we have food banks – a sign, according to one Tory politician, "we are a caring society". And he was not joking.

The harm being done to individuals is incalculable. But the politicians still plead for our vote and promise us happiness tomorrow.

28

THE LITTLE WHITE ROSE

I have a hand-written poem dedicated to me – well, that's an exaggeration. It is actually autographed to me, though written on the spot. The poet whose name I did not know until he put it on paper was invited to my guardian's flat [*apartment*] to talk about Scottish literature, an interview of sorts. She told me he was famous.

A child, I had never read a word of his work. I did not know then he was a founder of the independence movement, a gatherer of the Scots tongue, and a rebel. He said, "Yes, I am also a communist. I wear the red so that when people see me coming they know what I stand for." Hugh MacDiarmid was a nationalist and a communist; so much for the oft heard gibe 'Tartan Tories' poked at supporters of Scotland's rights.

When he entered the flat he was ushered hastily into an anti-room almost unseen. From my position at the end of the hall I caught sight of a shock of white hair, and a long black coat as he moved a short step from outer to inner door and the anti-room. I was barely of an age to tie my shoelaces and he, it seemed to me from that momentary glimpse, was very old. My guardian told me not to disturb him and her other guests while they were in conference. I was given a book to read, told to wait until the meeting was over.

Why had a poet come to our house? Had he not students to teach, a publisher to meet, an ode to compose? Should he not be striding over the stony crest of a scree-sided, ridge back, craggy Munro somewhere, rain lashing his face, he unperturbed jotting down giblets of verse, shouting it to noisy crows to check if it scanned?

Curiosity got the better of me. I had to know.

Adult counsel is of little value to children who are able to think for themselves. I ignored my guardian's good advice and, holding aloft pencil and a scrap of school lined paper, I rushed through the linoleum clad lobby in my stocking feet to the door at the far end, supposedly barred to my entrance. I entered behind a timid tap, tap on the old four-panel, varnish crackled, and brass handled door.

The elderly man stood back-lit against the tall Victorian lace windows. He stood motionless, taken aback at my unexpected appearance while he was in mid-speech. Silence. The people in the room waited as adults might a naughty child to stop talking. My guardian gave me a scowl. Down below, on the railway line than ran along the length of the Edinburgh tenement, a goods engine shuffled and puffed, stiffly, slowly, wagons heavy with coal taken from Niddrie coal yards to somewhere. In Pavlovian response the old man took a puff at his pipe. The smoke idled up to the rose on the ceiling.

His narrow shouldered frame was drowned in a long dark, serge blue, big buttoned overcoat that reached to his ankles, as if he was a municipal statue about to be revealed. The hair on his head was thick, unruly and impenetrable, a gorse bush swept back by gales not comb. It hovered suspended in the mid-air. He seemed to grow down from it until his feet touched the ground in shoes old and cracked. That head needed neither hat nor cap to stave off Edinburgh's cold winds. In contrast, his moustache was scraggy, immature, attached to a short lip and stained from years of tobacco smoke. His eyebrows, in line with the explosion of head hair, took the form of twin briar patches, his eyes lined and pouched, panda black. Tufts of hair grew out of his ears, and his lower lip that held the stem of his pipe, generous and distended, as if a roll of lava defying gravity.

I did not know then, not until years later, that he was the uncompromising architect of Scotland's literary renaissance, the man who wrote in broad Scots and not plain English to bamboozle Anglophiles and colonials, a co-founder of the National Party of Scotland.

For a very long minute we studied each other. I held up my stumpy pencil and paper.

He removed the pipe from his pursed lips and spoke down to my height, half of his.

"Ah dinnae dae autographs, son."

Crushed. Humiliated. Spurned. What an anti-climax. To screw up courage told no thanks, go away. In my head that's what I heard though he never spoke those words. What kind of person refuses the flattery of a request for their signature? The Scots actor Alan Cumming has a policy of not responding to autograph hunters. "If I give one to you, everybody here will want one." Conversely, George Bernard Shaw refused to give donations to worthy causes writing to him unsolicited. Instead he signed postcards and told the lucky recipient to sell it, "It is very definitely worth a pound or two to a collector." The poet in front of me had no such care for the conventions of fame. I said nothing, but my face must have said it all. He saw the hurt, the crumpled gait, for he stopped me as I reached the door.

"Ah tell yi what, son. Ah'll write yi a wee poem."

It took him a few minutes to complete. "Whit's yer name?" I gave it. He signed his barely legible scribble and dated the poem.

The Little White Rose

The rose of all the world is not for me.
I want for my part
Only the little white rose of Scotland
That smells sharp and sweet – and breaks the heart.

It is signed – Hugh MacDiarmid. I have it to this day, a little worn at the edges.

'Little White Rose' was first published by MacDiarmid anonymously in 1931 in periodical *The Modern Scot* and *Living Scottish Poets*, but with acknowledgement to Compton Mackenzie, who in a 1929 radio broadcast, part of which appeared in the *Scots Independent* later that year, said: "You know our wild Scots rose? It is white, and small, and prickly, and possesses a sharp sweet scent which makes the heart ache." The lyric then appeared in *Stony Limits and Other Poems*, in the 1934 first edition of which collection it, and 'Cattle Show' replaced the suppressed 'John Maclean (1879–1923)'. The sloppy Maurice Lindsay included the poem in his 1976 anthology *Modern Scottish Poetry* but published it under Compton Mackenzie's name causing confusion for years after for which MacDiarmid was not pleased.

Back then, MacDiarmid was already on MI5's list as a radical separatist to watch and of course, through various literary outlets, smear and defame as much as possible. A critic of wars conducted by the British state, a certain Major Buckley wrote to Scottish Command in Edinburgh on 12 June 1940 that he believed MacDiarmid to be "a rabid Scottish Nationalist who should be counted as an irresponsible fanatic". This description of MacDiarmid was applied to any and all supporters of Scotland's reinstatement as a nation state. MacDiarmid was well aware that he was being investigated. He made it public and that he intended to take legal action through the Civil Liberties Association. There was talk that sympathetic MPs might raise questions in the House of Commons over his case and the raiding of the Glasgow office of the Scots Socialist journal, from where manuscripts of his were seized. The British state is happy to brand any troublesome Scot as a would-be terrorist.

Later in life, nursing illness and still a heavy pipe smoker, he was considered spent and tame, consequently left to enjoy his final years in his Brownsbank Cottage near Biggar. I saw him interviewed by a group of enamoured fans, mostly writers, draped around his feet in his cottage chatting away for a television documentary of the couthy type BBC Scotland used to offer viewers north of the border as a cultural sop to the natives – rarely transmitted down south for the London glitterati to appreciate.

Those folk 'down south' got cathedral loving John Betjeman, Stephen Spender, and the drab library assistant, Philip Larkin, who, come to think of it, we were given too, just to remind us there existed poets of a greater stature, or so we were expected to assume by the attention they got compared to MacDiarmid or Norman McCaig, or any of the other Scottish poetic dominies.

The final image we have of MacDiarmid framed in a large wing-backed chair, pipe still lodged tight between stumpy, worn teeth, half-smiling, smug as potentate, heroic poet surrounded by minor literary figures, is probably due more to the tiny size of the cottage room than fans sticking close to him. In retrospect it seems almost religious iconography. It differed from my brief youthful meeting with him, when he espoused in school master terms a strict Presbyterian attitude to shallow celebrity. Did he enjoy fawning respect in his old age? Or was he as curmudgeonly about fickle fans and phoneys as he was before?

There is a post script to the meeting. Two decades later, his son, Christopher Grieve produced a television version of a musical I staged and directed with the Scottish National Theatre (SYT), written by novelist David Benedictus, the music composed by Guy Woolfenden, entitled '*What a Way to Run a Revolution*'. Young Grieve spotted a fellow traveller who could achieve. In the current political climate, one of suppression and self-censorship, do not expect to come across a similar all-Scottish production satirising the House of Commons, filmed for television, written by an Etonian. British broadcasters are chary of transmitting anything that smacks of political dissent.

Were he alive, MacDiarmid would be served by negative news columns and bulletins: "Scottish Communist Refuses Child His Autograph", this followed by a few thousand disillusioned fans abusing him on social network sites, and just as many cancelling his existence from their minds and bookshelves.

With former peevish television front man Jeremy Paxman cate-gorising Robert Burns as a poet who 'wrote doggerel', what chance would MacDiarmid have in our febrile McCarthyite atmosphere, Scotland's greatest Twentieth-Century poet, a radical republican? Special Branch and MI5 would appoint an operative to keep an eye on that 'subversive' just as they did back in the nineteen thirties.

Still, I must be one of the few people alive with MacDiarmid's signature poem written in his own hand, and that is fine enough for me.

29

HAPPINESS

Every individual has a right to happiness. The hard part is creating a society in which the majority can achieve a state of comparative happiness most of their existence. Happiness can add colour to a driech grey day.

Here I need to define 'happiness'; I do not mean *pleasure*, that is, hedonistic pleasure, food, sex, status objects, drugs or booze. What it is that keeps us jaunty and generally good natured, when not agitated or impatient? For me, I get high on happiness.

Unalloyed joy covers a lot of things: being with wife and children free of; watching a well-made film with beautiful images and a story line and characters that are plausible; cheering an exciting tennis match to see one's player win; having one's face licked madly by a loyal dog happy to see you – we can learn a lot from a dog's unconditional affection. I find it in designing and creating a garden from scratch to witness it blossom, mature over years; or listening to a great piece of music for the first time that inspires. It can be simple things, such as standing on a high observation point surveying a vast panorama on a hot summer's day feeling blessed at being alive, or giving a gift to a child and watching them overjoyed at the gesture with no demand to say thank you.

In youth, I liked nothing better than lying among grass and clover pastures looking up at cerulean blue sky focussed on a lark singing above and emptying my mind, my moment of Zen. These days, it is usually hearing a friend talk well of me! I could list more reasons to be cheerful, seeing this book take shape is one instance. There are so many activities which activate happiness in the human mind from friendships to creating art.

One looks at a country to see what inspires them. One counts their national composers. Finland has a lot: Jan Sibelius the most famous, Einojuhani Rautavaara, Eriki Melartin, Kaija Saariho, Swebastian Fagurland, Joonas Kokkonen, Orkar merikanto, Lotta Wennäkoski, Maria Kalaniemi, the list is by no means exhaustive. Finland has given rise to a great many composers enthralled with the people and the land. Music plays to the soul.

Being happy and spreading happiness is the least regarded state of mind. When all the senses are engaged, excitement, risk, intellect, participation, happiness is an intoxication. There is just not enough emphasis in our society on this wonderful state of being. We mistake it for hedonism or materialism.

For most of us the essentials of happiness are food, drink, and a roof over our heads. Owning lots of stuff is not happiness. We spend a lot of time satisfying pleasure buying things in shops which isn't happiness though it is a substitute for obsessive shoppers.

Can achieving political goals see contentment a reward? For some politicians who live to see laws enacted that they helped formulate for the common good and ultimately benefit the majority, I suppose political satisfaction must constitute happiness of a sort. Reinstating Scotland's constitutional autonomy is likely to secure opportunity for happiness for lots of people. A nation's renaissance opens up opportunity for individuals to develop to their full potential, new goals, new ideals, revaluating values, clearing out dead wood, rebuilding, creating jobs. The individual feels they are no longer a cog in a wheel. A heightened satisfaction is there to find through the democratically ages-established tradition of empowerment of the individual, participating in the democratic process. Then again, it can as easily attract headache and stress. Everything depends on personal motivation.

We cannot guarantee everybody achieves equality, no nation, no society can. What we can do is create a society where *equality* of opportunity is there for the taking, and the vulnerable without the means to better themselves, are protected from freefall. In a colonial reality the perceptive among us feel decisions are things people make elsewhere. For Scotland that means Westminster.

Are small countries places to find happiness? Greenland is worth a study. Greenland is the world's largest island but a very small nation. It has its own tribes, history, culture, art, topography, environment, and administration. After hundreds and more years ruled by Norway and then Denmark it achieved its ambition to become a self-governing country. Greenland retains Denmark's Monarchy, and monetary policy to some extent, something Scotland suggested for its autonomy by retaining the Royal family and the pound sterling.

With a tiny annual GNP a mere 1.3 billion, Greenland is not wealthy by any stretch of the imagination yet, by all accounts its 56,000 souls lead generally *happy* lives. They are as happy as circumstances permit. There is no unemployment. They talk openly of being contented, how communities look to each other's well-being and that in turn engenders harmony. Their lives are not boring. They don't look for passive amusements.

Greenland might be dismissed as a small community, easy to feel one large family; Scotland is much bigger and attached to an aggressive neighbour. Finland is another country that appears regularly atop the annual 'Most Happy' nation in the *World Happiness Report*. Why is this? The land is less dramatic than Scotland's topography, has a plethora of lakes and forests, but is similar in population number, roughly five-and-half million Fins. Crime statistics are low. Equality is generally the norm. They are blessed with a good education and universal health care system. Social support for the infirm and vulnerable is guaranteed and reliable. Those elements recognised and acknowledged, see a people who are not a competitive nation. Fins feel they enjoy a high standard of living and are generally content. Finland "ranked very high on the measures of personal well-being and mutual trust that have the population feel an homogenous community. Even instances of lost wallets were likely to be returned!" In Finland you sense a great feeling of solidarity.

Achieving any kind of social harmony is difficult if not impossible when the individual feels isolated, or separated from determining the things that matter in their daily life. Unionists warn Scotland of isolation as if our two nations should ever physically separate socially and geographically. Greenland can be described accurately as *extremely* isolated, particularly in its winter months, yet the people of Greenland are in control of their lives in large measure. They are empowered. Greenlanders are not freeloaders. They have an in-built sense of their own worth. One of the strongest instincts of human nature is the herd instinct, affinity with a group. Greenlanders have it in abundance. They are so confident in themselves that they readily embrace other races not indigenous, such as Americans and their air-craft base, a source of income until Greenlanders decides otherwise.

Westminster's patronising ethos is the United Kingdom contains all the qualities required to attain happiness, *ergo*, Scotland need only identify with those expectations, with England's best interests, values, culture. Their slogan is, colonial democracy is good for you. This might have an attraction were it not for adopting the ethics and motives of a dominant nation creates a faux, ersatz kind of domestic continuity. We are asked not to be overt Scots but rather imitation English, or at the very least, tenants of land that does not belong to us. We rent it via taxation. Worse, colonial rule *removes* responsibility from individuals. It stops the search for alternatives, for better societies and social structures. We become mere ciphers to the greater nation's goals, goals we don't share.

A nation in charge of its own destiny gives itself the chance to enact laws to govern behaviour that helps suppress our worst instincts, the venal and the avaricious and envy. It can construct a fairer distribution of goods and wealth than a bullying nation intent on keeping the best for itself. Colonial rule is a joyless creed. It survives by its tyranny. The natural inclination of any homogeneous society is to form and hold to its own ideals, to follow a moral language that is applicable to its people, to conduct itself by its own sense of values. Colonialism constricts joy and happiness.

The Scotland I want to see is a place where one individual cares about another as a natural state of affairs, where the individual develops unfettered and prospers, one's happiness bound up in the happiness of others. Happiness breeds objectivity. In a free society the spirit is alive, where work and play are joyous, a world in which we purge the ambition to dominate.

Let us work for a free Scotland. Let us join in the task and help the slow and the less able up that hill. In a shared pleasurable communal task there is a quiet, sure happiness that binds us together, with more joy to come when we attain the ideal. Our instinct is to construct; we are all reformers. When we are happy, we will, as a rule, adopt a happy creed. That's what independence means to me – the profound knowledge we are in the real stream of life pursuing happiness and hope for others and, by reward, for our self.

30

HARVESTING SCOTLAND

It is remarkable how land described as impoverished and infertile happens to hold vast riches for the few when it is freed of the many who thought it their own to till. The great myth of the Clearances is the one about landowners doing cotters, crofters, farmers and fishermen a favour by goading them into the modern age. 'Goading' is my term. They talk of *ushering*. The Clearances in the Highlands and the Lowlands saw progress, from a clan system to a civilised well organised society, opine hacks and apologists.

Read history books on Scotland's past and you will see references to 'modernising' a peasant society, the description accompanying photographs of abandoned villages in tourist journals, the smell of death and the excreta of brutal capitalist ideology conveniently scented. This is the justification for what amounts to theft by stealth and a disregard for human life akin to ethnic cleansing.

We are told had farmers and crofters not been forced off their small holdings many might have died of starvation. There is some truth in that, but self-serving truth from those who excuse barbarity and cruelty and call it progress. "We moved the gypsies on to better encampments" is one comparison, the Cherokee tribe were led to a reservation they could govern", is another racist solution to moving indigenous people off good land they lived on for generations, to bad land no one wants. The logic is obvious. Had Scots not been sent away to die on foreign battlefields for England's glory, or on over-stuffed immigration ships, or early deaths in Glasgow hovels, they would have died left on the land.

In reality, many European states and small provinces *existed as rural societies*, often relying on barter in order for people to gain the things they could not fashion or grow for themselves. In time, without any intrusion from another nation, they moved to a capitalist system of purchase while retaining farming or socialist system to feed the nation and share its wealth. The capitalist aspect allowed the governing body to buy and import food stocks, or indeed, sell surplus to a neighbouring nation. For those living off the land in Scotland, if the crop yield was low you could trade some of your cattle for grain to see you through the winter. What a cow was worth depended on the market value and the health of the beast. Cattle prices were not yours to control. If you had no cattle you could offer your labour, or borrow from a friendly neighbour, assuming they had surplus to give. And if you had nothing of value to trade you could subdivide your land and trade that.

Back in the 1830s and 40s I can see why landlords were at first against subdivision of small holdings. It may be trite, but it's reasonable to compare that transaction to renting an apartment which the tenant sub-lets without approval so he can subsidise his rent. Then again, proprietors were onto a good thing; the more subdivision that went on, the more labour you had at your disposal. Harvesting industries such as peat, wheat and kelp were labour intensive. That's how it must have seemed to land owners in Skye, Barra, and Loch Broom where kelping demanded a lot of labour, a strip of land and a but 'n' ben, the tied house in return for your work. However, this underhand policy has an accumulative counter effect which I'll come to shortly.

As a tenant your security was in permanent jeopardy. The more you gave away, the less you had to barter. No one paid you wages in money or grain. There were two bad harvests that most likely weakened the populace's resolve to withstand endless and sustained economic attacks from England. The English parliament exploited the situation. It needed to subdue Scotland to concentrate on war with France. In 1836 there was a similar fall in crop yield, potato and oats. The deficiency in crops was under half the expected yield. Now, this is where we have to remember Scotland was ruled from Westminster, and in *Victorian* times. England was the most powerful nation on Earth, unaccountably wealthy sucking millions of pounds from its colonial territories. Just like today, in almost every political issue you can think of, Scotland had too few MPs to win a vote that could direct finance to help Highland and Lowland crofters. The answer was to move people off the land into servitude in cities.

When English nationalists imply Scotland is ungrateful for their beneficence, we 'prospered' from the British Empire same as them, they omit detail. People can count; a tenth of MPs at Westminster does not constitute a balance of power. That the dice was loaded, and loaded still, is not a reason to dissolve the exploitative Union, argue British nationalists. This reasoning is a kind of madness, a dominant usurper not in the least caring his logic is dire.

The British parliament has a classic method of ameliorating public concern by doing nothing. It sets up a commission to 'look into the matter'. Westminster decided to show how much it 'cared' by sending an emissary to the western Highlands, Robert Grahame, an advocate of social medicine. Social medicine is distinct from the prescriptive service a general practitioner dispenses. It aims to assess a group's environmental circumstances, and any barriers to healthy living, by seeking out what is causing the hardship, suggesting ways to remodel habits. (There is a Robert Graham Policy Centre – spelled without the 'e' – near Chicago dedicated to this sort of study.)

Off went Grahame to the Highlands in carriage and on horseback to study the locals at close quarter and report back to the Treasury, facts and figures in a bound journal. According to records, he calculated there were just over 100,000 people subsisting in the worst poverty-stricken areas at risk of starvation. The Outer Hebrides and Skye were hit the worst, Ross-shire and Sutherland less so. Cottars (farm labourers) appeared to be the most vulnerable, but so too were many tenanting farmers.

What Grahame reported was something of a surprise. Though crop failure was a factor in the deprivation he encountered, the biggest agent of suffering and death was too many people sharing too small areas of arable land.

"*The population of this part of the country* [he meant Britain not Scotland] *has been allowed to increase in much greater ratio than the means of subsistence which it affords.*" [Note use of 'allowed'.]

The answer was simple. Move people off the land. The clan system had been attacked left right and centre by careful calculated English strategy and laws yet the majority of people held onto the land they and their forefathers had tilled rather than flee to the unknown. They were Gaels or Scots and had put their backs into it. Every rock moved to carve out a straight drill carried with it voices of their ancestor's toil. Life is precarious if you cannot save anything from your effort for bad times. There is nothing left to sell. Malnutrition stares you in the face. Lack of good nourishment sees rickets and scurvy. The Irish know how the rest of that story goes.

Outside charities, you were on your own. With starvation rife in the Highlands, the time it took to gather evidence and report back to London, left the destitute to suffer and die. It was stay, starve or emigrate. And if you were too underfed to work, the landlords would repossess your strip of ground and the house you lived in. The wealthiest nation in the world did not arrest the poverty of the Highlands, did not reverse its decline, but allowed its desecration; sharing the 'riches of the empire' was not parliamentary policy.

There is a silver lining to mass poverty – war, and that's exactly what England embarked upon for the next decade and more, strong men and boys rounded up, you might say 'harvested'. Highland soldiers the first to be sent into battle, Lowlanders to follow. There was an empire to subjugate. As a soldier you get to hold down a square meal if you manage to avoid a bayonet in the belly. Pick up that Union Jack, lad, your loyalty is to the English Crown.

With Scotland denuded of its men all but the old and infirm, the harvest of men folk dried up. After the Battle of Waterloo the remnants of Scottish regiments were stripped of their kilts and tartan badges because they could not be filled by true men of Scotland.

Meanwhile, back home, disaster capitalists were everywhere. Wife and children and the old were cleared off the land to make way for sheep, thousands of them, absent husbands unable to intervene. The protection of the clan system gone, families split up, told emigration was the way to prosperity, they were given a few bawbees and herded to the harbours to board the ships on which many never survived the journey to Canada, the Americas, Australia and New Zealand.

There is a fearful repetition to history when you're not in control of your own country.

31

SUZY WIGHTON

It's a measure of Suzy Wighton's modesty, of her steadfast commitment to her work first in Lebanon and then in the UK, and an avoidance of shallow celebrity, that I do not have a photograph of her. There are none I can find on the web. I used one from her book. *One Day at a Time* is part-diary, part a reflective account of her harrowing time as a nurse trapped in the clinic of a Lebanese refugee camp called Bourj al-Brajneh, in 1986. After it was over and she herself rescued, she was made a Member of the Order of the British Empire for services to the Palestinian people. For a short time she was a heroine to us all until the Tories kidnapped the ideological agenda, and Suzy slipped out of view.

You'd think every Scot knew of her. As well as the MBE, she was awarded the Star of Palestine, the UN Development Fund Woman of the Year, Scotswoman of the Year, and Nurse of the Year – perhaps that ought to be extended to As Long As She Likes.

The conflagration that is Lebanon is long forgotten in the miasma that is the Middle East Armageddon. Suzy was there when, compared to today's wildfire wars, it appeared an uncomplicated conflict, Jew versus Palestinian. Yasser Arafat was the Palestinian leader, idolised by his people. He tried hard to get a two-nation settlement as agreed by the United Nations, but there was always an objection to it by Israel, with the US acceding to Zionist Israeli's endless additional demands, particularly its appropriation of Palestinian land for Jewish settlements. On top of that there was an impotent UN constrained by vetoes from the big bully 'concerned' nations. Memories of that oppressed region fade as the next war monopolises media headlines, but Suzy's time there should not be expunged from the record.

I met a good humoured, fresh faced plump girl with blonde hair and an open smile. Behind the smile was a resolve of steel. Look closely and listen intently as I did, and there's something deeper – a sadness mixed with anger. When she returned home she came back to a disaster that was Thatcher and the Tories making. The Tories were attempting to privatise the NHS in England, and control the one in Scotland. Bean counters almost outnumbered nurses. "John Major and the Conservatives keep on telling us how there is more money than ever before going into the NHS but, if that's true, it's certainly not spent on looking after patients."

I recall my many conversations with her explaining the politics. She taught me a lot about what was happening, and who villains were, and who innocent casualties were. She had never lost her soft Edinburgh accent, nor showed any scars from her ordeal, not in public at least. And she was incredibly articulate.

Suzy is what we used to called a heroine. I think she'd dislike that term. She praises instead the medical staff around her, and the woman who life together. In fact, the only photograph of her in her book – reproduced here – is one with friends promoting the book when revisiting the camp; all the others are devoted to the people and the camp she found herself in. There she was surrounded by the people she saved from certain death by bomb, bullet or starvation, after all her medical colleagues had fled. There she remembered those she was unable to save.

I met Suzy after it was all over and her back safe in Scotland doing a brief round of radio interviews to promote her book, and draw attention to the plight of Palestine. She was studying for a Masters in Community Health at Liverpool School of Tropical Medicine which she obtained. I discussed the probability of turning her story into a cinema feature or dramatised documentary, but we both calculated the people who decide on such things, and who hold the purse strings, might not be well disposed to the Palestinian cause. My letters to BBC Scotland drama department were never answered. In one major Los Angeles talent agency, the bigwig literary agent turned the book over few times in his hands and handed it back to me with a wan smile, as if I'd given him sour milk to drink.

Thinking about the horrific experiences Suzy recounted, you realise nothing much has changed. Battles have turned into wars and invasions.

All the proselytising and all the pontificating of all the presidents and all the president's men since then failed to put Palestine together again. Indeed, the US, the most dogged in mouthing solutions whilst supporting Israel, remains the equivalent of the policeman who's not in the least impartial, yet insists on acting as referee in a dispute. Only one side trusts him, and it isn't the victim. The US is still sending billions of dollars of weapons to Israel to oppress the Palestinians, and help build Israel's Berlin wall.

Like all the individuals in the series of people who've impressed me or shaped my thinking, I cannot do justice to Suzy's experiences. I can only encapsulate them in a few hundred words. I offer a glimpse. For the real deal you should buy a copy of her book from Amazon. It's a hard read well written, but it will open your eyes to what goes on in God's own hell of the West's making.

Suzy was born in Edinburgh in 1959. In 1985, after completing a tropical nursing course, motivated by her earlier visits to occupied West Bank, Suzy found what she was looking for, an honourable cause for which she could use her medical skills. Ideals and training coalesced in the London office of Medical Aid for Palestinians. There she met Dr Swee Chai Ang, a surgeon who had survived the massacre of Sabra and Shatila. Dr Swee's commitment to the Palestinian cause, and her bravery along with that of Major Derek Cooper and his late wife Pamela, was inspirational to Suzy.

The Palestinian medical doctors and nurses in Beirut were being slaughtered in 1985 and 1986. They were dragged – along with their patients – from the hospital, which was on the edges of the Sabra and Shatila camps, and shot by militiamen. Health volunteers were required, and Suzy stepped forward, ending up in fated Bourj al-Barajneh camp in Beirut.

The Palestinian refugee population there had arrived from all over Palestine in 1948, mainly from the Galilee. They had left everything behind, locked their front doors, and moved over the border to wait for the fighting to end so they could return to their homes. When Suzy arrived none had managed to return to their homes all those decades before. Tents were replaced by corrugated tin shelters in which babies died sometimes of the heat and sometimes of the cold.

Six weeks after Suzy arrived, the war of the camps restarted, and she stayed for six months in the besieged camp. As the siege intensified the first to leave for safety were English doctors and surgeons. The pejorative term snowflake was not in fashion then. One day they were there, the next gone. They left death and destruction knowing it would never end.

The various factions fought on, Lebanese Forces, Amal, the Progressive Socialist Party, (PSP) and the communists. Getting food and medical supplies into the camp became a life and death act. Woman smuggled paper and torn bits of cardboard to Suzy for her diary of events, who needed what medical help, who died, and what was happening outside. In time food was so scare internees ate their pets and caught the rats. To get water women chanced the sniper's bullet dodging between collapsed buildings and debris strewn streets. Bodies were left to rot as a warning. Nobody dare collect them for burial.

A diary entry for two days before Christmas reads:

"Now the fuel is running out. There's supposed to be only enough to facilitate one operation of six hours duration. The internal squabbling and unwillingness to the hospital is leaving the only solution that each organisation pays for its fighter's operations in fuel."

Another entry reads:

"A young man, Bilal Shabati, hit by a large piece of shrapnel which fractured his spine. He was intubated and appeared to breathe spontaneously, but as soon as the tube was removed he started gasping and making tremendous efforts to breathe. We cannot evacuate him. He needs a respirator. The decision was taken to allow him to die. There is no morphine. He took a long time to do die."

And so it goes on, children and young adults, brought in for emergency aid on makeshift stretchers, limbs barely attached, leave Suzy and her nursing colleagues to administer heroic care until death is the permanent peace. A heartfelt diary entry reads:

"Dreamt last night I was not cut off from the world, and that many letters were given to me from Mum, Dad, and Poshie, and Ghillie, and Stewart – missing them all. A lovely old lady, Wafiqa's grandmother, asked where they all were today, and expressed concern at my being alone in a strange place with a war."

When Suzy was enjoying a return to mental and physical health here in her capital city Tony Blair took over the British Empire with a landslide victory. Then one day he backed George W Bush Junior on a pre-planned policy to invade Iraq with the public intention of shipping American style democracy to the Middle East, but in private, a long held doctrine of taming the entire region, Libya too. Suzy was outraged.

"I accepted my MBE on behalf of all my unsung Palestinian and Lebanese colleagues and comrades. I have now returned it, also in their name. It is an utter disgrace that the British prime minister refused to press for a ceasefire, remained on holiday while these war crimes were being carried out and that parliament has not been recalled. It is a disgrace that the US ambassador to the UN described a call for a three-day truce to assist in humanitarian relief and evacuation of the wounded as 'unhelpful'. It is a disgrace that this government ignored the concerns of the electorate and all other forms of lawful protest. I

have therefore come to the conclusion that to continue to hold on to my MBE, for which I was nominated by the parliamentary Labour Party, is also a disgrace. I have returned my MBE to St James Palace, with regret, in protest at the government's complicity in the prosecution of illegal wars and occupations. And I am returning it, above all, in the hope that this small gesture will add to the swell of support for action for the people of Lebanon and Palestine and to those who wish to see peace in Israel and other nations."

The last I heard of Suzy Wighton she was living in the bonnie village of Comrie, Perthshire, with her daughter. She doesn't work for the NHS anymore. If she ever reads this I hope I've honoured her memory, and that she knows an independent Scotland will not forget its outstanding citizens even if the UK does. Her bravery and that of her co-nurses was exemplary. I am proud to be her friend.

32

THINGS WE SHOULD NOT TALK OF

The Great Debate on freedom of choice that preceded the independence referendum of September 2014 was a tremendously liberating experience. Exhilarating is a better description. It lifted spirits and filled homes, pubs and streets with excited chatter about a new Scotland. It was the first time in anybody's memory we had *open* speech, not merely narrow 'free' speech.

It must have come as a surprise to many Scots *and* English too that Scotland had been an independent nation for centuries, and is a wealthy country now despite the lies of its tormentors. And boy did the enemies of liberty react badly. They've taken to calling a time of mass camaraderie, optimism and hope 'divisive'. Somebody was putting ideas of freedom into the heads of the natives. So speaks the colonial.

The situation made me to think about my state school education in the city that likes to call itself international but votes for English hegemony. Looking back on what I was taught of relevance to the world outside Britain disinters what was kept from sight.

We were steeped in Shakespeare, Wordsworth, Keats, Shelly, and Byron, Dickens too, more Shakespeare, and Jane Austen. Samuel Taylor Coleridge's *The Ancient Mariner* was thrown in for good measure. The absence of Scots poets was shocking: Hugh MacDiarmid, Edwin Morgan, Norman McCaig, Sorley MacLean.

Burns was evident. You can hardly hide a man the world quotes on a regular basis. I remember readings of Tam O'Shanter presented as a ghost story. Nobody told me about Burn's politics. Burns was presented in acceptable unionist form, a formulaic evening of bagpipes and haggis, toasts to the lassies, and then forgetting what he stood for the rest of the year.

I hailed from a low-income home, coats for blankets, cheap cuts of meat, white sliced bread, my mother unable to work, my father taken from her and another substituted, both poor as the fleas on church mice. Like thousands of other underprivileged kids I was singled out for an apprenticeship in woodwork or metalwork, or maybe sorting parcels in the head Post Office. I liked art and could read books without illustrations in them. Consequently, I was marked down as 'bright and creative', a boy with the gift of the gab, qualities considered of little value to society. "The boy has an imagination that should be curbed" ran a comment on a school report.

I can't remember any classes discussing RL Stevenson's novels but I found copies in a bookshop and read them there courtesy of the kind shop owner. I joined a library. My Irish grandfather was a literate man. When I marvelled at Disney's film of *20,000 Leagues Under the Seas*, (*Vingt mille lieues sous les mers*), it was grandfather who told me who the writer was, Jules Verne, and how far ahead he was in his time. Television gave us the works of the second-rate Thomas Hardy as if idealised English rural life was a dream shared by Scots. His novellas were dramatised for television, thatched cottages, twee cottage gardens, woven baskets of handpicked herbs, and white picket fences sold as an idyllic British life, but nothing of hard grafting gardeners having a steamy affair with the lady of the manor. *Lady Chatterley's Lover* was left to D.H. Lawrence and Penguin paperbacks, the novel wrapped in a plain brown paper cover.

The scathing critical satire of Lytton Strachey writing of flawed Victorian heroes was never mentioned, no essays taking apart the avarice and buttoned-up nature of Queen Victoria and Florence Nightingale, both delivered to young impressionable Scots as saintly.

The Bloomsbury set was waved in our faces by the British media as a confluence of outstanding talents to which only the English can give birth. The weirdly witch-like figure of poet and critic Dame Edith Sitwell was thrown in for good measure. Who could live with such a woman, I thought, as I watched her pose, fingers dripping in heavy rings, hair pull tight at the scalp and then released like a bursting bomb, dressed all in black, an elderly Goth before her time, all to answer questions on writers she knew. Oh how the BBC loves eccentrics but not the Scottish nationalist type.

Discussing the work of contemporary Scots poets meeting in an Edinburgh spit and sawdust pub was unthinkable. Edwin Morgan, William Edminstone, Norman MacCaig did not exist, though MacCaig lived up the road from where I first lived in Fountainbridge. The school I attended was busy lining us up in twos in the playground each morning and marched us in to the stirring patriotic theme from the British film of *The Dam Busters*. There was not a sausage about any of the great Irish writers, Joyce, O'Casey, O'Brien. Beckett was never mentioned, but Jonathan Swift was because he was the author of Gulliver's Travels, considered a children's story and anyhow, Swift was Anglo-Irish. We were told about Oscar Wilde. He had written one of the most popular English of English plays, *The Importance of Being Earnest*. No one seemed to know it was a satire on English mores. I discovered the republican Brendan Behan myself.

European authors didn't exist. The riches of Proust, Zola, Victor Hugo, and Sartre were yet to be discovered. I found them in bookshops, and soon was acquainted with American authors by adaptations of their novels for films. Wole Soyinka had no place in my school learning, or the struggles of other African writers. I came to know the powerful anti-apartheid message of Athol Fugard by his plays.

War poets Sassoon and Owen were chief among the standard bearers of England's sacrifices. There was always a corner of a far away field forever England, never Scotland, or the British isles. I read of the meeting between Wilfred Owen and Siegfried Sassoon in Edinburgh; two poets whose lives momentarily entwined in 1917 in Craiglockhart's military hospital, there to convalesce. Both were celebrated for their anniversary year in a series of special events in Edinburgh organised by none other than the Scottish Poetry Library, there being no Scots poets to include of any status of that vintage, apparently.

In my school days we didn't read Blake but we sang *Jerusalem* in Friday service. Samuel Taylor Coleridge's *Ancient Mariner* was an annual event almost as much as Burns night, but no one told me he was zonked on laudanum and probably opium when he wrote his naval narrative ballad. What I learned of the outside world beyond the Saxon shores of street party England I got from television through the prism of the BBC. There was a British Commonwealth out there, full of happy carefree Jamaicans, and an Australia open to economic migrants.

No matter what was happening in the world it took second place to each and every Royal event commentated upon in reverential tones by Sir Richard Dimbleby, progenitor of an Etonian broadcasting dynasty. When he was not available the imperious Scots actor Tom Fleming took over, rewarded with a knighthood presumably for services to British propaganda. In cinemas you were expected to watch Pathé News narrated by Bob Danvers-Walker, and at the end of the main film remain standing when *God Save the Queen*, was played over the tannoy system, allegedly a national anthem but not of Scotland. As the years wore on cinema-goers ignored the dirge and left. It took a lot of courage to push your way out of a line of seats while others stood to ram-rod attention or searched for a lost umbrella or purse.

What strict attention to the traditions of England's literature and film heritage does is remove resistance to British rule. George Orwell states in a letter how easy it is to suppress free thought in his England. He wrote that although England is "relatively free", unpopular ideas can be suppressed without the use of force. "English education instils that there are certain things it simply wouldn't do to speak about."

Control of our educational syllabus is only one method of containment and influence. Control of the media is another. Advertising slogans and images – Union Jacks replacing Saltires on buildings and Scottish produce – remind us we must not only do as colonials do, we must think like them.

The cries of protest when the Scottish National Party asked for greater teaching of Scottish history and literature in schools was a warning from a unionist mindset not to meddle in the source of their influence. For those who know an independent country is a confident country, knowledge of your own land and people severs ties to your oppressor. Shuttered windows to the world are opened wide.

Scotland's quest for relevance isn't a call for English-style isolationism but rather the recognition national liberation is *the very core* of internationalism. Continuation of the neo-colonial state is the negation of progress. Forced into being second-rate isn't modesty. A free Scotland liberates our national wealth, resources, and the entire productive forces of Scotland; it takes us into the 21st century, the modern world, whereas the British establishment want us to remain locked in the 19th century, paralysed, an immobility that keeps Scotland at the service of the British state. Then we are berated for retaining the mentality of last century, and not appreciating the benefits of English xenophobia.

Whatever I was taught was taught in the name of British patriotism, sold as if Britain was one country called England. I accept there existed exceptions to intellectual imperialism. The lucky ones attended state schools of a higher standard where teachers were better informed, freer to speak their mind. Those teachers should be regarded as the best type of anarchist, educational revolutionaries. The unlucky ones attended private schools where the teaching of Scottish history was banned. How important to stay alert to class ideological assumptions of what is healthy and what is bad for children to learn.

Critics of free choice don't have a problem with the drivel of unionist politicians. Nor do they see anything wrong in the emptiness of Tory parliamentarians telling the Scottish people to reign in ambition. We should stick to being shop assistants, or beating heather to scatter grouse for the laird's income. After all, in Tory eyes Scotland is the crap end of North Britain. Who are we to question the status quo? When I look at what is happening now, for the life of me I can't think what has altered in colonial coercion these last decades.

Yes, there are things we really shouldn't speak of.

33

POSTCARDS OF WISDOM

Essays take a lot of time and thought. Some flow like honey over bread, urged on by some unseen hand motivated by a political ideal that has to be expressed. Memorable phrases appear fully formed. I have no idea why or how, they just do. Others require a ton of scholarly research from which I can eke out a gem. Now and again, epigrams and a bon mot or two materialise unsolicited. Proverbs sound teacherish, pretentious. I try to avoid them.

My one-liners are a subconscious manifestation issuing from my beloved guardian. Her name was Honora Emmula Louise, Edwardian nomenclature of another time. She died when I was eighteen. I was there at her moment of passing. The vision affects me to this day. She wrote sayings in a wee red note book, knowledge stored, sayings of sages she picked up on her travels, Chinese proverbs, a Shakespearian quotation, or something a friend said *en passant*. "You can't fasten a door tightly enough to keep out trouble" was one I remember. "Best not be disturbed at being mis-understood; be disturbed rather at not being understanding", was another. I liked, "A red-nosed man may be a teetotaller but no one will believe him."

Like an artist with a book of sketches, studies to develop into paintings or prints, a few epigrams inspire an essay, the core of an idea; others become a paragraph in an essay, a number are leaden and junked. Most remain philosophy in miniature, an aphorism. I hope they are passed easily one person to another, *a postcard of wisdom*.

Here is a small selection:

There is a major difference between the Scot and the Irish. The Irish are prepared to die for their country. The Scot dies for other people's countries.

I have a maxim I try to live by religiously: never write anything about a person things you would not say to their face. Thus, I always begin with a warm compliment before going straight for the jugular.

Personalities and fame pass; a mass movement intent on a nation's liberty may pause for a while, but momentum is always inexorably forward, pushed onward by people who seek natural justice. Revolutions are unstoppable.

The colonial is incapable of understanding why the country he has invaded wants rid of him. The brutalities, the cruelties, the authoritarian rule, the theft of wealth, are justified to help make the country a better, more Christian place.

When a unionist boasts of how much Scots benefitted from the British Empire, remind them of the slum tenements in Glasgow, and how 'all the empire's riches' were never used to reverse the plunder and desecration of the Highlands.

When a group or an individual advises you to look away from wrong doing in order to 'keep your eye on the prize', they are asking you to swallow your critical faculties and your conscience. You must ask yourself if you can live with the immorality of the act.

When you speak truth to power, expect retribution. It will arrive sooner or later if you dare stand up to authority. The first words you will hear are liable to be, "What is *your* name?"

Apologies Defined: "I did the thing. I am sorry" – is an apology. "I am sorry you're offended" – is *not* an apology. "I am sorry you feel hurt" – is *not* an apology. "I will do better" – is *not* an apology. "I did it because..." – *is not even close to an apology*!

Intelligence is not the same as rationality. For the latter you need an open mind free of leaden prejudices. This in turn relies on a well-adjusted personality. Hence, a person considered a clever academic might be someone who votes for the Tory party.

A 300 year old Treaty, severely deficient when signed, its conditions are bound to gather more and more breaches as years and decades go by, controls and constraints out-dated, dropped or forgotten, until it reaches the point when all meaning is lost.

No nation in history has invaded another and held it fast in colonial servitude as an act of philanthropic kindness, or to help the indigenous population prosper. The invader is there to plunder resources and taxes for as long as profitable.

Scots are so inured; numb to decades of Anglophiles and colonial English belittling them with insult and scorn, we do not perceive the abuse as racism, but that is what it is – racist.

When I use the word 'liberty' I use it in its oldest form; the absence of alien domination. The Tory party would have us believe it means little more than obeying the police.

We like to think we live in a tolerant society. Look how easily in Scotland some feel able to persecute men and women of ability. We know about Socrates, Joan of Arc and Thomas Paine, yet the same happens to individuals here once regarded as unusually admirable.

What is new in my time is the increased power of the authorities to impose their prejudices. In that I include the SNP. The police, while their job is to solve everyday crime, are just as apt to suppress our civil rights. Those developments must be resisted.

By a natural authority, some men, and women too, are able to restore calm and dignity to a troubled nation, guiding our energy to seek the greater good, a strong, steadying presence whose skill lies in the old-fashioned virtue of quiet competence.

Modern industry has made our lives easier in many ways. But we need elected governments to control the excesses of capitalism. Why praise mass manufacturing of tweed while putting out of work the tradition of hand-weavers of the Highlands and Hebrides?

When the journey from means to desired end is not too long the means are enjoyed. Watch happy children drag sledges up snow slopes to the top for a few moments joy on the way down. No one forces them to do it. There lies the essence of the human spirit, overcoming obstacles for an ideal.

We elect representatives, not kings or queens. I am not building a pharaoh's pyramid, doing as told fearing the lash of a team supervisor; I am building a new society to free the slaves.

A Scotsman's worst enemy is not an Englishman, but another Scotsman who prefers to spend his life as a facsimile of an Englishman.

Life is short; better to tell someone they made you better than you are, and to tell them while they are alive than wait to express it at their funeral.

Never speak in a forthright manner to governance – you might upset a politician ill-acquainted with honesty.

My English tutor believed there existed 'fine' writing. Ask and one finds hardly anyone knows what good prose is and what bad prose is.

Those in power attack fluency. They wish the conventionally-minded to think elegance and precision anarchic and undemocratic.

The French have a phrase: 'l'*esprit de l'escalier*', which means, literally, 'the wit of the staircase'. It refers to all those marvellous things you did not say at the society gathering which occur to you as you descend the staircase on the way home.

Women were once the possession of their father and then the possession of their husband. They fought to be free citizens, individuals. Now weak men are given carte blanche to be a woman and so feel stronger in a female society and not a failure among men.

Asked if I hate the English I reply, no, I envy the English. I envy England because it has a voice in the world and a seat at the United Nations. Scotland has neither. What I dislike is our voice and rights actively suppressed by England.

What makes an outstanding person? I cannot be over-weaning self-confidence. I think the rebel in us, issues from persecution. Thinking of men and women who sacrificed their time and energy to gain justice, they are usually spurred on by personal jeopardy.

We like to advance the principle that a fundamental right of a democracy is freedom of expression, but in reality it comes with responsibilities. We are free to buy a hammer, but we are not free to use it to smash the windows of someone we dislike.

When life is between Nazis and non-Nazis, declaring oneself resolutely 'impartial' or 'neutral' is not smart nor a civilised attitude. You are allowing evil to grow. In time you will become a casualty of it, or forced to join it as a means of self-preservation.

It's remarkable how politicians discover God soon after elected to high office. Non-believers or agnostic previously, they feel compelled to walk to church with their wife on Sundays and chat with the minister after the service, making sure they are photographed doing it.

Scots must be alone in the world of nations taught we produce great thinkers, scientists, engineers, medical men, explorers and adventurers, in fact, we helped create the British Empire, and yet we are told we are singularly unqualified to run our own country.

For the most part, history will judge England's colonial rule of Scotland a disaster. This is because history is written by middle-class liberal English who would not know where Achiltibuie is, and assume the Highland Clearances is a sale at the House of Bruar.

The colonised subject, known in Scotland as a 'House Jock', finds it nearly impossible to accept their mind is colonised. They think they are making free will choices. Some want to sit at the coloniser's table, to be a 'winner'. This is how they are educated to think.

It does not matter that you cannot speak Gaelic, or your mither tongue was educated out of you leaving you with a few dialect words and phrases. What matters above all else is that you *think* like a Scot and not like a colonial Englishman.

Each time I convince one person to see the blazing light in independence restored I count that as a tiny revolution.

A unionist will explore every avenue and every alternative until only common sense is left.

Better a friendly Scotland self-reliant than an angry one coerced.

No nation ever rose up to demand its abolition.

Tonight, at the chimes of midnight, I danced a spirited step to a Celtic drum beat, fiddle and pipes, my heart beat faster, carefree and exhilarated. I danced as if my mortality was so distant I had life in abundance. For a few minutes I was liberated.

34

DO NOT COME TO SCOTLAND

Don't come to Scotland because England isn't to your liking anymore. You once ruled almost all of the green earth, and the seas too. Your nation grew rich on the resources of other nations, and off the backs of indigenous people that you ruled. You told those people they were British. But you didn't mean British like you, that is, English. Now riddled with vast debts and a corrupt parliament, your first obligation is to make your own nation a better place, to rid it of the unreason England has embraced. Granted, it is a difficult task, but not impossible. Youth will drive change if you cannot. They will rebel if you have not the energy.

Don't come to Scotland thinking no world is better than an English world. If you think England the greatest nation on the planet, that's where you belong. Don't search for a Little England enclave where you can play cricket on the green, read the Times in an all-English pub decorated with Union Jacks, and talk warmly of Thatcher, Brexit or Empire. We want none here.

Don't come to Scotland looking for an idyllic cottage in the Highlands to closet yourself away from life, or pretend you are English landed gentry, all tweeds and Barber outfits. It does nothing for Scotland's democratic progress. Incidentally, *loch* is not pronounced 'lock'. Try and get it right. And we have burns here not brooks, and glens not dales. We have our own language, two when you count Gaelic.

Don't come to Scotland to promote English cultural mores. That's patronising. We need no colonials. Come to learn about Scotland's history and culture, to get involved in it, Gaeldom too. Scots admire, indeed were educated on English culture and heroes. Please return the compliment.

Don't come to Scotland hoping to mould our structures and institutions in the image of England. That way lays conformity and resentment. We've managed, just about, to resist invasion by genocide and now by stealth and yet still be a separate country. You're here because you acknowledge we are different.

Don't come to Scotland thinking you must become Scottish. We don't ask that of you. In time your children will be, and their children too. Be yourself, but remember you're in another country. Treat us as you would wish to be treated. Delight in the differences.

Don't come to Scotland hoping to avoid Italian, Polish, Chinese, Indian, or Irish communities. They've been here for generations, Polish as early as 1850. Bonnie Prince Charlie's mother was Polish. Those people have contributed to Scotland's intellectual thought and economy in ways we can never fully repay. We have an international outlook and proud of it.

Don't come to Scotland thinking the standards of southern England are the standards by which all things must be judged. That really gets up our nose. London-centric is for Londoners, or wealthy Saudi Arabians and Russians buying gazillion pound properties with massive tax and rates exemptions.

Don't come to Scotland and treat it as a dominion of England's aristocracy. Dukes and lairds are not to be envied. The duke's great grandfather probably got a chunk of Scotland over a game of cards, 'validated' by fake property deeds written by an alcoholic lawyer. We detest the English class system and all its stands for.

Don't come to Scotland to use its great glens and mountains as a play park for hunting, shooting, fishing and climbing while littering the place with garbage. Don't clog our roads with caravans and our mountains with old trainers and plastic bags and bottles.

Don't come to Scotland to buy Highland property to make a quick killing and go south again. And don't buy land and fence it off. Everywhere is a right of way except your home. Ultimately, we want the land back in the ownership of the state – us.

Don't come to Scotland to tell us self-governance is a risky business. Scotland wants *inter*-dependence with England to continue, but on a healthier basis, on *equal* terms.

Come to Scotland ready and willing to help build a happy, thriving, exalted society that will endure, one in which challenging authority is not considered subversive. Scots see themselves first as a human being, then a Scot, and a citizen of the world. Know the grass roots momentum that is termed 'Scottish nationalism' expresses those humane values – together with small nation pride. Come prepared to elevate what is good in human nature. Exercise an open mind; be curious and wise, able to contribute to our society in joyous, positive ways. Jettison the habit of comparison. Suppress envy, and train anger to right injustice, not to demoralise others. Be compassionate, good humoured, happy to be part of a new era in civic camaraderie and open government. Let your affection have free play. Come to Scotland released from fear; celebrate the vigour of our Enlightenment.

35

OUTLAW KING

Outlaw King teaches us Scotland, one of the world's oldest nation states with hundreds of years of history, has been harassed and plundered by an aggressive neighbour and remains shackled to it, desperate to regain liberty. It reminds us of the sacrifices our fore-fathers made to keep Scotland a free country. It reminds us that a handful of weak earls sold a nation into servitude, not because Scotland was a poor place, but because the earl's had made bad investments, desperate to take English bribe money to sign a treaty. England was, and still is, an imperialist nation. Imperialism is trans-national nationalism, an aggressive, violent form of nationalism. Scottish nationalism is an expression of national consciousness, a protective pride of place and culture. Scotland has no wish to rule another country either by force or financial inducement. England once ruled the globe. *Outlaw King* encapsulates those ethics and ideology.

This exciting film is a Brueghel canvas; so many interesting things happening at once for the eye to take in you hardly know what to concentrate upon. One unexpected and gratifying surprise, I was proud to see so many of my graduates from Scotland's Youth Theatre in major roles, the company I founded and ran as artistic director. One of the earliest, Tam Dean Burns, I auditioned. He was a tall, gangling, eccentric figure with a marvellous face. I asked him why he wanted to join a theatre company. His answer was swift and to the point, "Ah'm an accountant. I dinnae want tae dae it aw' ma life". He plays a villain in *Outlaw*.

A depressing number of English critics gave the film a few stars and glossed over the history it rakes over because they know so little of Scotland, and the few who have rubbished the work as worthy, plodding, fit "only for nationalists". The colonial mentality lives on. Let the bigots eat dirt. This is a gloriously energetic and intelligent epic, gripping from start to finish. And it has the wonderful, spirit-raising dividend of Highland panoramic images, a host of them adding a rich backdrop to the drama of the story.

When the film was premiered in the Toronto Film Festival it was 20 minutes longer – three hours – the first section of a movie being where you lay out the back-story of the main characters. The current release has severed – the correct word for a film oozing in blood and gore – a lot of exposition, verbal and visual, in some cases leaving a vacuum of character detail on combatants pre-eminent in the history of a nation's defiance. A few minor roles are left high and dry, at least to the practiced eye.

David Mackenzie is emerging as a highly skilled director; co-founder of the Glasgow based Sigma Films. *Outlaw King* cements his reputation beyond his superb Texas cops and robbers *Hell or High Water*. The last film he made set in Scotland was in 2003, *Young Adam*, a sombre adaptation of the novel set in 1950s Glasgow. Tackling Robert the Bruce's disasters and triumphs, one of Scotland's most revered heroes, is courageous, all the more so since Mackenzie follows the Oscar winning *Braveheart* with its similar theme of Scotland's bloody struggles to retain its nationhood against the belligerence of a mighty neighbour state.

The film begins with a statement, 'Based on the life of Robert the Bruce', a gentle reminder to the philistine and Union Jack waving Anglophile that creative licence is the very stuff of drama. *Outlaw King* begins where *Braveheart* left off, with an uncertain Bruce (Chris Pine) pledging allegiance to Edward I (Stephen Dillane) knowing his father (James Cosmo) would not trust the English Crown as far

as he could kick it into the Clyde. Then again, Edward has promised to give back seized lands to Scotland's nobility in return for
homage. Equated with modern Scotland we see token powers given
back to Scotland in the infamous 'Vow' so long as the union is
respected, that is, Scotland defers to England in all things. Think on
it, why would you be thankful if a thief demanded all you earned
in return for handing back some property they stole? Was co-writer
Mackenzie conscious of these parallels?

Bruce is needled into a sword bash with the spoiled Prince of
Wales, (Billy Howle) a well educated dolt, the precursor to every
Etonian toff ever. What follows is a scene of medieval laddism, the
equivalent of who can piss highest up a tent pole. Bruce is mature
beyond his years and doesn't let himself be ensnared by junior
rivalry. He beats the gauche prince, easily. England's anxiety-prone
royal sports the worst pudding bowl haircut in the whole of merry
England, a copy of Lawrence Olivier's in the 1944 propaganda
version of *Henry V*. The effete prince is no fighting match for a
swarthy posh Scot, one of two potential contenders for Scotland's
crown, a man who eats thistles for salads. After leaving the prince
humiliated in the mud, Bruce strides back into Edward's tent to be
given the hand in marriage of Edward's goddaughter, Elizabeth de
Burgh, (Florence Pugh) the daughter of one of the most powerful
Irish nobles around, the Earl of Ulster.

The betrothal is the seal on a permanent truce, Scotland with
England. Throughout all this Bruce remains decidedly phlegmatic,
a man of few words. This is a leader of men who doesn't need to
say very much to make his feelings known. From there it's back
outside the Royal tent once more. Pulling back, Mackenzie reveals
a gigantic catapult – Edward's latest war toy – and has him cut its
rope, swinging a massive flaming projectile straight at us, we recoil,
before it cuts through the air in the opposite direction exploding
on the ramparts of a distant castle, but Scotland's future king is
unimpressed with Edward's bravura.

Before continuing this critique I must add that this entire opening sequence is filmed in a single take, the conceit of ambitious

directors since Orson Welles first managed the feat of perfect timing for the opening of his classic 1958 noir, *Touch of Evil*. The technique is easier to achieve these days – hand-held cameras are as light as a bag of crisps. One requires only actors who won't muff their lines and be on their mark at a precise moment in time.

With his second wife, Elizabeth, now looking after the child of his dead first wife, Bruce begins an uneventful life as a jobbing earl with estates to look after. Two events turn his and Scotland's future upside down. On a day in town he comes upon an angry rioting mob braying for blood at the capture and killing of William Wallace, sentenced hung drawn and quartered by Edward, though Wallace carried a letter of Royal protection when arrested on his way to negotiations in London. Bruce is shocked to see the severed arm and shoulder of Wallace strung up on the town's Mercat Cross, a warning to enemies of England's power.

The crass and criminal act echoes David Cameron's overweening bumptiousness when in September 2014 he strode balls high to a Downing Street microphone and announced the parliament of the United Kingdom was dropping pretence of being a four nation's assembly. He told us it was England's Parliament, so suck it up. Alas, Scotland lost the vote to reinstate its independence; see how weakness is punished.

Bruce's second error is the killing of a rival. He knives his opponent for the Scottish Crown, Sir John III Comyn, Lord of Badenoch, (Callan Mulvey) in Greyfriars Kirk, Dumfries. He had met him to seek support for a campaign of insurrection but was refused. History is unsure exactly what happened in the kirk. It is said the long-time enemies had a fight; Bruce only wounded 'Red' Comyn in the shoulder in a fit of pique. Ooutside, Bruce's his friend, Roger de Kirkpatrick is reputed to have said 'You doubt. Ise mac siccar' (I'll make sure), and finished the job with a thrust of his sword. Bruce as sole killer is acceptable – it tells us he's capable of homicidal violence.

Expecting retribution from fellow Scots and English soldiers, Bruce gathers his resolve to free his land of foreign power. He assembles clan support to help rid Scotland of English garrisons and plundered land but is caught unawares while camping with his men late at night. After the defeat at the Battle of Methven on 19 June 1306, Bruce, now crowned King of Scotland with the blessing of the Church, sends Elizabeth, his nine year-old daughter Marjorie (Josie O'Brien) by his first marriage, and sisters Mary and Christina to Kildrummy Castle, under the protection of his brother Niall. The English lay siege to the castle containing the royal party. (In reality, the siege succeeded when the English bribed a blacksmith with "all the gold he could carry" to set fire to the corn store.) The victors hang, draw and quarter Niall Bruce, along with all the men from the castle. However, under the escort of the Earl of Atholl the women flee. They are taken from the sanctuary of St. Duthac at Tain by the Earl of Ross, a supporter of the Comyns, and dispatched to King Edward. He imprisons Bruce's sister Mary and Isabella MacDuff, Countess of Buchan, in wooden cages erected on the walls of Roxburgh and Berwick castles respectively, and then sends Bruce's daughter Marjorie to the nunnery at Watton. Hamlet would have approved.

Elizabeth is held under poor conditions of house arrest in England for eight years, released after the battle of Bannockburn is won. The Earl of Atholl was hanged and his head displayed on London Bridge, English justice and hospitality then, character assassination and tabloid denunciation nowadays. From here on war between Scotland and England is assured and Bruce runs from one hiding place to another as English chase him down and Scottish clans betray his whereabouts.

Chased from mountain to glen, from forest to island, these sequences give cinema-goers around the world satisfying confirmation that Scotland is a country of unparalleled topographical grandeur, blessed with a unique light. Scene after scene makes you proud to live in a land of plenty though scarred by invasions and treachery. Verdant braes and crag and scree lie under dramatic skies. All this and boats on crystal lochs are captured in the sensitive lens of cinematographer Barry Ackroyd and his Second Unit.

Credit is also due to the crew who moved actors, extras and equipment from one mountainous location to the next. Almost every castle that can be reached is used to its full extend, including Blackness Castle, home to many a film shoot, Mel Gibson's Hamlet one example. Mackenzie has the luxury of a big budget that allows him to reach places normally out of geographical bounds.

Chris Pine gives us a Bruce who is made of Scots pine, he stands tall, hard, tough, and a great place to shelter when the storm is raging. His large forehead is perfect to get bespattered with mud and blood. His Bruce is a thinker. There are key moments where we know he has come to a profound decision conveyed by a slight shift in his gaze. Bruce is a tactician who learned his trade from the hit and run tactics of the guerrilla, and step by step brought them together in arguably Scotland's greatest victory over England's power, at Bannockburn. Pine carries just enough authority and a decent Scots accent – not localised in any way – to grow into the role of the King of Scots. Is there a Scottish actor who could have taken on the role? Most certainly, but not sufficiently popular to secure a Netflix budget, another downside of being a colonised country where one's culture is sidelined, our thespians lacking experience of film work.

There are too many supporting cast to single out them all, suffice to say Stephen Dillane is plausible as a workaday world weary Edward I, free of the mannered eccentricities of Patrick McGoohan's version in *Braveheart*. Each and everyone give fully rounded characterizations; all seem able to ride a horse well and wield a broadsword or swing a sharp-pointed stave. In fact, there's not a weak link in the chain, not even a glaiket extra staring at the camera as it passes him, or wearing a watch. By all accounts the shoot was a happy affair and it shows in the cohesion of ensemble acting. I can add that it was good to see James Cosmo move from his role in *Braveheart* to Bruce's father in *Outlaw King*. Not once did I feel he was selling me a bank account, his pension earner from a number of television commercials selling the Bank of Scotland. He has had a good career ever since he starred in my production of *Brond*, a contemporary political thriller set in Glasgow.

Had she been given more scenes, Pine would have been matched in acting chops by Florence Pugh as Elizabeth his wife. Pugh (why no poetic surname?), has only one scene in which she asserts her personality over male misogyny. After that she is the harassed wife, the fate of acting in male scripted films. That said, very little is known of Elizabeth. She was imprisoned for much of the time Bruce was baiting English regiments, so Mackenzie can't be blamed for the brief chances we get to see this fine actress grace the screen.

The final battle is not Bannockburn, but the last in Bruce's hit and run guerrilla campaign, a modest battle by Bruce's standards, at Loudoun Hill in Ayrshire in 1307. Violent and blood curdling it surpasses the tense, doom-laden opening sequence in Ridley Scott's *Gladiator*. It was a battle reminiscent of Stirling Bridge, boggy ground opened up and spiked to filter English horsemen into a narrow pass, a line of soldiers easy to pick off. You hold your breath as you witness the carnage. As victory becomes clear, Bruce shows his magnanimity as a general. He is no Butcher Cumberland, murderous aristocrat of Culloden. Wounded English are allowed to go home.

I *did* miss Bannockburn, a twinge of regret we could not see how Bruce pulled together everything he had learned to show his war craft in full glory against the most powerful army of his time. His greatest weapon was his intimate knowledge of the Scottish countryside, which he used to his advantage. Perhaps that is for another film, the planning of it, the battle itself, and the aftermath. To be appreciated, hats are doffed for the stunt men and the horses in particular. Horses pack almost every scene in the film, a major organisation in itself. Cinema is always the better off for the muscular magnificent steeds.

Jane Petrie deserves an Oscar for her costume design. I found myself inspecting boots for rubber soles and things as small as the stitching on a battle dress for any sign of a sewing machine. Extras are suitably grimy, as if they'd lived in a Scottish croft village all their life.

Of weaknesses, there are a few. A candlelit soft porn scene between Bruce and Elizabeth supposedly to tell us their marriage is consummated; a few too many characters too swiftly introduced and then given too little to say, sacrificed for pace of storytelling. And there is a truly cringe-worthy long distance shot on a sandy beach straight out of Hollywood's *Ten Worst Hackneyed Images*. Sad to report, Jim Sutherland's music does not quite grab the emotions. Mackenzie gives us a thoroughly modern costume drama; Sutherland gives us an old fashioned score without a melody to take away, a disappointment.

Patrons in the packed cinema I attended in Edinburgh stood to their feet and cheered. How odd to see that reaction in the capital city that voted 'No' to reinstating Scotland's self-governance. Far too many critics awarded *Outlaw King* a grudging three star acceptance. Those reviewers are brain dead or envious. *Five* stars. No doubt about it.

36

THE SCOTTISH HEALTH SERVICE

I could begin and end with the statement that the Scottish Health Service is second to none and not bother to fill in the middle because that's the flat-out truth. There are other nations, such as Thailand, where the health service is of a high standard too, but though massively overtaxed by England, Scotland has a free health service to all intent and purpose. England is well on its way to a pay now or poor house service. Yes, children in England play 'Doctors' same as children in Scotland, only the rules are different. One says 'you operate and I'll sue'.

Scotland is this strange thing, a nation with its own health service yet allied to its bigger neighbour which is undergoing brutal and underhanded privatisation. Scotland is doing all it can to remain true to the principle of universal care for all irrespective of personal wealth, ethnicity or religion. The wealthy have recourse to private clinics but get the same doctor and surgeon who is employed by the main hospital, the equivalent of buying an Audi which is a VW in a dinner suit, as admitted by a past CEO of that over-priced car maker. Scotland keeps our health service separate from the private sort.

No one wants to face the sharp end of the surgeon's scalpel, my fate of late, a man of revoltingly good health and physique ever since I abandoned adolescent dandruff, pimples and zits, enjoyed strong lungs, a non-smoker, the heart beat of a twenty-one year old, teeth that can still demolish a hard apple, who never needed to wear a shirt three sizes too large to hide his corpulence. I can take two stairs at a time, tuck away four scoops of ice cream in one sitting, yet suddenly struck down by the smallest of evils, an incurable cancer cell with the look and the dimensions of a pearl of tapioca. Awe, crap!

Why me? Why bloody me? Well, why not? Cancer doesn't discriminate. Take solace knowing it couldn't happen to a nicer person.

A great smile and vaulting ambition does nothing to hide the fact that we are all dying, one way or another, just that some are given an approximate date. I have a theory that the most ruthless drug lords and dictators spot that irony when they reach middle age and assume a fatalistic attitude to their fellow men, and then decide they have nothing to lose by signing a pact with the Devil.

There is no getting around it, the sum total of life for the human biped amounts to being born tiny, getting big, procreating, and then getting small again, swiftly. In between we screw up relationships, ourselves and the planet. Thankfully, the Scottish health service is here to keep us positive and cheery if not exactly doing chorus girl high kicks.

Scotland's NHS – it should be renamed the SHS – gets kicked from pillar to bed pan by the scrofulous servants of Tory and Labour neo-liberal England, each dreaming of an OBE and an earldom announced in the *Scottish Times*.

I go to see my doctor once in a blue moon. Don't ask why, not to change my car tyre. I accept I am getting old but not as old as my doctor thinks. Inside my head is a thirty-five-year-old drama and philosophy student of easy sensuality. Which old guy are they staring at? Incarcerated in hospital, should I expect to see a sign hanging on the bed end, 'Not to be resuscitated'?

What Celticphobes and carpetbaggers forget in their quest to pacify the natives, is how many of us are reaching late middle age or our dotage. We *use* the health service regularly, from doctor's surgery to operating theatre via the local chemist. Unionists should drop the daily crap of claiming it is falling apart.

We know it works, we know it is a good thing. And although the quality of the service can depend on where you live, it comes free and with an ambulance and a wheelchair if needed, and a pair of crutches thrown in for good measure. You have to pay when dead, the coffin, the carriage, the service, burial or cremation. When ill, you can enjoy bad health for free.

Living in Edinburgh, I used the Royal, the Western, and finally, St John's Hospital in Livingston. There is a rivalry between them, a bit like football teams; who offers the most efficient care, the best meals, the most comfy recuperation facilities, the easiest way to bypass the ward nurses to an exit for a fly drag on a fag.

When told you have cancer, facing your mortality, every sense becomes acute. You see things sharper, can pick out sounds like a dolphin, and achieve a heightened awareness of the scent of flowers and the strength of birds on the wing. Hearing becomes acute; you can pick out a blackbird's song a mile distant. There's no need to take up Buddhism to achieve deep contemplation, everything stops around you; life stands still. You can hear your heart beating.

Back in St John's hospital, on the stretcher Americans call a gurney, counting the overhead strip lights pass by, a cliché image on television soaps, you try to look cheery on your way to the operating theatre. I decided to wave to people as if the Queen. That got a few muffled laughs from folk cloaked in face masks, humanity hidden.

Gallows humour is a useful tool to aid stress when the patient is wheeled in his bed out of the ward, off down the corridor to the operating theatre. To the American with the gammy leg, "Don't let them amputate! Those surgeons are lazy. They want home early for a game of golf with their cronies at the Royal Burgess. They'll take the quick solution!"

Hospitals are indeed places of comedic inspiration, but the joke is on mankind, we keep finding reasons to use them. On arrival at the outer surgery facility, staff in the anaesthetist's room wore masks too, faces hidden, but I could tell they were smiling. I warned them that I was quality and charged them with selling my body parts for the highest price. That got another laugh. Doctors and surgeons enjoy gallows humour. I wish I'd worn my T-shirt on which I had printed: "The Complete Works of Gareth Wardell".

From that moment until waking up in the ward, all is a blank. I was out at the time.

Nurses work like Trojans: twelve hour shifts, patients in, patients out, adhering to strict procedures, checking and rechecking and checking again your blood pressure, blood sugar count, tempera-ture, dressings, changing your beds clothes, dishing out pain killers, bringing food, bedpans, jabs to stop blood clots and uppercuts to stop clots who think verbally goosing a nurse is smart.

To this add the cleaning staff straight out of a Brueghel painting, on their hands and knees disinfecting every part of the bed carcass, the side tables, floor and toilet, never a complaint as they suffer their own aches and pains while getting up again from the floor, a task so much harder than getting down. Whatever they get paid, it isn't enough.

My ward saw men of various ages and backgrounds come and go, forget their social standing and play roles of equal measure, bed ridden, walking wounded. The patient with nose cancer and more tattoos than cigarettes smoked; the American with an infected leg wound happy to engage in political discussion; the semi-retired ophthalmologist, the first to identify I was Grouse Beater, the com-pulsive essayist and Twitter fanatic, he with a hole in his thigh and a drip; the bus driver whose bus no passenger would board knowing how jittery a person he was; and the drug addicted youth just out of prison for a serious assault. And then there was the poor pensioner, thin as a celery stick that needed craned in and craned back inside his Sheltered home. For all his screaming in the night he responded to my humour with the laugh of a child.

One bed held a succession of men who had sliced their finger, by band saw, drill, door slam, and a dustbin man who didn't move his hand quick enough to stop the wind crash the wheelie lid on three fingers, he himself feeling ready for the rubbish bin. We were as one, equality restored, at the benevolent mercy of nurses and consultants.

What is the collective noun for a group of consultants and their attendant retinue of trainees and registrars all dressed in green scrubs – a scrub of consultants? There is a kindness in the way the chief consultant explains your medical condition, the outcome and the consequences, his demeanour caressing, nothing like the stertorous authority of James Robertson Justice playing Sir Lancelott Spratt in a *Carry On Nurse* caper.

The group are a mixture from a dozen nations, from China to Ireland via Nigeria and France, the surgeon Scots, Irish or English. Nigel Farage won't sleep nights. The head Royal College of Surgeons consultant and his troupe arrive punctually at 9 am, gather around your bed, drapes pulled shut, his students listen intently in strict hierarchy, as quiet as fish while he explains what has been done to you and the consequences of it.

I made sure I had at least two questions to ask, but not once felt patronised by the answers. The one question they never answer is how long you have left on this earth, no morbid exchanges of doom. Crack a joke in the midst of this medical throng and you can see the young registrars who get the punch line bite their lip to avoid getting sucked into frivolity while the chief consultant is holding forth.

The plastic surgeon who carved his initials on my breast popped in to check his handy work. He knelt to inspect the wound and the staples holding the skin floes together, stood up and with a broad grin under his Covid mask, said, "Textbook", and disappeared for his holidays. Thank you, sir, whoever you are, for the extra time.

An inept doctor can be lethal. Mine, one of the best in Edinburgh, like me, an Italo-Scot, spotted my skin cancer on my upper arm at the primary stage. It lies *under* the skin, not the melanoma type on top, a rare type contracted by people who live in very hot countries, or as I did, work seven years in Los Angeles wearing sleeveless tops, and for it, forever getting hit on by gay guys. The doctor is the start of the medical chain, the nurses at the far end, but all are magnificent in the sacrifices they make for their duty.

Scotland's health service is home to folk of far greater integrity and compassion for Scotland's citizens than any grovelling unionist politician. We must protect it from the carrion crows of the right and the left who wear ermine.

Let no House Jock or second class Scot proud to be a colonial tell you the Scottish health service is on its knees. It is a triumph of care over shoestring budgets. I owe whatever time I have left to those who serve in St John's hospital and latterly the Western in Edinburgh, especially the Department of Oncology. The Scottish health service exists so the terminally ill do not have to crawl under a hedge to die like a wild animal.

With all the time I had to lie in bed looking out the window at the voluminous cumulus clouds that remind us we live in a wet country, I came to the conclusion only hypochondriacs enjoy bad health and they have none. For my part I think death sucks. I am definitely against death, and will *not* vote for it at the next election.

Death comes in many forms, one of them is telling a joke to the wrong people at the wrong time, but I'll risk more black humour: What's grey, sits at the end of a hospital bed and takes the piss? A kidney dialysis machine.

Thank you, thank you; I'm here all week… or whenever the ward sister lets me out.

37

THE STORY OF CIRCUS LANE

I am about to relate the tale of how, by accident, I changed a forgotten backwater lane in the centre of this nation's capital to a thriving, beautiful place to live, and how it proved to be not only a microcosm of society, but a fable not unrelated to the fate of Scotland's hopes to reinstate its self-governance. I could have shot a television soap opera there. The place was full of characters, from the young couple with twins to the antique dealer, from the widow to the boor with the arrogant swagger, as if his fly zip was undone, ready for a selfie, a village within New Town, within a great city. It is the story of empowerment, people power, and how easily it can be lost.

It began when I was homeless and gardenless. (There's a magazine as antidote for that.) I was living in a single room offered by a kind friend. A bedroom is not an address that impresses prospective employers. In my forties and married, I had to find a proper place to live, to function as a well-adjusted adult. With only a few pounds in my pocket my choice was limited to a skip (US – *dumpster*, a rubbish or garbage bin), or a cardboard box in a warm shop doorway. A small-time estate agent suggested I look at Circus Lane; some properties for sale there, tiny rooms but cheap.

I arrived confronted by a shabby crescent-shaped lane at the rear of the illustrious Royal Circus, a beer and Bollinger comparison one with the other, Royal Circus soon to provide the first £1 million pound property in Edinburgh, whereas the dilapidated mews lane offered a scruffy one-room office space with toilet for as little as £45,000.

The 9-feet wide cobbled lane had no footpath, two-way traffic using it as a shortcut at an average of 25mph, a plethora of run-down buildings fixed with plastic windows and corrugated roofing. You could just about discern it was the remnants of a Georgian set of modest dwellings, most old stables converted to various uses over the decades. The street was a forgotten rat run, ignored by the city council since the Thirties.

As I walked along its length, dejected, 'For Sale' signs nowhere to be seen, one window was open, inside a joiner was hard at work sawing a length of timber on his trestle, one knee on the wooden plank. I bent down to look inside.

"Excuse me, do you know if there are properties for sale in the street?"

He straightened his back, pushed his cap off his forehead and stared at me.

"Ye kin have this one, if ye want."

"Sorry? This is yours, you're renovating it," I answered, puzzled.

He moved to the window.

"Ah'll be straight with ye. I wis buildin' this fir ma mistress, but she's dumped me."

You could have knocked me down with a feather.

Within minutes the owner offered a price within my poverty limits sufficient to afford a deposit. Fate sealed, I spent the next twenty-odd years there, encountering good people and malicious, envious and reticent, taking life and adventures as they came, while improving everything around me. I stayed about five years too long, the core of this tale.

The dangerous proximity of speeding vehicles to homes along a narrow mews lane, with two blind corners, was alarming. What to do? One big truck parked right across my door and windows for an hour, blocking egress and light. I had an idea, one that would start a revolution of reformation. I removed a few cobbles (sett stones) and dug a small trench on both sides of my front door to plant large yew shrubs. Their bulk gave me extra 18-inches of a safety zone. The shrubs warned speeding drivers someone lived in the lane.

A troubled neighbour asked what I was doing removing the cobble stones, council property. I pointed out we owned the soil three feet from the wall. We have to reach foundations, gas main, electricity, sewage pipes for repair. True, the council owned the cobbles, but I had replaced them around the yew bushes. There was a long pause while my explanation sunk in. "Can you do that for my place?" she asked, and that was the start of landscaping the entire lane from one end to another.

Homeowner and tenant, one after another, asked for my help to make their place safer to enter and leave. Over the years, in consultation with each resident, I planted something different at front doors and under windows for the sake of variety and individuality, from plain box hedging to magnolia trees, via rose bushes, taking care to ensure the shrub could withstand winter weather and freezing rain and slush chucked at it by passing cars. I chose evergreens whenever possible. Where there was a manhole cover, I added a large container of flowers on top.

I am relieved to say, a mews lane ignored by the council was, in this instance, a good thing. The mews never saw road salt guaranteed to kill all living flora, the reason so few trees line city centre streets.

The next task I decided to tackle was a monstrous telegraph pole one-foot from a wall in the middle of the lane. People kept to the walls to avoid on-coming taffic only to find a whopping big, tar-injected British Telcomm (BT), pole smack in their path. From it hung thirty-nine phone lines running in all directions, and, as if the way of lazy convention, tacked across the front of buildings, disappearing bored through window casements to get access to rooms inside.

I made the phone call to BT.

"Hi. I'm calling from Circus Lane. Can you remove an old telephone pole?"

"Depends where it is," was the instant reply.

"Right in the path of pedestrians," I answered.

There was a long pause. "There are no poles in that lane."

"You're kidding me. I'm looking at one now."

"Our records show no standard telephone poles there since 1932."

"If you find none when you come here I'll buy you a bottle of whisky."

When he arrived he eyed the monster of a telephone pole, cables and wires attached all over it. "Hell! How did that get there?"

"Folk here have little money. How much to shift it?"

"We can remove it free of charge," he said.

"In that case, can you remove the one over that garden wall too?" I asked. "And while you are at it, how many of the cables are actually in use?"

He opened a box of electronic gizmos from the back of his van and used it to check what lines were alive and which were dead. One was in use. Thirty-eight were dead.

Thirty-eight redundant cables. I asked him to replace the one still in use along and under gutters and remove all the others. To his credit, BT did that and removed all the redundant telegraph poles free of charge and both poles. The neo-liberal creed is to give everything with a financial value, free is not a choice today. Everything has a price. Aye, we used to laugh at cans of Edinburgh air sold to gullible tourists, but look at us now; we can even buy and sell our place in a queue. But I digress.

My first great achievement was a doddle – visual clutter removed from the lane in an instant. I felt triumphant. I had beaten the system. There was nothing beyond my capacity to make things better! Over the next two decades, aided by enthusiastic residents, I began a campaign of alterations and restoration. The list I recount is not comprehensive.

One of the best moves got rid of the Fifties orange illuminated concrete lampposts and substituted them with Georgian lanterns affixed to the buildings. Half the money came from the folk in the lane, matched by half from the council. The poorest folk, usually retired, paid a few pounds, the well-heeled, £500. Soon as the lamps were installed, people came out their house smiling with pride. They had improved their surroundings, added quality, thrown off what was crap for what was quality – the first glimmer of people power. Very soon after, residents began improving the *interior* of their homes, modernising kitchens, bathrooms and electrics.

Next, I had plastic windows removed, Georgian 12-paned windows installed. The thick yellow No Parking line was relayed as a thin yellow conservation line. (Yes, there is such a thing, if you ask the council nicely.) I divided property block units visually (three properties), with an architectural line, roof to street level, delineating individual houses, so that owners could paint their exterior walls and doors a conservation colour to kill dead the monotonous grey facades. I put doors under strict Georgian conservation colours – exterior eggshell, not gloss! My wife is a painter; she knew which front door needed a sharp hue or a muted 18th century tone, advice from a world expert on colour.

I replaced ugly areas of brick inserts with sandstone as original, painted ingoes, lintels and sills a contrasting colour from the wall in the old Scottish style. I got chimneys rebuilt, concrete additions removed, proper Scottish slate put back on roofs, asked owners to remove satellite dishes, and often landscaped their small back gardens to achieve places of peace in the southern sun. Finally, I had the council make the lane one-way, west to east, the direction least used by rat-run drivers. This added a huge measure of safety and tranquillity to life in the mews of mews. Drivers began to slow down, inhibited about using a residential mews as a race track.

When the council widened the footpath around the chapel at the end of the mews, opposite the St Vincent Bar, I got permission to plant a mature tree there to soften the area, an indigenous variety, a multi-stemmed silver birch. I surrounded it with Georgian railings to give it pride of place and keep it safe from vandals No sooner were the railing installed than cyclists used them to chain their bicycles – I then added three cycle racks nearby.

To the branches of the tall silver birch I added a hardy white Scottish climbing rose. One day, when both were in full leaf, the rose blooming, I heard a young girl say to her boyfriend admiring the roses in the branches, "Ah never kent them birch trees grew flooers."

I left the lassie blissful in her ignorance.

In short time the lane was awarded full conservation status, a great thing for preserving its best elements, dissuading Barbarian incomers from sticking Magnet and Southern doors on their house to make it look 'different'. All that and a ton more alterations achieved by rustling up resident support to see their environment a superior place than before. And it was all pushed ahead by a change in council attitude to community participation: let people propose ideas, not council impose them. Gradually, a visual harmony took shape followed by a shared pride.

Wherever there is human activity, there is money to be made, and so it was with Circus Lane, until then overlooked. Developers and opportunists moved in, but I beat them to the threat of demolition and desecration. After negotiations with the council the mews was designated an A Listed conservation lane. It curbed the worst excesses of would-be architectural vandals. This is the stage where the residents began to flex their civic muscles. If they did not like a planning proposal out of character with the surroundings, they let the council know. Plans modified, gap sites were filled-in with sensitive contemporary renditions of mews properties. It was not long before house prices rose.

Everyone was happy. Police women on horseback used the lane as if of old. The sun shone on Circus Lane.

By then I had organised residents into an association, people power, which I did without much effort. There was unity of purpose. To my responsibilities, largely assumed because no one set down what a 'secretary of the Association' should do, I added a monthly newsletter. I sent it to every resident that lived in or used the mews, and to council officials to keep them up-to-date and to use as a platform to exchange ideas. By that protocol I left the city authorities with the honest impression of a cohesive community.

Lest folk think I exaggerate the tasks undertaken and achieved, I emphasise the lane renovations, the improvements, the renaissance of the mews, and the verdant landscaping admired today, were accomplished over many years, augmented when I had surplus money from film commissions, and time to put my back into the work, local friendly guerrilla gardener and landscape artist. I received no reward for my work nor looked for any, no accolade, no remuneration. I did it because it was a great thing to do, a gift to the community, thanks were enough from residents.

We met once a month to discuss moans, groans, neighbour disputes, and what we had in the bank, amassed from an annual donation. Solutions to stop vehicles using the lane and parking was the most regular topic, followed by dog walkers who thought the plant were for their dogs to cock a leg and pee on. In one incident, a drunk lawyer used a plant container as a toilet, showing no shame when I shamed him as he peed.

"A man has to relieve himself," he said, swaying unsteadily in judicial pronouncement.

"Is that so? Tell me where *you* live so I can crap at *your* door!"

Membership of the Association was a modest £25 a year, more if you could afford more. Often, I paid the sum myself for the few on welfare benefits. Most paid eagerly, one or two were always 'out' when I called. Residents paid what they could towards items for improvements, but not the work involved.

Not all went swimmingly to plan. Some owners had to be encouraged to make things better, cajoled, schmoozed, short-term incomers made to understand they had no entitlement to destroy improvements, knock holes in walls for windows, or cut down shrubs. Nevertheless, the quality of the lane went from strength to strength. By 2010 the lane had become internationally famous, an Internet site to itself, voted '*The Most Beautiful Street in Edinburgh*', the destination of film and stills shoots the world over, from Japan to Australia, from the USA to Italy. Fashion designers love it as a backdrop. A Mercedes Smart Car advert said, "Small is beautiful". Movie stars marvelled, Julia Roberts took her coffee break on the stone bench I had built outside my windows. Jack Vettriano kept his muse there in a property he bought – his muse nested in a mews.

Mike Hart, founder of the Edinburgh Jazz Festival, lived there most of his life.

Circus Lane was one way to make my mark on my country even if there is no plaque on a wall to say I was the architect. When I left the lane to live elsewhere, residents added to the landscaping, though not always with enough attention to the Georgian vernacular, Edwin Lutyen's Victorian benches out of character, and some plants veering to the twee. But the residents will full of pride of place enough to protect my legacy.

At this point I should mention something of the lane's history. Most visitors think the lane the result of indiscriminate placing of stables. To a quick study, buildings are usually seen as stables to house horses of the wealthy of Royal Circus, now homes for the hoi polloi. There is only one stable, at the west end entrance and what we see in the lane is the *rear* facade. The front, the best side, a clever miniature of Georgian composition, faces Royal Circus and the owner who built it. Because of the angle it is built, on a curve, it is nicknamed 'The Squinty House'. Properties were built on once fertile cattle fields from the early 1800s, but in an haphazard fashion, one, here, another there, numbered consecutively as they were built. Postmen and delivery drivers are forever flummoxed, Number 6 is at one end, and number 7 at the other, number 25 in the middle, number 24 is down a short alley.

Lane buildings are often assumed to be stables. A lot of the buildings were built by Hansom cab owners, the middle-class of their day. Horse and cart stayed below, hay bales on the first floor, the cabby and his family in two rooms next to the food store.

One of my last ambitions was to add a Georgian stone archway at the lane's entrance; one side marked 'Circus Lane', the other 'Stockbridge', the stonework adorned with etched silhouettes of Hansom cabs, wagon wheels, and horses. That was a costly project, and I was on the point of moving out. I still think the lane needs a monumental architectural marker at the entrance, an arch the perfect boundary.

A census record from 1891 tells a story of cab proprietors, and cab drivers who were not owners, a widow, a teacher, a general merchant, a confectioner, and one hapless 'unemployed'. To the mews lane's modern history should be appended a plaque on Number 11, 'Here lived the eminent Royal Academician Painter Dr Barbara Rae CBE RA RSA RE, and her Writer and Producer Husband, Gareth, who wrote volumes of stuff'.

Shortly before I moved home, an annoying thing happened. Two years earlier I had responded to resident complaints about parked cars blocking the narrow lane, a common occurrence. I asked the council to consider double yellow lines *only at certain narrow points*. Many months later the council's roads department popped up with a proposal to place double lanes *the entire length of the mews*. I got wind of the proposal two days before it was to be passed by the Council. What to do? I decided here was the test for the residents. Rather than me, Association Secretary, take the hit, rushing off to the council and arguing the original case for short lengths of lines, I thought it a good experiment to see how the residents handled it themselves, standing on their own two feet.

The gossip went round like lightning: whose idea what this? Only one resident picked up the baton, the selfish one who left her car in the street, her garage used for her son as a gymnasium. She got the no parking lines proposal stopped, but did not consult a soul about it. The community democracy I had taken pains to engineer was broken in one fell swoop. One council official gloated, "I see Circus Lane is not all unity, sweetness and light as it's made out to be." My cover was blown.

One day I woke up to find the lane had its own Internet site and had become internationally famous. It was a place to visit when in the capital, after you had seen the Edinburgh Castle. Tourists flocked to take photographs. Some of my happiest memories are talking to excited Japanese tourists, and visiting performers there for the great arts festival.

There were happy times, getting together with neighbours to share a chinwag and a beer on a warm day, meeting people taking the lane as a shortcut and getting to know them with a cheery "How're you doin' today?" Back would come the reply, "All the better for a walk through the lane!" After I left the lane it began filling up with English incomers: "I knew this was the place I wanted to live." For a time, I remained the go-to man for film and stills photographers to contact, a fee negotiated, donated to the Residents Association fund for the upkeep of the mews. But I noticed the Residents Association was nowhere to be seen. I protested, gently, democracy had to be protected, and then withdrew completely.

Did my experiment fail? I had planned a Georgian archway at the lane's west entrance but left the idea too late to achieve fruition. I have the drawings to this day. More importantly, I learned it is harder to alter human behaviour than to alter buildings, but altering buildings for the better can have a positive effect on human behaviour.

From May to September you will find Circus Lane ablaze in colour, at night music and laughter from an open window, the hoot of a barn owl, the scud of rust red hair belonging to a shy urban fox. In winter it affords a wind free walk among evergreens beneath the illuminated church steeple. Life for me has moved on. I am almost finished creating a Roman garden on strict Venetian lines at my new home. My biography states essayist, educationist and *creator of spaces and places*. It is satisfying to make one's mark on society for the common good. Circus Lane was a milestone in an eventful life.

37

I AM A MAN

I am a man. I am a man who is fighting for his rights.
I fight for the rights of every man in my homeland.
And every woman and every child, and those who want none,
The apathetic that will be richer from my struggle.
I am the sun's balm, and the blood that flows within us.
I am the breeze that caresses the rocks and stones,
Whispering chapter, verse, the stories of our ancestors.
I am the scriever and the dominie and the wisdom of ages,
The planter of barley and the harvester of fruit.
I am the protector, and the bringer of hope.
I am your reflection in the flinty peat pool.
I am forever vigilant, the passing shadow of the eagle
Gliding ghost-like across the frost at your feet.
And when I die I shall be the seed in the earth.
I am a man. I am a man who is fighting for his rights.
I am the thistle in the conscience of my oppressor.
I will not be ignored.

ACKNOWLEDGEMENTS

Most of the essays appeared under the *Grouse Beater* banner, a dozen published in the unparalleled *iScot* magazine, an example of a genuine free press flourishing in the modern age that has issued from a mass movement for greater democracy. A few essays are new to this collection. The hard graft of compiling and designing a hardback belongs to my patient typesetter Laura Kincaid, with whom it has been a pleasure to collaborate. Finally, I must thank the thousands of readers who enjoy my scrievin' each week and find meaning in it.

ABOUT THE AUTHOR

Gareth Wardell's '*Grouse Beater*' essay site is as provocative as his opinions, "never expressed arrogantly and always with modesty". This collection of essays, some new, span from 2015 to 2021. He is not just a political polemicist. This collection contains reminiscences of his youth in Edinburgh and his teaching days in Glasgow. For the most part, the essays are preoccupied with Scotland's return to an independent nation state.

Born in Edinburgh into a large family of Irish pioneering professional musicians, he is half-Sicilian, the latter on his father's side, "a combination that works wonders for poetic prose". He trained at the Royal Scottish Academy of Music and Drama, Jordanhill College of Education and Glasgow University, moving into theatrical writing and direction, and teaching and lecturing. He founded and became the first Artistic Director of the Scottish Youth Theatre which nurtures actors, writers and performance musicians. After a spell as an executive producer for the BBC in Northern Ireland and then Scotland, he established his own film production company, *Jam Jar Films*, which produced a number of highly praised original dramas, the political thriller *Brond*, and the film *Conquest*, the most notable, before moving to Los Angeles as a screenwriter and script doctor. He returned to Scotland permanently in 2014 to take part in the independence referendum.

He founded and edited the educational magazine *Information for Drama*, has written countless columns for magazines and newspapers, published movie reviews, and written books for the Royal Academy of Arts. He broadcast regular radio programmes on classical music. Described as a polymath, and given the accolade of "Scotland's foremost intellectual on independence" by Professor Alfred Baird and "Scotland's Mark Twain" by readers, he is one of the few polemicists with insight into human nature.

Currently, he is working on a humorous book of his Hollywood adventures. Married to the Royal Academician painter and master printmaker Dr Barbara Rae, he has two daughters, Emma and Nora, and no pets. As a 'relaxing hobby' he designs and plants large gardens.

INDEX OF NAMES